T0280545

FORMAL SPECIFICATION AND DESIGN

Cambridge Tracts in Theoretical Computer Science

Titles in the series

1. G. Chaitin *Algorithmic Information Theory*
2. L.C. Paulson *Logic and Computation*
3. M. Spivey *Understanding Z*
4. G. Revesz *Lambda Calculus, Combinators and Functional Programming*
5. A. Ramsay *Formal Methods in Artificial Intelligence*
6. S. Vickers *Topology via Logic*
7. J-Y. Girard, Y. Lafont & P. Taylor *Proofs and Types*
8. J. Clifford *Formal Semantics & Pragmatics for Natural Language Processing*
9. M. Winslett *Updating Logical Databases*
10. K. McEvoy & J.V. Tucker (eds) *Theoretical Foundations of VLSI Design*
11. T.H. Tse *A Unifying Framework for Stuctured Analysis and Design Models*
12. G. Brewka *Nonmonotonic Reasoning*
14. S.G. Hoggar *Mathematics for Computer Graphics*
15. S. Dasgupta *Design Theory and Computer Science*
17. J.C.M. Baeten (ed) *Applications of Process Algebra*
18. J.C.M. Baeten & W. P. Weijland *Process Algebra*
23. E.-R. Olderog *Nets, Terms and Formulas*
26. P.D. Mosses *Action Semantics*
27. W.H. Hesselink *Programs, Recursion and Unbounded Choice*
29. P. Gärdenfors (ed) *Belief Revision*
30. M. Anthony & N. Biggs *Computational Learning Theory*
33. E.G. Manes *Predicate Transformer Semantics*
34. F. Nielson & H.R. Nielson *Two Level Functional Languages*
35. L. Feijs & H. Jonkers *Formal Specification and Design*

FORMAL SPECIFICATION AND DESIGN

L.M.G. FEIJS & H.B.M. JONKERS
Philips Research Laboratories
Eindhoven

CAMBRIDGE UNIVERSITY PRESS
Cambridge, New York, Melbourne, Madrid, Cape Town, Singapore, São Paulo

Cambridge University Press
The Edinburgh Building, Cambridge CB2 2RU, UK

Published in the United States of America by Cambridge University Press, New York

www.cambridge.org
Information on this title: www.cambridge.org/9780521434577

First published 1992
This digitally printed first paperback version 2005

A catalogue record for this publication is available from the British Library

ISBN-13 978-0-521-43457-7 hardback
ISBN-10 0-521-43457-2 hardback

ISBN-13 978-0-521-43592-5 paperback
ISBN-10 0-521-43592-7 paperback

Contents

List of figures

List of tables

Preface

This book is about formal specification and design techniques, including both algebraic specifications and state-based specifications.

The construction and maintenance of complex software systems is a difficult task and although many software projects are started with great expectations and enthusiasm, it is too often the case that they fail to achieve their goals within the planned time and with the given resources. The software often contains errors; attempts to eliminate the errors give rise to new errors, and so on. Moreover, the extension and adaptation of the software to new tasks turns out to be a difficult and tedious task, which seems unsuitable for scientific methods.

This unsatisfactory situation can be improved by introducing precise specifications of the software and its constituent parts. When a piece of software P has a precise specification S say, then 'P satisfies S' is a clear statement that could be verified by reasoning or that could be falsified by testing; users of P can read S and rely on it and the designer of P has a clearly formulated task. When no precise specifications are available, there are hardly any clear statements at all, for what could one say: 'it works' or more often 'it almost works'? Without precise specifications, it becomes very difficult to analyse the consequences of modifying P into P', for example, and to make any clear statements about that modification. Therefore it is worthwhile during the software development process to invest in constructing precise specifications of well-chosen parts of the software system under construction. Writing precise specifications turns out to be a considerable task itself. In many situations the use of natural language, pictures and pseudo-code does not yield specifications of the required level of abstractness and precision. *Formal specification* is an approach to writing precise specifications, building on concepts from mathematical logic. During the past decades, much research and development concerning formal specification techniques has been conducted. Well-known results in this field are the techniques of 'abstract data types' and of 'pre- and postconditions'.

What is the role of 'language' in connection with formal specifications? One can say that, in many respects, the practical progress in software engineering is language-driven: it is hard to introduce methodological concepts unless these are concretely available as constructs in the language in use. This is a major motivation behind the introduction of formal specification languages. In practice it is not enough to have good methodological concepts for writing formal specifications: one needs a language as a vehicle. Throughout this book, the language COLD-K is employed as a vehicle. COLD is an acronym for *Common Object-oriented Language for Design.* This book explains the constructs offered by the language and shows how to use them. The use of formal specification techniques at certain well-chosen points in the design process is one of the key factors – though certainly not the only one – in increasing the quality of the software development process.

A formal specification language is a language whose constructs are derived both from mathematical logic and from programming languages and which has a precise syntax and semantics. If, furthermore the language allows for descriptions at several levels of abstraction, it is called a *wide-spectrum* specification language. The language employed in this book is such a wide-spectrum specification language; other wide-spectrum specification languages are VDM, CIP and RSL. One could also call it a *design language* to emphasise that the language can be used for recording a software system in its intermediate stages of design, ranging from *specification* to *implementation.*

Many techniques such as 'abstract data types', 'abstraction functions', 'invariants', 'pre- and postconditions', 'modular specification' and 'information hiding' can be explained using the constructs offered by COLD-K [1]. The language is in the tradition of VDM [2, 3] and Z [4, 5], but has been influenced by ASL [6], Module Algebra [7], Harel's dynamic logic [8], Scott's E-logic [9, 10] and object-oriented languages. Furthermore it contains a novel notion of 'design' comparable with the structuring mechanisms provided by e.g. HOOD [11].

The language was developed at the Philips Research Laboratories in Eindhoven within the framework of ESPRIT project 432 (also known as METEOR). It has been designed mainly by H.B.M. Jonkers, with technical contributions from C.P.J. Koymans, G.R. Renardel de Lavalette and L.M.G. Feijs. The fact that its well-formedness and semantics are defined mathematically guarantees that descriptions in the language leave no room for ambiguity and that a high level of tool support can be provided. Actually, COLD-K is one out of a sequence of language versions, in which it plays a special role: it is a *kernel language*, serving as a point of departure in the further development of the language. It is meant to be used as the kernel of user- and application-oriented language versions, to be derived by syntactic extensions. All essential semantic features are contained in this kernel language, as well as high level constructs for modularisation, parameterisation and designs. It is important to realise that this language is the forerunner of versions which are much more user-friendly – at least from a syntactic point of view. Indeed, certain aspects of the language are somewhat Spartan, but for the purpose of this book this is hardly a disadvantage.

One of the main goals of this book is to treat the basic concepts underlying algebraic specification techniques. The book shows how algebraic specification techniques can be effectively used in the software development process. Yet, the approach of this book goes far beyond algebraic specifications: it shows how algebraic and state-based techniques can be combined in an integrated approach. The main motivation for using COLD-K is as follows. It is a *formal* language, with a well-defined syntax and semantics; it can be used as an *algebraic* specification language; furthermore, it is an *integrated* language, unifying algebraic and state-based techniques.

The book is divided into three parts. The first part is concerned with algebraic specifications, the second part with state-based specifications. The first and the second part have essentially the same structure, beginning with an introduction of the basic concepts followed by methodological guidelines about setting up a specification. After that the the topics of *large* specifications as well as *implementation* strategies are treated – each in one chapter. In the third part we have three chapters, each of a different nature. In Chapter 9 a number of existence proofs and theoretical discussions are presented. These are related to the earlier chapters, but are not presented there in order not to distract too much from the main line of these chapters. In Chapter 10 a number of additional language constructs are presented informally. In the last chapter (Chapter 11) a pictorial representation of module structures is explained as well as a systematic approach for putting specifications and implementations together in a top-level language construct called *design*. The structure of the book is as follows.

I
1. Introducing the basic concepts,
2. Setting up algebraic specifications,
3. Structuring algebraic specifications,
4. Implementing algebraic specifications.

II
5. From algebras to states,
6. Setting up state-based specifications,
7. Structuring state-based specifications,
8. Implementing state-based specifications.

III
9. Theoretical topics,
10. Additional language constructs,
11. Towards large systems.

Since the goal of the book is not to serve as a language reference manual, we decided not to present *all* language features. Instead of that we restricted ourselves to the most essential aspects of the language. These are covered in depth by the Chapters 1–9, and additional language features as well as constructs for building systems from components are dealt with briefly and informally in Chapters 10 and 11. The syntax of the full language COLD-K is contained in Appendix A.

This book developed from the course material for a post-graduate course given by the authors at the Technical University of Eindhoven and at the University of Nijmegen. Special thanks go to J.A. Bergstra, R.J. Bril and C.A. Middelburg for their contributions, reviewing and discussions supporting the creation of this text.

Part I
Algebraic specification

Chapter 1

Introducing the basic concepts

1.1 Introduction

The conception, construction, maintenance and usage of computer-based systems are difficult tasks requiring special care, skills, methods and tools. Program correctness is a serious issue and in addition to that, the size of the programs gives rise to problems of complexity management. Computers are powerful machines which can execute millions of instructions per second and manipulate millions of memory cells. The freedom offered by the machine to its programmer is large; often it is too large, in the sense that the machine does not enforce order and structure upon the programs. Computer-based systems are artificial systems and therefore there are no natural system partitionings and interface definitions. All structure is man-made and all interfaces must be agreed upon and communicated to all parties involved. The description and communication of system structures and interfaces turns out to be a non-trivial task and 'specification languages' have become an active area of research and development in computer science. When discussing 'language' we must distinguish explicitly between *syntactic* objects and *semantic* objects. Wittgenstein [12] has expressed this idea as follows:

Der Satz stellt das Bestehen und Nichtbestehen der Sachverhalte dar,

i.e. the proposition represents the existence or non-existence of certain states of affairs. The propositions are syntactic objects and in this text we shall call them *specifications*. To describe a state of affairs concerning the natural world and concerning human interaction, natural language is the tool par excellence; to describe a state of affairs concerning computer-based systems, special languages are required in addition to that. The situation is typical: special restricted domains require special languages and this is also the case for the domain of computer-based systems. Programming languages belong also to this domain, but they are not meant for communication between designers. They are meant for instructing machines, and using them for other purposes often leads to problems – such as descriptions not being abstract enough. Therefore 'specification languages' have been created. They serve to describe artificial systems and therefore they are rich in logical constructs and structuring mechanisms, but they are poor with respect to their built-in vocabulary. Specification languages are artifacts themselves and the meaning of the language constructs must be documented and learned explicitly.

We explain the notion of a 'specification language' as follows. If we write $\mathcal{P}(\mathcal{A})$ to denote the set of all subsets of a set $\mathcal{A}$ (its powerset), a *specification language* is characterized by:

1. a set $\mathcal{S}$ of *syntactic objects*, or *specifications*;
2. a set $\mathcal{A}$ of *semantic objects*;
3. a *meaning function* $\mathcal{M} : \mathcal{S} \to \mathcal{P}(\mathcal{A})$.

If $S \in \mathcal{S}$ is a specification and $A \in \mathcal{M}(S)$, then A is called a *model* of S.

This chapter is organised as follows. Section 1.2 deals with the question 'what is an algebraic specification?' Section 1.3 is concerned with names and signatures, both being elementary syntactic notions. Section 1.4 gives a formal introduction to the notion of an 'algebra', which is a semantical notion employed throughout the text. Sections 1.5, 1.6, and 1.7 introduce several syntactic constructs, together with their meaning. Section 1.8 gives an example of a specification. Section 1.9 is about initial algebras; this is a theoretical concept, but it is interesting when comparing the COLD-K approach with the *initial algebra* approach, used in several other algebraic specification languages. Section 1.10 and Section 1.11 add more examples.

1.2 What is a(n algebraic) specification?

The syntactic objects of *algebraic specification languages* are referred to as *algebraic specifications*, or *specifications.* Specifications are constructed from keywords, user-declared identifiers, operators etc. according to a certain grammar, in much the same way as computer programs are constructed. The main difference between a specification and a computer program is that a specification is an abstract description, whereas a computer program contains a concrete recipe (= algorithm) which can be executed by a computer. To give a first impression, we show a simple specification which introduces a sort name `Set1` together with two function names `nil` and `id`. This `nil` is a nullary function, i.e. a constant whereas `id` has type `Set1 -> Set1`. There is one axiom, which is a simple equation.

```
CLASS

  SORT Set1
  FUNC nil : -> Set1
  FUNC id  : Set1 -> Set1
  AXIOM id(nil) = nil

END
```

The semantic objects of *algebraic specification languages* are *many-sorted algebras*, which we most often call just *algebras*. These are a kind of mathematical structure based on the viewpoint that things (objects/data values) should be organised into sorts. For example the sort of natural numbers is considered disjoint with respect to the sort of character-strings, which in turn is disjoint with respect to the sort of stacks, etc. One of the simplest algebras one can imagine is the algebra which has one sort, where this sort in turn has exactly one element. Figure 1.1 depicts such an algebra which, as it happens, is a model of the above specification.

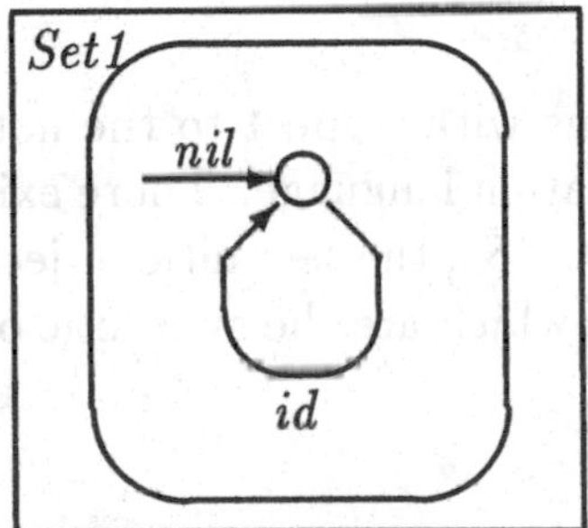

Fig 1.1. Algebra with sort *Set1* and one object.

In general, the algebras can be much more complicated than the one given above. There may be several sorts, each sort having several or even infinitely many objects. Such a more complicated algebra is shown below. The many-sorted algebra of this figure has two sorts, denoted by T and V. Each sort is drawn as an oval, like in a Venn diagram; note that the ovals do not overlap, which models the fact that in a (many-sorted) algebra the sorts can be considered disjoint. The sort T has five elements whereas the sort V has four elements. The elements of a sort are also called *objects* or sometimes *values*. In this algebra there are two functions f and g. The first function, f, maps T objects to T objects, a situation which we formulate as $f : T \to T$. The second function g, maps T objects to V objects, formulated as $g : T \rightarrow V$. The details of this mapping process are shown by means of the arrows in this figure. For example, there is an arrow labelled g to indicate that the function g maps the lowest T object to the lowest V object.

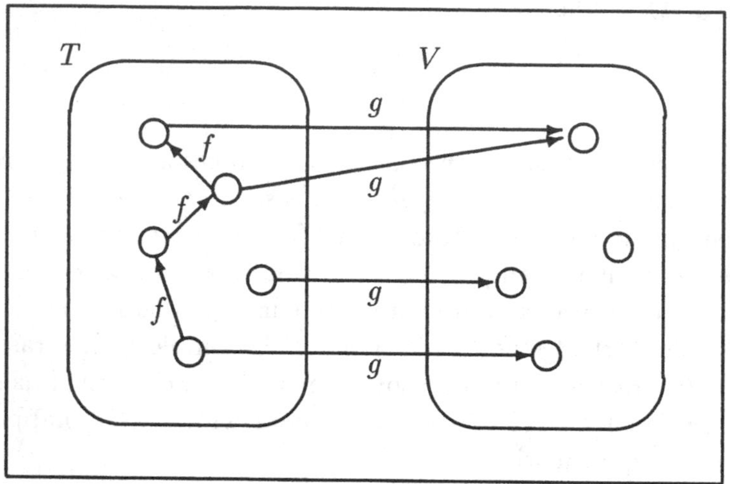

Fig 1.2. Algebra with two sorts.

There are several variations with respect to the notions of algebraic specification and algebraic specification language. There exist distinct options with respect to the syntactic objects ($\mathcal{S}$), the semantic objects ($\mathcal{A}$) and the meaning function ($\mathcal{M}$). *Specifications*, which are the syntactic objects, can for example be based on:

- equational axioms,
- conditional equational axioms,
- first order axioms,
- first order axioms + inductive definitions,

although the last option goes beyond what most authors would call 'algebraic'. Let us add a few lines of explanation to these options. Equational axioms are well-known from algebra, and a famous example of algebraic specification, the stack, can be described by means of equations such as

```
pop(push(x,s)) = (x,s)
```

Conditional equational axioms are a generalisation of this where each equation may be provided with a condition. For example:

```
is_empty(s) = false => push(pop(s)) = s
```

First order axioms are a further generalisation, allowing the use of quantifiers, i.e. the special operators FORALL and EXISTS. Usually these are written as $\forall$ and $\exists$ or sometimes as **.A.** and **.E.** respectively. First order axioms have certain limitations with respect to their expressive power and they cannot be used for stating induction principles and certain minimality properties of sorts. To add such expressive power requires the addition of a kind of 'fixed point operator'.

With respect to the nature of the *algebras* serving as semantic objects, there are also a number of options.

- sorts + total functions;
- sorts + partial functions;
- sorts + predicates + partial functions.

To adopt total functions means that for every function f and every argument x the function value $f(x)$ must exist. This gives rise to simple kinds of algebras. On the other hand, it leads to somewhat artificial situations, e.g. when considering the value of $1/0$ when dealing with rational numbers, or of pop(empty) when dealing with stacks. The option to add predicates is convenient; for example when considering numbers, it is natural to consider $<$, $\leq$ etc. as binary predicates. On the other hand, predicates can be avoided by using Boolean-valued functions – although this introduces new problems in connection with partial functions.

Finally, let us present the various choices existing for the meaning function $\mathcal{M}$. The *meaning function* can, for example be such that for a specification S:

- $\mathcal{M}(S)$ consists of a single algebra;
- $\mathcal{M}(S)$ may contain arbitrarily many algebras;
- $\mathcal{M}(S)$ contains only *minimal* algebras.

The first option, i.e. that the meaning $\mathcal{M}(S)$ of a specification S is a single algebra, can only be chosen for very restricted kinds of specifications. This is the case when using (conditional) equational axioms. Then there is always a special algebra: the so-called initial algebra. This is a kind of 'canonical' model which arises in a natural way. For other kinds of specifications (e.g. using first order axioms) no such canonical model exists in general. In that case, the second option where $\mathcal{M}(S)$ may contain an arbitrary number of algebras is better. This second option is referred to as *loose semantics.* The third option, where $\mathcal{M}(S)$ contains only *minimal* algebras, is intermediate between the other two options. The idea is that the sorts of the algebra contain only those objects which can be denoted by terms. So when considering the specification of a number system, the introduction of `0` and a successor operation `succ` is sufficient to guarantee that all numbers can be represented by one of the terms `0`, `succ(0)`, `succ(succ(0))`, etc. The advantage is that the language does not need special constructs for expressing minimality; on the other hand, if this minimality is *not* desired in special cases, there is no way to express this. The approach taken in COLD-K and in this text is based on specifications employing

- first order axioms + fixed point operator,

algebras consisting of

- sorts + predicates + partial functions,

and a meaning function according to

- loose semantics without implicit restrictions on the algebras.

These choices guarantee a large expressive power and flexibility (for example when compared with an equational approach with total functions and initial semantics). We shall come back to one of these alternative options in Section 1.9. The choices reflect design decisions made when the language COLD-K was developed and they are closely related to the wide-spectrum nature of the language – as explained in the preface. The language is even more wide-spectrum than being a powerful and flexible algebraic specification language: it is also possible to model state-based systems. However, all state-based aspects are postponed until Part II of this text.

In the next section we shall discuss names and signatures, both of which are topics related to the syntactic objects ($\mathcal{S}$) of a specification language. It will not be until after Section 1.7 that we will have gathered enough syntactical and semantical machinery to write complete examples of algebraic specifications in COLD-K.

1.3 Names and signatures

The introduction and usage of names is one of the most fundamental and universal mechanisms that play a role in the construction of syntactic objects in general and in our specifications in particular. To express a certain property of rational numbers, one could write

```
FORALL x:Rat ( add(x,0) = x )
```

but this only makes sense if we know that Rat is a sort, that 0 is a constant (a function taking an empty list of arguments) and that add is a function whose first argument must be an element of sort Rat.

COLD-K specifications are about (many-sorted) algebras containing sorts, predicates and functions; therefore we need names of three kinds, viz. sort names, predicate names and function names. In the above example, Rat refers to a sort, and 0 and add refer to functions. We shall employ a fairly general notion of 'name', where the kind of the name (sort, predicate or function) is *part of* the name. For predicates and functions it is relevant to know the number of arguments and their sorts. In addition to that, functions also have one or more results and again the number of results and their sorts are relevant. All this information is considered part of the name. By an *identifier* we mean a non-empty string of letters, digits and the six special characters ", ', ., /, \ and _. For example, Rat, 0 and add are identifiers.

Definition. A *sort name* consists of:

- an identifier S

and the notation for this is

SORT S □

Sort names are unstructured, but predicate names and function names also contain information concerning the number of arguments and their sorts. Such information is put together in a *type*.

Definition. A *type* is a sequence of sort names $S_1, \ldots, S_m$ ($m \geq 0$). The notation for this is

S_1 # ... # S_m □

A predicate name has an identifier and a 'domain type', which is the type of its argument list.

Definition. A *predicate name* consists of:

- an identifier r;
- a type S_1 # ... # S_m, called the *domain type* of the predicate name.

The notation for this is

PRED r : S_1 # ... # S_m □

Unlike a predicate, a function name has also a range type. Although in many situations functions yield just a single result, the approach chosen in COLD-K is more general in the sense that a function can yield a tuple of results. In this way the situation with respect to input arguments and output results is symmetric.

Definition. A *function name* consists of:

- an identifier f;
- a type S_1 # ... # S_m, called the *domain type* of the function name;
- a type V_1 # ... # V_n, called the *range type* of the function name.

The notation for this is

FUNC f : S_1 # ... # S_m -> V_1 # ... # V_n □

Two names are equal only if they are of the same kind (sort, predicate or function) and have the same components. In an applied occurrence of a name we only write the identifier of the name. It should be possible to reconstruct the other components of a name from the context; this is a task which can be done mechanically by a tool called *type checker*. This explains why we can write `FORALL x:Rat ( add(x,0) = x )` rather than the full

```
FORALL x:SORT Rat
( FUNC add: SORT Rat # SORT Rat -> SORT Rat
   (x, FUNC 0: -> SORT Rat ) = x )
```

which is far less readable. Once the full names are reconstructed, the type checker can perform its main task, which is to perform a *check* on the correct usage of names.

Usually algebraic specifications are not concerned with one sort, predicate or function. They introduce a sort together with a number of predicates and functions which operate on that sort. In an algebraic specification all names must be introduced formally and one or more properties (propositions, facts) must be stated. Often it is interesting to know which names are introduced in a given specification – disregarding the stated properties. This gives rise to a notion called 'signature'.

Definition. A *signature* Σ is a set of sort, predicate and function names such that each sort name occurring in a name in Σ is also a member of Σ. □

This means that if the name PRED r : S_1 # ... # S_m is an element of a given signature, then all sort names involved ($S_1, \ldots, S_m$) must be in that signature as well. Similarly, if the name FUNC f : S_1 # ... # S_m -> V_1 # ... # V_n is in a signature, then $S_1, \ldots, S_m$ and $V_1, \ldots, V_n$ must be in that signature as well.

We shall give two examples of signatures. The first example is the signature of an algebraic specification concerning integer numbers.

```
SORT Int,
FUNC 0   : -> Int,
FUNC 1   : -> Int,
PRED lss : Int # Int,
PRED gtr : Int # Int,
FUNC add : Int # Int -> Int,
FUNC sub : Int # Int -> Int,
FUNC mul : Int # Int -> Int,
FUNC div : Int # Int -> Int
```

Fig 1.3. Signature of the specification of integers.

The only sort name in the signature of Figure 1.3 is SORT Int. In informal texts we shall be somewhat sloppy, saying simply 'sort' rather than 'sort name' and we shall use identifiers instead of full names. So, the only sort of this signature is Int and there are six functions and two predicates. The functions 0 and 1 are nullary functions, by which we mean that their domain type is empty. Nullary functions are also called *constants*. The functions add, sub, mul and div are binary: they take two arguments. The predicates lss and gtr are binary as well. Note that a signature consists of name information only: the signature as such is not concerned with properties of the sorts, predicates and functions. The names are suggestive and we expect that add refers to normal addition but formally speaking, this is not yet stated anywhere.

Our next example is the signature of an algebraic specification concerning stacks.

```
SORT Item,
SORT Stack,
PRED is_empty : Stack,
FUNC empty    : -> Stack,
FUNC push     : Item # Stack -> Stack,
FUNC pop      : Stack -> Item # Stack
```

Fig 1.4. Signature of the specification of stacks.

There are two sort names in this signature: `Item` and `Stack`. Note the function `pop`, which has a composite range type.

We shall leave the syntactic issues for a moment and in the next section turn our attention to the semantic objects, which are algebras.

1.4 Algebras

Signatures are the starting points for writing specifications in COLD-K. Just as for classical algebraic specifications, the main mechanism is to write equations between terms constructed from sort names and function names. Throughout the text we shall gradually introduce more and more sophisticated expressions and assertions.

In this section we shall present a class of structures that will play an important role in the semantical analysis of our specifications. These structures are algebras, or algebraic systems, and one can think of them as 'models' or 'possible worlds'. For COLD-K we need special kinds of algebras which we shall call 'partial many-sorted algebras'.

Although the specifications in COLD-K are suitable for describing real-world situations as well as computer-based artifacts, digital systems and physical systems, it is too great a task to take all these 'possible worlds' into account. We replace them by suitable mathematical structures (algebras) built from sets, functions and relations, all of which are constructions whose existence in mathematics is widely accepted. This approach of abstracting from the real-world situations and systems is customary in the branch of mathematical logic called 'model theory' and in the branch of computer science called 'denotational semantics'. It has the advantage of enabling a semantical analysis of the COLD-K language constructs but avoids ending up in general philosophy.

In mathematical logic, an algebra is usually just a set with a collection of functions and relations. Since we have adopted a notion of signatures that can contain more than one sort name, we must employ *many-sorted* algebras. In particular, for each signature Σ a many-sorted Σ-algebra is a collection of sets

– one for each sort name in Σ – with a collection of functions and relations – one for each function and predicate name in Σ. In Section 1.2 we showed two examples of many-sorted algebras by means of Figures 1.1 and 1.2.

A complication arises because we want to have special provisions for dealing with definedness and undefinedness. Undefinedness arises when popping from an empty stack, when dividing by zero and when invoking ill-defined recursive functions. Therefore the functions of each many-sorted algebra A will be *partial* functions, i.e. functional relations viewed as sets of pairs, where not necessarily every object occurs as a first element. In this way we arrive at a many-sorted algebra which will be called *partial many-sorted algebra.*

In the formal definition below we use the (right-associative) operator '$\times$' to construct Cartesian products, writing $S_1 \times S_2$ where S_1 and S_2 are sets. We use parenthesis to denote certain elements of such Cartesian products. For example, if $x_1 \in S_1, \ldots, x_m \in S_m$ then $(x_1, \ldots, x_m) \in S_1 \times \ldots \times S_m$. For tuples of length 1 we sometimes write x_1 instead of (x_1).

Definition. A *partial many-sorted algebra*, or *algebra* A with signature Σ is a system of sets S^A, functions f^A and relations r^A for S, f, r in Σ, such that:

1. For each sort name S in Σ we find that S^A is a set. The elements of S^A are called *objects* of sort S.
2. For each function name f : S_1 # ... # S_m -> V_1 # ... # V_n in Σ we find that f^A is a partial function from $S_1^A \times \ldots \times S_m^A$ to $V_1^A \times \ldots \times V_n^A$.
3. For each predicate name r : S_1 # ... # S_m in Σ we find that r^A is a relation on $S_1^A \times \ldots \times S_m^A$. □

So a Σ-algebra A has one set of objects for each sort name in Σ, one partial function for each function name in Σ and one predicate, i.e. a relation, for each predicate name in Σ. The set is said to be the *interpretation*, or *carrier* set of the sort name, the partial function is said to be the interpretation of the function name and the relation is said to be the interpretation of the predicate name.

We can define mathematical notions such as homomorphisms and isomorphisms for Σ-algebras; we shall return to the notion of a homomorphism in Section 9.3. We give an example of an algebra with the following signature.

```
SORT V,
SORT W,
PRED r : W,
FUNC f : -> V,
FUNC g : V -> W
```

Fig 1.5. Signature Σ with two sort names `V` and `W`.

This signature contains two sort names `V` and `W`, a predicate name `r` defined on `W`, a constant function name `f : -> V` and a function name `g : V -> W`.

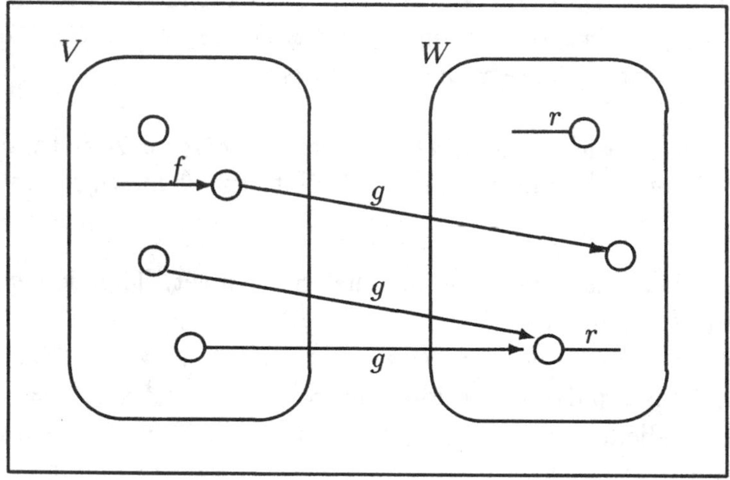

Fig 1.6. Algebra with signature Σ.

The Σ-algebra A in Figure 1.6. has two sorts, denoted by V and W. They correspond to the sort names `V` and `W` in the signature. Referring to the formal definition of a Σ-algebra, we have $\mathtt{V}^A = V$ and $\mathtt{W}^A = W$. This means that the set V shown as the left oval in the figure serves as the interpretation of the sort name `V` in Σ and similarly the set W, which is the right oval, serves as the interpretation of `W`. Figure 1.6 shows the functions f and g, serving as the interpretation of `f` and `g` and the predicate r interpreting the name `r`. The figure indicates that in this particular Σ-algebra, r holds for two objects of W (the upper and the lower object in the picture). Clearly this is not the only Σ-algebra; *every* algebra with two sets V and W, relation $r : W$ and functions $f :\rightarrow V$ and $g : V \rightarrow W$ is a Σ-algebra for the signature Σ of Figure 1.5.

This concludes our introduction to algebras (the semantic objects) and in the next section we turn our attention to the syntactic objects again, i.e. to the specifications themselves.

1.5 Flat algebraic specifications

In general, algebraic specifications have a flexible modular structure. In this chapter we shall restrict ourselves to specifications of a simple fixed modular structure, the *flat specifications.* These consist of essentially *one* module, indicated by the matching keywords `CLASS` and `END`.

Definition. A *flat algebraic specification* consists of a list of definitions, where each *definition* defines one of the following items:

- sort;
- predicate;
- function;
- axiom.

The set of names thus defined should constitute a signature Σ. Our notation for this is as follows:

```
CLASS
  definition_1
      ⋮
  definition_n
END
```

□

The meaning of such a specification is the class of all Σ-algebras satisfying the definitions *definition*$_1$ ... *definition*$_n$, where Σ is the set of names introduced by the sorts, predicates and functions in these definitions.

Of course we still must explain the syntax and semantics of the sort definitions, predicate definitions, function definitions and axiom definitions. This is the subject of the remainder of this section. Our notation for sort, predicate and function definitions is as follows:

```
SORT S                                      body
PRED r : S_1 # ... # S_m                    body
FUNC f : S_1 # ... # S_m -> V_1 # ... # V_n body
```

In other words, to introduce a sort, predicate or function, one must write its full name, including keyword, domain type and range type followed by a defining *body*. According to their body, the sort, predicate and function definitions can be subdivided into:

- *explicit definitions*, which uniquely characterize a sort or operation in terms of other sorts and operations (we use the term 'operation' as a general name for functions and predicates),
- *implicit definitions*, which introduce a sort or operation that is characterized (not necessarily in a unique way) by axioms.

For the time being we restrict ourselves to implicit definitions, *which have an empty body*. Explicit definitions will be presented in Chapter 2 and Chapter 4. So, to introduce a sort S by means of an implicit definition, we write

`SORT` S

To introduce a predicate r with domain type S_1 # ... # S_m we write

`PRED` r : S_1 # ... # S_m

Finally, to introduce a function f with domain type S_1 # ... # S_m and range type V_1 # ... # V_n we write

`FUNC` f : S_1 # ... # S_m -> V_1 # ... # V_n

In addition to sort, predicate and function definitions, it is possible to define *axioms*, which are propositions concerning a certain state of affairs in an algebra. Axioms have the following form:

`AXIOM` *assertion*

where an *assertion* can be built from terms by means of equations, logical connectives, quantifiers etc. We present assertions in the next section.

1.6 Terms and assertions

Terms are used in assertions to denote tuples of objects. As usual, terms are built from names by using function application, parentheses, etc. Before giving the precise definition of 'term', we must introduce another kind of names called *object names*. These serve as logical variables which arise for example in connection with quantifiers; they are used to give names to tuples of objects.

Definition. An *object name* consists of:

- an identifier x;
- a type S_1 # ... # S_m, called the *type* of the object name.

Our notation for this is

x : S_1 # ... # S_m □

Object names are introduced in assertions by *quantifiers*, to be discussed later in this section, and by *declarations*, to be discussed in Chapter 4. Let us begin with a simple example first. Using the function names from the signature of Figure 1.4. and assuming that `i` is an object name of type `Item`, the following is a term

```
push(i,push(i,empty())).
```

More precisely, it is a term of type `Stack`. Similarly,

```
pop(push(i,push(i,empty())))
```

is a term of type `Item # Stack`. We give a survey of all terms first (Table 1.1) and after that we shall go into the details.

x
X,Y
$f\ X$
(X)
()

Table 1.1. Survey of all terms.

So, first of all, object names are terms and secondly, terms can be composite, where ',' serves as a tuple constructor. Furthermore terms can be obtained by means of function application and terms can be put in parentheses. We give a simultaneous inductive definition of both terms and their types.

Definition. The notions of *term* and *type* of a term are inductively defined by the following rules:

1. if x is an object name of type T, then x is a term of type T;
2. if X is a term of type T and Y is a term of type V, then X,Y is a term of type T # V;

3. if f : T `->` V is a function name and X is a term of type T, then f X is a term of type V;
4. if X is a term of type T, then (X) is a term of type T;
5. `()` is a term of the empty type. □

In the above definition T and V denote referring to general types, built from sort names and the '#' type constructor. The definition is *inductive*, by which we mean that the set of all terms is the *smallest* set satisfying the rules 1, ..., 5. Note that the third rule says that terms can be obtained by means of function application, provided the domain type of the function and the type of the actual argument match. The fifth rule introduces a particularly simple term, which has the empty type. It should be noted that types contain sort names and the '#' type constructor, but do not contain parentheses.

We relax the rule for function application for functions with an empty domain. Instead of f`()` we usually write f. This is convenient: it allows us to write e.g. `push(i,push(i,empty))` instead of `push(i,push(i,empty()))`.

The following definition serves to relate terms to signatures and to introduce the notion of a *closed term*.

Definition. A Σ-*term* is a term X such that each sort and function name occurring in X is contained in Σ. A *closed* Σ-*term* is a Σ-term not containing any object names. □

Let us explicitly discuss the interpretation of the various kinds of terms. The interpretation of object names (x) can only be understood in connection with binding operators like `EXISTS` and `FORALL`, which provide for the contexts in which a term x gets its meaning.

If X is a term of type S_1 # ... # S_m and Y is a term of type V_1 # ... # V_n then the interpretation of X,Y in M equals

$$(x_1, \ldots, x_m, y_1, \ldots, y_n)$$

where $(x_1, \ldots, x_m)$ is the interpretation of X and $(y_1, \ldots, y_n)$ is the interpretation of Y in M, provided that both X and Y are defined. Otherwise, if X is undefined or Y is undefined, then the interpretation of X,Y is undefined. This interpretation makes the COLD-K operator ',' associative.

If X is a term of type S_1 # ... # S_m and f is a function name whose domain type matches the type of X and whose range type is V_1 # ... # V_n then the interpretation of f X in M equals $f^M(x_1, \ldots, x_m)$ where $(x_1, \ldots, x_m)$ is the interpretation of X, provided the latter is defined. Otherwise, if X is undefined, then so is the interpretation of f X in M.

If X is a term of type S_1 # ... # S_m then the interpretation of (X) in M is the same as that of X – as expected. Finally the term () has as its interpretation the empty tuple () which is the only object of the empty Cartesian product, i.e. the product of zero sets.

We give a survey of all assertions (Table 1.2) before giving further details. The entries in the table are organised in three blocks. The first block contains the logical constructs. The second block contains the constructs related to built-in predicates and user-defined predicates. The last block concerns constructs with parentheses.

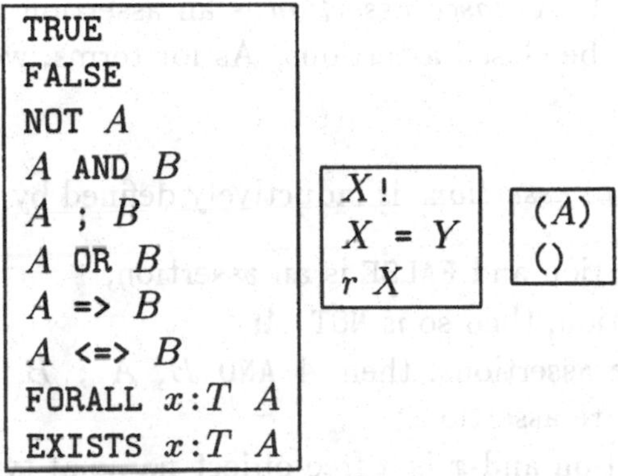

Logical constructs	Predicates	Parentheses
TRUE	X !	(A)
FALSE	X = Y	()
NOT A	$r\,X$	
A AND B		
A ; B		
A OR B		
A => B		
A <=> B		
FORALL x:T A		
EXISTS x:T A		

Table 1.2. Survey of all assertions.

The TRUE and FALSE assertions are logical constants, whereas NOT, AND, OR, => and <=> are propositional logic connectives. The symbol ';' is available as an alternative for AND. The difference lies in the priority of the connective when an assertion is parsed. The ';' connective has a very low priority. The other connectives have their usual priority, where NOT binds stronger than AND which in turn binds stronger than OR, etc. For the details we refer to appendix A. Because of the low priority of ';' we can write

A OR B ; C OR D

instead of (A OR B) AND (C OR D).

We refer to the FORALL and the EXISTS constructs as *universal* and *existential* quantifiers respectively. They introduce an object name which is said to be *bound* by the quantifier.

The symbol '!', called 'definedness', is a built-in predicate written in postfix notation. The concepts of definedness and undefinedness are an addition of the assertion language to standard first order predicate logic. When discussing stacks, we could write `NOT pop(empty)!` to indicate the fact that it is an error to pop from an empty stack and write

```
FORALL s:Stack (NOT s = empty => pop(s)! )
```

to indicate that popping from a non-empty stack always yields a defined result.

Equations are simply written as X = Y. Assertions of the form r X are predicate-applications; r must be a predicate name and X a term whose type must match the domain type of r. Finally one is always allowed to put an assertion in parentheses and an empty pair of parentheses is the same as TRUE. Object names occurring in an assertion A and not bound by a quantifier are said to occur *free* in A. A *closed assertion* is an assertion without free object names. Axioms must be closed assertions. As for terms, we give an inductive definition.

Definition. The set of *assertions* is inductively defined by the following rules:

1. TRUE is an assertion and FALSE is an assertion;
2. if A is an assertion, then so is NOT A;
3. if A and B are assertions, then A AND B, A ; B, A OR B, A => B and A <=> B are assertions;
4. if A is an assertion and x is a free object name of type T, then FORALL x:T A is an assertion and EXISTS x:T A is an assertion;
5. if X is a term, then X! is an assertion;
6. if X and Y are terms of the same type, then X = Y is an assertion;
7. if r is a predicate name with domain type T, X is a term of type T, then r X is an assertion;
8. if A is an assertion, then so is (A);
9. () is an assertion. □

Now let us discuss the interpretation (the meaning) of assertions. In order to determine whether a certain Σ-algebra M is a model of a specification S, we have to *interpret* the axioms of S with respect to M. The interpretation of the propositional and quantified assertions is as usual. For example, consider the conjunction assertion: A AND B which is the same as A ; B. The interpretation of this assertion is that it holds in M if A holds in M and B holds in M. Similarly NOT denotes negation, OR denotes disjunction, => denotes logical implication whereas <=> denotes bi-implication or logical equivalence.

The assertion FORALL x : S_1 # ... # S_m $A(x)$ holds in a model M if for all values $x_1 \in S_1^M, \ldots, x_n \in S_m^M$ we have that $A(x_1, \ldots, x_m)$ holds in M.

The assertion EXISTS x : S_1 # ... # S_m $A(x)$ holds in a model M if there are values $x_1 \in S_1^M, \ldots, x_m \in S_m^M$ such that $A(x_1, \ldots, x_m)$ holds in M.

The assertion X ! holds if the term X is defined, i.e. if it denotes an existing value.

The COLD-K assertion X = Y holds in a model M only if both X and Y are defined and equal. More precisely, if X is a term of type S_1 # ... # S_m and Y is a term of the same type then X = Y holds in M if

$$(x_1, \ldots, x_m) = (y_1, \ldots, y_m)$$

provided that both X and Y are defined. Otherwise, the equation does *not* hold in M.

The assertion r X holds in M if $r^M(x_1, \ldots, x_m)$ is true, where $(x_1, \ldots, x_m)$ is the interpretation of X. We must make a special provision for the case that X is undefined: in that case r X does not hold in M.

Finally the meaning of the assertion (A) is the same as the meaning of A. The meaning of the assertion () is just *true*, i.e. it holds in any model M.

1.7 Undefinedness and strictness

In this section we shall explain the philosophy behind the definedness and undefinedness notions. In COLD-K functions are viewed as *partial* functions. The idea that a function might be partial is consistent with the way we draw our pictures of models. Consider a term f X and a model M where X denotes an object x and $f^M(x)$ is not defined. The corresponding situation is shown in Figure 1.7 where f^M simply does not map the A object denoted by x to any B object.

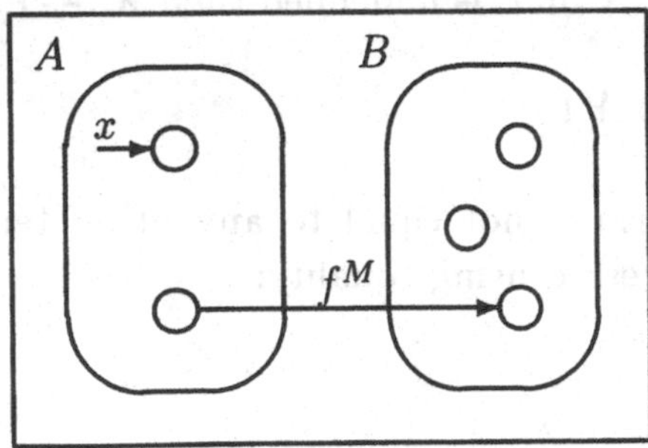

Fig 1.7. Algebra where $f^M(x)$ is not defined.

Writing X! is a way of explicitly mentioning the definedness of a term, but apart from the '!' operator, most COLD-K constructs have been designed so as to deal with definedness and undefinedness in an *implicit* way. This is motivated by the following philosophy with respect to undefinedness. In many practical situations, the undefined terms can be viewed as errors or as problematic terms. Therefore we should not encourage statements involving undefined terms. This is reflected in the *strictness* property, consisting of three sub-properties. The first and the second of these regulate the propagation of undefinedness, whereas the third one guarantees most propositions concerning undefined terms to be false.

1. *tuple construction* is strict: if X or Y is undefined then so is (X,Y). Therefore the following always holds:

   `(X,Y)! => X! AND Y!`

2. *function application* is strict: if we apply a function to an undefined argument the result will be undefined. Stated otherwise, if X is undefined then so is $f(X)$. Therefore the following always holds:

   `f(X)! => X!`

3. *predicates* are strict: if we apply a predicate to an undefined argument, the predicate will be false. Stated otherwise, if X is undefined then $r(X)$ is *false*. As a consequence, we always have:

   `r(X) => X!`

The strictness property also holds for equality when viewed as a built-in predicate of the language: if X or Y is undefined then $X = Y$ is *false*. Conversely:

`X = Y => X! AND Y!`

Hence an undefined term is not equal to any other term, or to itself, and definedness can be expressed using equality:

`X! <=> X = X`

For details concerning the approach to undefinedness, see Section 9.2.

Let us also explain the motivation for having predicates as a special language construct in COLD-K. There is an alternative, which is to always use Boolean functions. But a Boolean function r applied to an argument X can give three possible outcomes: $r(X) = $ `true`, $r(X) = $ `false` and $r(X)$ is undefined. In many applications this is a nuisance, and therefore predicates are added, which have only two possible outcomes: `TRUE` and `FALSE`. This fits in with the traditional way of reasoning and complies with the two-valued logic underlying COLD-K.

1.8 Example: specification of switches

This section is devoted to an example of a flat algebraic specification. It concerns a two-valued sort of switches. The specification will be constructed incrementally, beginning with an incomplete and naive specification which is improved step by step. In the first attempt there are only one sort definition and three function definitions – but no axiom definitions.

```
CLASS

  SORT Switch
  FUNC on     : -> Switch
  FUNC off    : -> Switch
  FUNC toggle : Switch -> Switch

END
```

This specification has many models, and Figure 1.8 below depicts one particular algebra which formally satisfies the above specification of switches. In this model the set *Switch*, interpreting the sort name `Switch` is shown to be empty. The functions `on` and `off` are both undefined, for what else could their result be when the set is empty? This explains why the functions `on`, `off` and `toggle` are not visible in Figure 1.8: no arrows can be drawn.

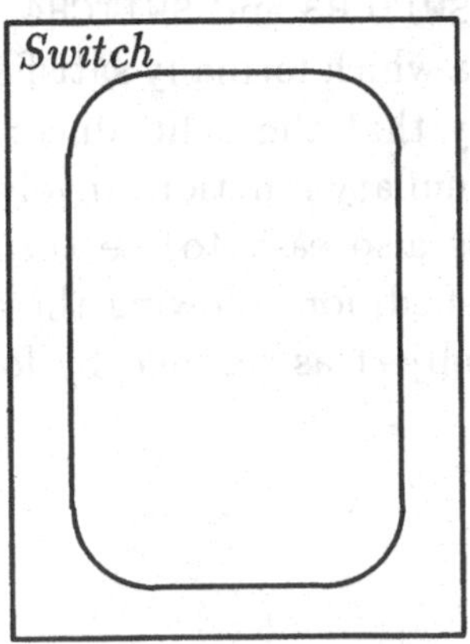

Fig 1.8. Algebra with empty sort *Switch*.

This model is certainly not what we intend and the obvious way out is to add axiom definitions to the CLASS ... END part of the specification.

```
CLASS

  SORT Switch
  FUNC on     : -> Switch
  FUNC off    : -> Switch
  FUNC toggle : Switch -> Switch

  AXIOM
  {SWITCH1} on!;
  {SWITCH2} off!;
  {SWITCH3} toggle(on)  = off;
  {SWITCH4} toggle(off) = on

END
```

Let us add one more remark about the concrete syntax. After the keyword AXIOM an assertion is given which is built from four smaller assertions, viz. on!, off! etc. These four assertions have been combined by means of the ';' connective, which is an alternative for AND.

The newly added axiom contains one assertion, whose four conjuncts are labelled SWITCH1, SWITCH2, SWITCH3 and SWITCH4 – using the { and } comment convention. SWITCH1 and SWITCH2 are definedness assertions, whereas SWITCH3 and SWITCH4 are equations.

In fact the definedness assertions for on and off are not needed because they follow by strictness from SWITCH3 and SWITCH4.

Figure 1.9 depicts an algebra which formally satisfies the above specification of switches. It is easy to verify that the definedness assertions SWITCH1 and SWITCH2 are satisfied, for both nullary functions involved yield an object which exists in the sort *Switch*. It is also easy to see that the equality assertions SWITCH3 and SWITCH4 are satisfied, for following the arrows *on* and *toggle* (in that order) leads to the same object as reached by following the *off* arrow in

Figure 1.9.

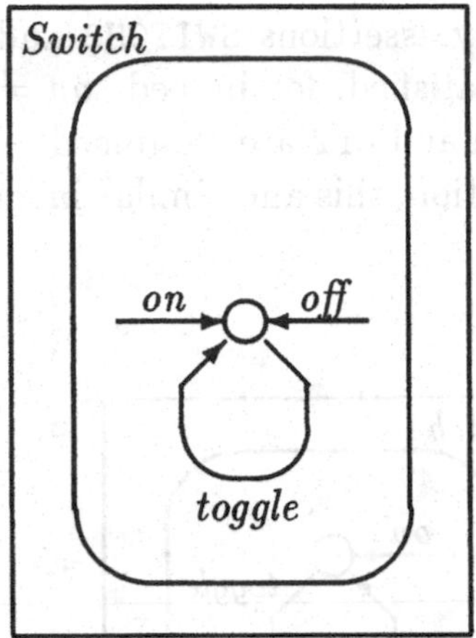

Fig 1.9. Algebra with sort *Switch* and one object.

The algebra of this figure has only one object, which acts as the interpretation of both **on** and **off**. Clearly, this was not the model we had in mind when mentioning a two-valued sort of switches. We can try and remedy this by adding an additional axiom. In this way we get the following specification. (We use two conventions for *comment* in COLD-K, viz. { ... } and % ..., as will be explained in Appendix A.)

```
CLASS

  SORT Switch
  FUNC on     : -> Switch
  FUNC off    : -> Switch
  FUNC toggle : Switch -> Switch

  AXIOM
  {SWITCH1} on!;
  {SWITCH2} off!;
  {SWITCH3} toggle(on)  = off;
  {SWITCH4} toggle(off) = on

  AXIOM  % "no confusion"
  {SWITCH5} NOT on = off

END
```

Figure 1.10 below depicts an algebra which formally satisfies the above specification of switches. It is easily verified that the definedness assertions `SWITCH1` and `SWITCH2` and the equality assertions `SWITCH3` and `SWITCH4` are satisfied. Also the axiom `SWITCH5` is satisfied, for indeed, $on \neq off$. The latter axiom avoids the situation where `on` and `off` are 'confused' – as they were in Figure 1.9. In view of this interpretation, this and similar inequality axioms are called *no confusion* axioms.

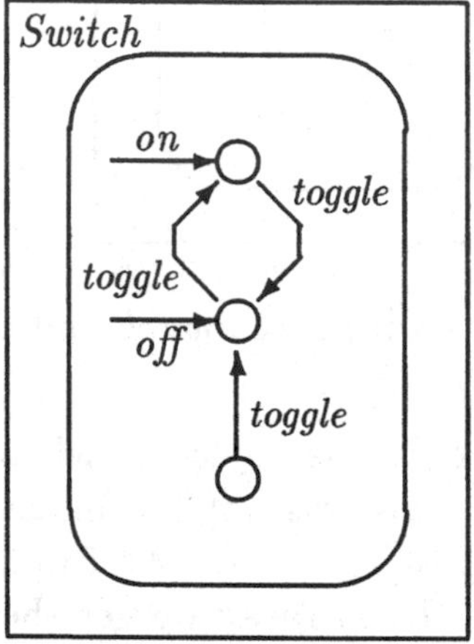

Fig 1.10. Algebra with sort *Switch* and three objects.

This algebra has distinct objects to interpret `on` and `off`. Yet there is something peculiar about this model: the existence of a third object. Again this was not the intended model. We give an improved specification, which is obtained from the previous one by adding one more axiom.

```
CLASS

  SORT Switch
  FUNC on     : -> Switch
  FUNC off    : -> Switch
  FUNC toggle : Switch -> Switch

  AXIOM
  {SWITCH1} on!;
  {SWITCH2} off!;
  {SWITCH3} toggle(on)  = off;
  {SWITCH4} toggle(off) = on
```

```
    AXIOM  % "no confusion"
    {SWITCH5} NOT on = off

    AXIOM  % "no junk"
    {SWITCH6} FORALL s:Switch ( s = on OR s = off )

END
```

Figure 1.11 below depicts an algebra which formally satisfies the above (final) specification of switches. It is easily verified that the definedness assertions SWITCH1 and SWITCH2, the equality assertions SWITCH3 and SWITCH4 and the 'no confusion' axiom SWITCH5 are satisfied. Also the axiom SWITCH6 is satisfied, for indeed, this *no junk* axiom excludes the existence of objects other than on or off.

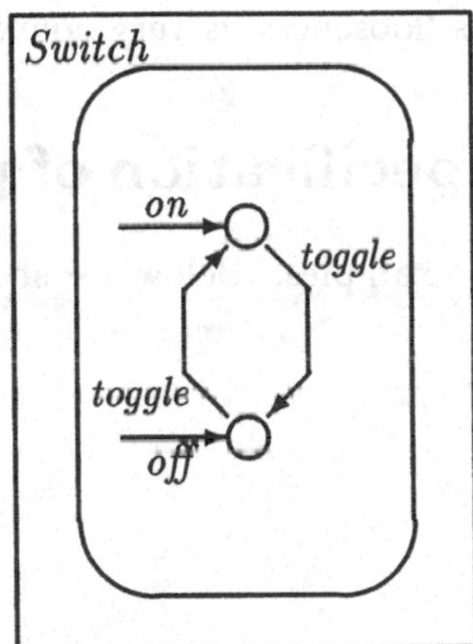

Fig 1.11. Algebra with sort *Switch* and two objects.

The algebra of this figure has precisely two objects, which are the interpretation of on and off. This is the intended model and in fact it is the *only* model satisfying our strengthened specification. As the reader probably will have noticed, the specification of switches has in fact boiled down to a specification of the Booleans.

1.9 Initial algebras

When suitable syntactic restrictions are imposed on algebraic specifications, an interesting option with respect to the meaning of the specifications arises. In that case, the meaning $\mathcal{M}(S)$ of a specification S can be defined as a single algebra. Roughly speaking, when restricting the axioms to equational axioms only, there is a unique special algebra satisfying the specification: the initial algebra. This approach has been used as a starting point for defining many algebraic specification languages (ASF [13], PLUSS [14], CLEAR [15], Act-one [16], OBJ-2 [17]). The technical details about the initial algebra approach are worked out in Section 9.3.

Readers who are familiar with the initial algebra approach might already have noticed that the COLD-K specifications given so far, seem more complex than their initial algebra counterparts: in the initial algebra approach, automatic no-junk and no-confusion principles apply, implying that fewer axioms are required. In return for that, COLD-K has a greater flexibility: one specification can have two or more essentially different models. In Section 9.3 it will be argued that sometimes this 'looseness' is very convenient.

1.10 Example: specification of pairs of switches

We proceed with a few more examples. Below we show how to describe the concept of *pair construction.*

```
CLASS

  SORT Switch
  % ...

  SORT Pair
  FUNC pair  : Switch # Switch -> Pair
  FUNC first : Pair -> Switch
  FUNC last  : Pair -> Switch

  AXIOM   FORALL s:Switch,t:Switch (
  {PAIR1} first(pair(s,t)) = s;
  {PAIR2} last (pair(s,t)) = t )

  AXIOM   FORALL p:Pair
  {PAIR3} EXISTS s:Switch,t:Switch ( p = pair(s,t) )

END
```

An object of sort `Pair` can be viewed as a 'pair of switch values'. More precisely, each object of sort `Pair` is a two-tuple (s_1, s_2) where s_1 and s_2 are objects of sort `Switch`. There are projection functions `first` and `last` to take the first and the last switch of a pair. Starting with the introduction of the sort `Switch`, we assume the full list of definitions used in our earlier specification of switches with the axioms `SWITCH1` ... `SWITCH6` (see Section 1.8). The dots (`%` ...) are used by way of abbreviation.

It should be noted that there is no need for a 'no confusion' axiom. Suppose e.g. that 'confusion' would arise in the sense that

```
pair(on,off) = pair(off,off)                                    (*)
```

then, because `first` is total, we can apply the function `first` to both sides of this equation which gives

```
first(pair(on,off)) = first(pair(off,off))
```

which can be further reduced by means of `PAIR1`. We apply this axiom twice which yields the following equation

```
on = off
```

which is in direct contradiction with the 'no confusion' axiom `SWITCH5` which states that `NOT on = off`. Therefore the assumption $(*)$ is false, i.e. the 'no confusion' property is already implied by the other axioms. In the same way we can reason for all other conceivable 'confusion' cases.

1.11 Example: specification of natural numbers

From a software engineering point of view there seems to be not much progress in specifying data types like natural numbers, integers etc. Yet, let us see if the specification language introduced so far is powerful enough to describe them. It is interesting here to quote L. Kronecker (1823-1891) who stated [18]:

> God made the integers; all the rest is the work of man.

As it will turn out, from the COLD-K point of view there is no distinguished position of the integers amongst other data types such as stacks, switches, queues, etc. We shall not address the question whether natural numbers really exist, and who made them, but we shall just give a flat algebraic specification which has the natural numbers as (one of its) model(s). The good thing about specifying natural numbers formally is that subtle questions like 'do we consider zero as a natural number?' are answered very explicitly. Furthermore, there is an advantage from a language-design point of view. One can argue that it is better to have a simple but powerful language with the data types put in a standardised library, than a language which has to include its data types as built-in constructs.

The specification below focuses on the constant zero and a successor operation. The other constants and the operations for addition etc. are not included here yet. We shall come back to these later. The following specification is a first attempt.

```
CLASS

  SORT Nat
  FUNC zero : -> Nat
  FUNC succ : Nat -> Nat

  AXIOM  FORALL m:Nat,n:Nat (
  {NAT1} zero!;
  {NAT2} succ(n)!;
  {NAT3} NOT succ(n) = zero;
  {NAT4} succ(m) = succ(n) => m = n )

END
```

Note that `NAT1` and `NAT2` are definedness assertions. `NAT3` is a 'no confusion' assertion. `NAT4` is essentially a 'no confusion' assertion as well; this is seen best by applying a simple logical transformation (known as *contraposition*) to `NAT4` which turns it into `NOT m = n => NOT succ(m) = succ(n)`. The above specification contains a tricky flaw, in the sense that the model with an empty sort is not excluded. This is due to the fact that for an empty sort T, the assertion `FORALL` x:T A is true for *any* assertion A. So the algebra of the following picture is a model as well.

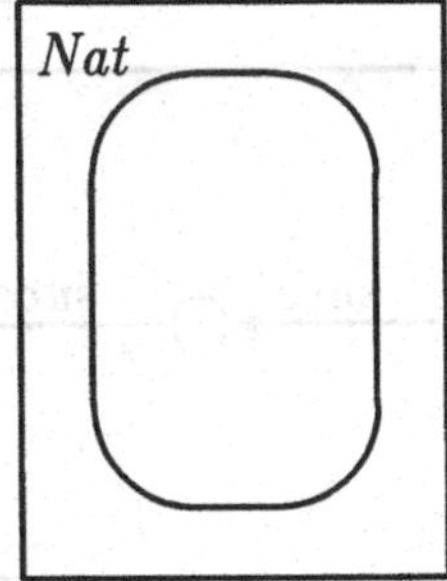

Fig 1.12. Algebra with empty sort *Nat*.

The problem is easily remedied by keeping NAT1 out of the scope of the FORALL quantifier.

```
CLASS

  SORT Nat
  FUNC zero : -> Nat
  FUNC succ : Nat -> Nat

  AXIOM
  {NAT1} zero!;
         FORALL m:Nat,n:Nat (
  {NAT2} succ(m)!;
  {NAT3} NOT succ(m) = zero;
  {NAT4} succ(m) = succ(n) => m = n )

END
```

The following algebra is a model of the above specification. It is the *standard model* of NAT1 ... NAT4 and this is the structure we had in mind when we set out to specify the natural numbers.

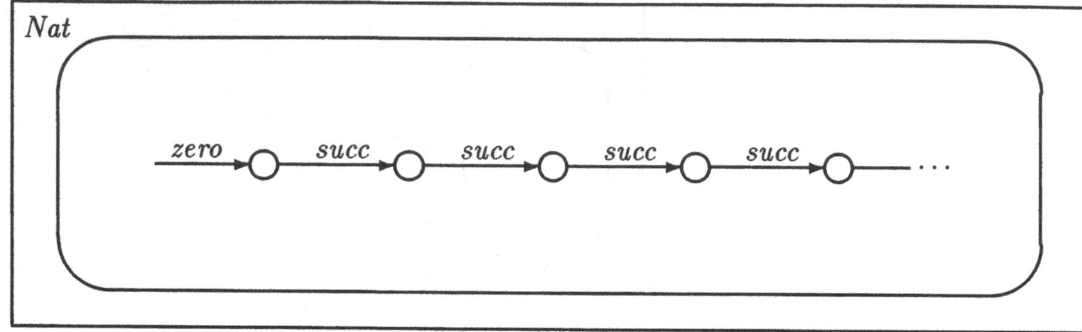

Fig 1.13. Natural numbers as a model.

But unfortunately there are still 'non-standard models' of the above specification such as the one given below.

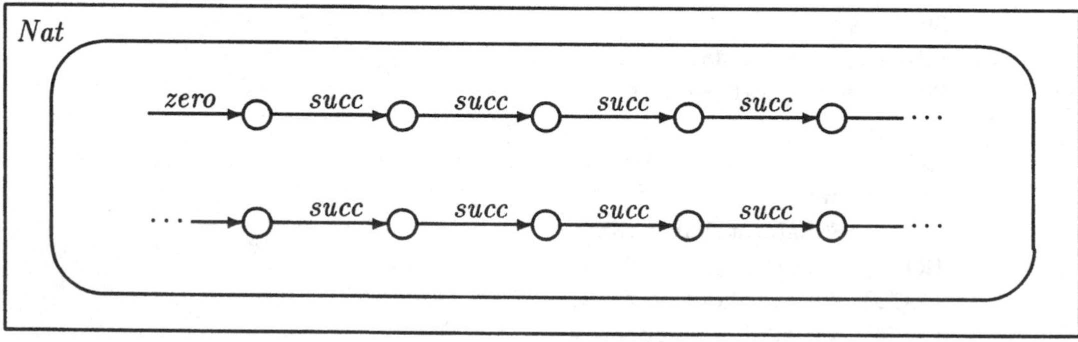

Fig 1.14. Non-standard model satisfying `NAT1`, `NAT2`, `NAT3` and `NAT4`.

The solution is to add a 'no junk' axiom. We postpone the formulation of such an axiom since difficulties arise from the fact that `Nat` is infinite. In the next chapter we introduce *inductive definitions* providing the expressive power to enforce the 'no junk' property.

Chapter 2

Setting up algebraic specifications

2.1 Introduction

This chapter is about setting up flat algebraic specifications. This involves the introduction of more COLD-K constructs and the formulation of various methodological guidelines. At the end of the previous chapter we had to conclude that we almost succeeded in specifying the natural numbers, the only problem being that the expressive power to express the minimality of `Nat` was lacking. This expressive power will be available after we have introduced the *inductive* predicate definitions below. We shall complete the example of the natural numbers and we shall investigate various technical aspects of inductive definitions - which unfortunately are quite non-trivial. In addition to inductive predicate definitions, we shall also have inductive function definitions. We address issues like 'proof obligations' for inductive definitions, consistency and completeness. Finally we give a number of complete examples of flat algebraic specifications: queues, stacks, bags and symbolic expressions.

2.2 Inductive predicate definitions

An inductive predicate definition defines a predicate as the *least* predicate satisfying some assertion (provided that this predicate exists). Before turning our attention to the syntactic machinery available in COLD-K for expressing this, we ought to explain this notion of 'least'. Therefore we shall formulate what we mean by one predicate being 'less than or equal to' another predicate.

Definition. A predicate r is *less than or equal to* a predicate q if for each argument x we have that $r(x)$ implies $q(x)$. □

We illustrate this definition by means of two unary predicates p1 and p2. We assume the sort Nat with its operations zero and succ as specified before.

```
PRED p1 : Nat

AXIOM FORALL n:Nat ( p1(n) <=> n = zero )

PRED p2 : Nat

AXIOM FORALL n:Nat ( p2(n) <=> ( n = zero OR n = succ(zero) ) )
```

In this example, the predicate p1 is less than or equal to the predicate p2. It may be helpful to think of the predicates as sets. In that case we think of p1 as the singleton set {zero} and of p2 as the set {zero, succ(zero)}. Since {zero} $\subseteq$ {zero, succ(zero)}, we clearly see that p1 is less than or equal to p2.

Recall from Section 1.5 that a predicate definition consists of a full predicate name including keyword and domain type, followed by a defining *body*. Until now we have only presented *implicit* definitions – with an empty body. Now we shall also present a form of *explicit* predicate definitions, which serve to characterize predicates in terms of other sorts, predicates and functions. The explicit definitions presented in this section are called *inductive* definitions. There is also another form of explicit predicate definitions, called *algorithmic* definitions, but the introduction of these is postponed until Chapter 4.

The body of an inductive predicate definition consists of the keyword IND followed by an assertion; so the structure of such a definition is as follows:

PRED r : S_1 # ... # S_m IND A

where A is a closed assertion. We give an example. The following inductive definition defines a predicate alt, where alt(s,t,u) expresses that the switches s, t and u 'alternate':

```
PRED alt : Switch # Switch # Switch
IND  alt(on,off,on);
     alt(off,on,off)
```

This definition is equivalent to the following axiomatic definition:

```
PRED alt : Switch # Switch # Switch
```

```
AXIOM FORALL s:Switch,t:Switch,u:Switch
      ( alt(s,t,u) <=>
        ( s = on  AND t = off AND u = on  ) OR
        ( s = off AND t = on  AND u = off )
      )
```

Inductive definitions are a versatile tool, but there is one frequently used standard application of them, which is to express the minimality of a sort. In order to eliminate the 'junk' from the models of the specification of the natural numbers, we have to express that all natural numbers belong to the set { zero, succ(zero), succ(succ(zero)), ... }. This set can be characterized by means of the inductive predicate definition:

```
PRED is_gen : Nat
IND  is_gen(zero);
     FORALL n:Nat ( is_gen(n) => is_gen(succ(n)) )
```

By adding the axiom:

```
AXIOM FORALL n:Nat ( is_gen(n) )
```

we guarantee that all natural numbers belong to the above set. In contrast with the definition of the `alt` predicate, there is no equivalent axiomatic definition of the `is_gen` predicate. This shows that the possibility to have predicates inductively defined really adds expressive power to the language. It should be noted that the definition of the predicate `is_gen` alone is not sufficient to guarantee the 'no junk' property. For this the axiom is required.

By way of methodological guideline, let us formulate a procedure to express minimality of a sort:

1. Choose a number of functions that *generate* all values of the sort; these are called the *generators* or the *constructors* of the sort.
2. Inductively define a predicate characterizing the set of all objects generated by the constructors.
3. Add an axiom expressing that all objects of the sort satisfy this predicate.

We conclude this section by giving a complete specification of the natural numbers. After the above discussion, it should be clear that the specification given below has exactly one model, which is the algebra of Figure 1.13. The algebra of Figure 1.14. fails to satisfy the last axiom and hence is not a model.

```
CLASS

  SORT Nat
  FUNC zero : -> Nat
  FUNC succ : Nat -> Nat

  PRED is_gen : Nat
  IND  is_gen(zero);
       FORALL n:Nat ( is_gen(n) => is_gen(succ(n)) )

  AXIOM
  {NAT1} zero!;
         FORALL m:Nat,n:Nat (
  {NAT2} succ(m)!;
  {NAT3} NOT succ(m) = zero;
  {NAT4} succ(m) = succ(n) => m = n );
  {NAT5} FORALL n:Nat ( is_gen(n) )

END
```

The next section is devoted to a further study of inductive definitions. In general, it is quite a task to analyse the interpretation of an inductive predicate definition with body `IND` A, when A is an arbitrary assertion. For details the reader is referred to [19] and [20]. In practice certain well-defined patterns are used for structuring A. The definition of so-called Horn clauses, to be presented in the next section, provides for such a pattern.

2.3 Horn clauses

Recall from the previous section that an inductive predicate definition defines a predicate as the *least* predicate satisfying some assertion (provided that this predicate exists). We shall not specify the meaning of an inductive predicate definition if this least predicate does not exist; our approach is that the COLD-K writer better makes sure that this least predicate exists. Below we shall provide a practical approach to this existence problem.

When defining a predicate inductively as in

`PRED` r : S_1 `#` ... `#` S_m `IND` A

we have to *prove* that there exists a least predicate r satisfying the assertion A. Let us first show that some care is indeed needed. For example, there is no least predicate r : `Switch` satisfying the following assertion:

r(on) OR r(off)

To see this, let r be the least predicate satisfying the above assertion. Since the predicates {on} and {off} both satisfy the above assertion, we have that $r \subseteq$ {on} and $r \subseteq$ {off}, and hence $r = \emptyset$. However, $\emptyset$ does not satisfy the above assertion, hence there is no least predicate.

We cannot give a simple syntactical rule to characterise precisely those assertions A which assure the existence of a least predicate. But we can give a *sufficient* syntactic rule, guaranteeing the existence of a least predicate. If we write A as a *Horn clause*, the least predicate r satisfying A always exists.

Definition. An assertion A is an r-Horn clause iff it has the form of a conjunction, where each conjunct is a universally quantified assertion of the form:

t_1 AND ... AND t_m => $r(x_1, \ldots, x_n)$

Here $x_1, \ldots, x_n$ are object names (introduced by the universal quantifiers) and each t_i is either:

- an assertion not containing r,
- or an assertion of the form $r(y_1, \ldots, y_n)$ where $y_1, \ldots, y_n$ are object names. □

There is an important proposition stating that if one adopts the syntactic pattern of Horn clauses, the least predicate is guaranteed to exist. For its proof we refer to Section 9.4.

Proposition. Let A be an r-Horn clause, then there exists a least predicate satisfying A. □

The remainder of this section is devoted to some examples of Horn clauses. First, let us have a look at the definition of the `is_gen` predicate on `Nat`:

```
PRED is_gen : Nat
IND  is_gen(zero);
     FORALL n:Nat ( is_gen(n) => is_gen(succ(n)) )
```

It is not in Horn clause form but can be rewritten to the equivalent form:

```
PRED is_gen : Nat
IND  FORALL m:Nat
     ( m = zero => is_gen(m) );
     FORALL n:Nat,m:Nat
     ( is_gen(n) AND m = succ(n) => is_gen(m) )
```

which is in Horn clause form. In order to prove the equivalence of both definitions we need axioms NAT1 and NAT2.

We proceed to a second example concerning a 'less' predicate on Nat, which can be defined by:

```
PRED less : Nat # Nat
IND  FORALL m:Nat,n:Nat
     ( less(m,succ(m))
     ; less(m,n) => less(m,succ(n))
     )
```

which is equivalent to the following definition in Horn clause form:

```
PRED less : Nat # Nat
IND  FORALL m:Nat,p:Nat
     ( p = succ(m) => less(m,p) );
     FORALL m:Nat,n:Nat,p:Nat
     ( less(m,n) AND p = succ(n) => less(m,p) )
```

Finally let us discuss a few examples of non-Horn clauses (in r):

```
FORALL s:Switch,t:Switch
( s = on AND t = off => r(s) OR r(t) )
```

This assertion does not have the syntactical pattern of a Horn clause (because of the OR construct). As it happens, no least predicate satisfying it exists, for the same reason why there is no least predicate satisfying r(on) OR r(off). The next example of a non-Horn clause is:

```
EXISTS n:Nat ( r(n) )
```

which again does not have the right syntactic pattern – because of the EXISTS quantifier. For this assertion there is no least predicate: the only candidate would be $\emptyset$, but that does not satisfy the assertion.

```
FORALL m:Nat,n:Nat ( n = succ(m) => NOT r(m,n) )
```

This is not a Horn clause because of the NOT operator, but there is a least predicate satisfying it, viz. the predicate $\emptyset$.

2.4 Inductive function definitions

In addition to inductive predicate definitions we also have inductive function definitions. These look very much the same as the inductive predicate definitions. An inductive function definition defines a function as the *least* function satisfying some assertion (provided that this function exists).

Definition. A function f is 'less than or equal to' a function g if for each argument x with $f(x)$ defined, we find that $f(x) = g(x)$. □

The body of an inductive function definition consists of the keyword IND followed by an assertion; so the structure of such a definition is as follows:

FUNC f: S_1 # ... # S_m -> V_1 # ... # V_n IND A

where A must be a closed assertion.

We give an example concerning the 'addition' function on Nat, which is inductively defined by:

```
FUNC add : Nat # Nat -> Nat
IND  FORALL m:Nat,n:Nat
     ( add(m,zero)     = m
     ; add(m,succ(n)) = succ(add(m,n))
     )
```

We give another example concerning the 'predecessor' function pred on Nat where each natural number has exactly one predecessor, except for zero whose predecessor we expect to be undefined. This function is inductively defined by:

```
FUNC pred : Nat -> Nat
IND  FORALL n:Nat
     ( pred(succ(n)) = n )
```

Inductive function definitions can be explained in terms of inductive predicate definitions, as shown below. Consider the above definition of the predecessor function on `Nat`. We associate an inductively defined predicate `is_pred` with `pred`, with the intended meaning that:

`is_pred`(m, n) iff `pred`$(m) = n$.

In other words, `is_pred` is the interpretation of the function `pred` as a predicate. We rewrite the inductive definition of the function `pred` in the obvious way to an inductive definition of the predicate `is_pred`:

```
PRED is_pred : Nat # Nat
IND  FORALL n:Nat
     ( is_pred(succ(n),n) )
```

The function `pred` can now be characterized as follows: `pred`(m) is the unique object n such that `is_pred`(m, n) holds. If this object does not exist or if it is not unique, the function is undefined. We have to *prove* that the second case cannot occur, i.e., that the predicate associated with an inductively defined function is indeed functional. In this way we arrive at a notion of 'proof obligations' for inductive definitions, which we shall summarise in the next section.

2.5 Proof obligations and applications

Consider the following inductive predicate definition:

PRED r : S_1 # ... # S_m IND A

which gives rise to the following proof obligation:

Show that there is a least predicate r satisfying A.

The corresponding proof technique is to rewrite A to an assertion A' in Horn clause form and show that A is equivalent to A'. For functions, the situation is slightly more complicated. Consider the following inductive function definition:

FUNC f: S_1 # ... # S_m -> V_1 # ... # V_n IND A

which gives rise to the following proof obligation:

Show that there is a least function f satisfying A.

The corresponding proof technique consists of three steps. The first step is to rewrite the definition of f to an inductive definition of the predicate:

PRED is_f: S_1 # ... # S_m # V_1 # ... # V_n

with the intended meaning:

is_$f(x,y)$ iff $f(x) = y$.

The second step is to show that the inductive definition of is_f is correct (see above). The third step is to show that is_f is functional in its first m arguments.

Inductive definitions can be used, among other things:

- for expressing minimality properties (cf. is_gen);
- as an alternative to axiomatic definitions (cf. pred);
- for definitions by induction over the structure of objects (cf. add);
- for defining 'tabular information' (see below).

We give an example which fits into the last category (tabular information). The program of a four-player chess tournament can be specified by means of a predicate game : Nat # Nat # Nat, where the intended meaning of game(k,m,n) is that, in round k, player m will play white against player n. The definition of game could read:

```
PRED game : Nat # Nat # Nat
IND  game(1,1,2); game(1,3,4);
     game(2,1,3); game(2,2,4);
     game(3,4,1); game(3,2,3)
```

If we have an application of the first category (cf. is_gen), then the minimality property of a sort, expressed by means of an inductively defined predicate, provides an *induction principle* for proving properties of objects of that sort. This means that besides definitions we can also give *proofs* by induction over the structure of objects.

In fact the approach of inductive definitions is slightly more general than presented here in the sense that it is allowed to have inductive (predicate and function) definitions which are mutually recursive.

2.6 Consistency and categoricity

A specification is *consistent* if it has at least one model. Intuitively, this means that the specification does not contain contradicting statements. In general inconsistencies require correction of the specification. Yet it happens quite frequently, when writing a formal specification directly from customer requirements, that the latter requirements are inconsistent, resulting in an inconsistent formal specification. Once the requirements are formalised, it is usually much easier to point out the inconsistencies, which in turn are useful input for a further dialogue with the customer about his requirements. In [21] it is argued that surprisingly, the most frequent inconsistencies cannot be considered errors; they are manifest contradications, but anybody knows how to resolve them, because a kind of implicit exception mechanism is assumed. Formal specification helps in making implicit assumptions explicit.

A specification is *categorical* if it has at most one model (modulo isomorphism). Intuitively, this means that the set of axioms is 'complete' in the following sense. When adding one more axiom a to a categorical specification, there are only two possibilities: either a is redundant, or a makes the specification inconsistent. We use the word *categorical* rather than *complete* because this is the usual terminology in mathematical logic.

Whereas consistency is a desired property of *any* specification, categoricity is only a desired property if we have a fixed model of the specification in mind, as e.g. with the switches and the natural numbers. As a rule of thumb, mathematical data types must have a categorical specification, whereas specifications of 'real-life' systems and specifications leaving implementation freedom need not.

Proving consistency amounts to constructing a concrete model (an algebra) and showing that it satisfies the specification. For example in Section 1.8 the specification with axioms SWITCH1 ... SWITCH5 is consistent because it has at least one model – as shown by construction of the algebra of Figure 1.10 with sort *Switch* and three objects.

Pointing out an inconsistency amounts to deriving a contradiction. For example if we specify the price-performance relation between the maximal speed of cars (in km/hour) and the price of cars (in K$) as

```
FUNC speed : Car -> Nat
FUNC price : Car -> Nat
AXIOM FORALL c:Car ( less(150,speed(c)) => less(20,price(c)) )
```

and add to this the customer requirement

```
FUNC my_car: -> Car
AXIOM speed(my_car) = 200 AND price(my_car) = 15
```

then this is inconsistent. To see this, note that the first axiom applies to `my_car`, whence `less(150,speed(my_car)) => less(20,price(my_car))` and so by a simple substitution `less(150,200) => less(20,15))` which yields the contradiction `TRUE => FALSE`.

Now we briefly turn our attention to *proving categoricity*. Categoricity of a specification can often be proven by means of a *normal form* lemma. For example, for the natural numbers we can prove the following lemma.

Lemma. Let A be a model of the specification of the natural numbers as given in Section 2.2. Each $x \in \mathtt{Nat}^A$ can be denoted in a unique way by a term of the form:

$$\mathtt{succ}^n\mathtt{(zero)} \quad (n \geq 0)$$

Proof. The fact that each x is of the form $\mathtt{succ}^n\mathtt{(zero)}$ follows directly from axiom `NAT5` and the inductive definition of `is_gen`. It remains to be shown that n is unique, so we assume $\mathtt{succ}^n\mathtt{(zero)} = \mathtt{succ}^m\mathtt{(zero)}$ from which we shall have to derive that $n = m$. If $m = 0$ then our assumption turns into $\mathtt{succ}^n\mathtt{(zero)} = \mathtt{zero}$ and by `NAT3` we get $n = 0$. If $m > 0$ and hence $n > 0$, we have $m = m' + 1$ and $n = n' + 1$ for suitable m' and n'. Our assumption becomes $\mathtt{succ}^{n'+1}\mathtt{(zero)} = \mathtt{succ}^{m'+1}\mathtt{(zero)}$, so $\mathtt{succ(succ}^{n'}\mathtt{(zero))} = \mathtt{succ(succ}^{m'}\mathtt{(zero))}$. Now we can apply `NAT4` to get $\mathtt{succ}^{n'}\mathtt{(zero)} = \mathtt{succ}^{m'}\mathtt{(zero)}$. In this way we can proceed, applying `NAT4` m' more times until we are in a position to apply `NAT3` again. This shows that $n' = m'$ and hence $n = m$. □

Using this lemma we can prove that two models A and B of the specification of the natural numbers are 'essentially' the same. Therefore we consider a mapping ϕ from $\mathtt{Nat}^A$ to $\mathtt{Nat}^B$ which is defined by:

$$\phi((\mathtt{succ}^A)^n(\mathtt{zero}^A)) = (\mathtt{succ}^B)^n(\mathtt{zero}^B)$$

Note that this is an acceptable definition for ϕ only because of the uniqueness of n. We shall show that this ϕ 'preserves structure'.

There is one nullary function (`zero`), for which preservation of structure by ϕ means $\phi(\mathtt{zero}^A) = \mathtt{zero}^B$ which follows immediately from the definition of ϕ (take $n = 0$). Furthermore there is one unary function (`succ`), for which preservation of structure boils down to

$$\phi(\mathtt{succ}^A(x)) = \mathtt{succ}^B(\phi(x)).$$

Let $x = (\mathtt{succ}^A)^n(\mathtt{zero}^A)$. Then $\phi(\mathtt{succ}^A(x)) = \phi((\mathtt{succ}^A)^{n+1}(\mathtt{zero}^A))$ which by definition of ϕ equals $(\mathtt{succ}^B)^{n+1}(\mathtt{zero}^B) = \mathtt{succ}^B((\mathtt{succ}^B)^n(\mathtt{zero}^B))$ which again by definition of ϕ equals $\mathtt{succ}^B(\phi(x))$.

We also claim that ϕ maps each object from A to exactly one object of B and conversely. These properties follow from the definition of ϕ and the lemma. Altogether this shows that there is a one-to-one correspondence between objects of A and B such that this correspondence preserves all equalities that hold in A and B. So A and B are essentially the same.

For readers which are already familiar with the mathematical notion of homomorphism, we can explain the situation as follows: A and B are isomorphic, which is demonstrated by the isomorphism ϕ (an isomorphism is a homomorphism which is surjective and injective). The so-called 'structure preservation' of ϕ just means that ϕ is a homomorphism.

2.7 How to set up an algebraic specification

Below we give a list of steps that can be followed when setting up an algebraic specification. This list is not *prescriptive* but it is just meant as a methodological guideline and certainly other useful approaches exist as well.

1. Give the signature of the algebra and the intended interpretation of the sorts, predicates and functions in the signature.
2. For those sorts intended to be minimal, choose a minimal set of *constructors*, i.e., a set of functions sufficient to generate all objects in the sorts to be defined.
3. Formulate axioms specifying the definedness and equality predicates on the sorts in the proper way. If necessary, add auxiliary sorts and operations.
4. For each minimal sort to be defined, add an inductively defined auxiliary predicate expressing that an object of that sort can be constructed by means of the constructor functions.
5. Use the above predicates to add axioms expressing that the sorts to be defined are minimal.
6. Define the remaining operations inductively or by means of axioms.

When mentioning the *intended interpretation* we clearly refer to an informal notion. It is important to have at least some informal understanding of the sorts, predicates and functions involved before trying to formalise them – just to avoid ending up with formal nonsense.

Referring to the theory of Horn clauses of Section 2.3 and the definitions of the notions consistency and categoricity of this section, we have the following points which are to be checked:

1. *Validity:* does the formal specification correspond with our intuition about the subject matter?
2. *Correctness:* are the inductive definitions OK?
3. *Consistency:* is there a model satisfying the axioms?
4. *Categoricity:* should there be at most one model satisfying the axioms and, if so, is there at most one such model?

2.8 Example: specification of queues

In this section we shall give an algebraic specification of queues. These occur frequently in connection with operating systems and other systems that regulate the dynamic allocation of scarce resources to users. When a user has requested a resource that is not available yet, the user's request is temporarily put in a queue, which serves to administrate the waiting line of users for that resource.

In the formal specification to be set up below we abstract away from the particular details of the user requests and instead we just introduce a sort of items, i.e. the things that can be put in a queue. Therefore we shall introduce two sorts `Item` and `Queue`. We also need the sort `Nat` of natural numbers, for we want to have a notion of *the length of a queue*. We adopt the following signature:

```
SORT Nat,
FUNC zero : -> Nat,
FUNC succ : Nat -> Nat,
----------------------------------------
SORT Item,
SORT Queue,
FUNC empty : -> Queue,
FUNC put   : Item # Queue -> Queue,
FUNC geti  : Queue -> Item,
FUNC getq  : Queue -> Queue,
FUNC len   : Queue -> Nat
```

Fig 2.1. Signature of the specification of queues.

The intended interpretation of the elements of this signature is as follows. `Item` is the set of items to be stored in queues and `Queue` is the set of queues. `empty` is the empty queue and **put**(i, q) is the new queue obtained by putting item i in queue q. **geti**(q) is the item obtained by getting an element from queue q whereas **getq**(q) is the new queue obtained after getting an element from queue q. Finally **len**(q) is the number of items in queue q.

We give the specification below, but we do not repeat all formal details of **Nat**.

```
CLASS

  SORT Nat
  % ...
  SORT Item
  SORT Queue
  FUNC empty : -> Queue
  FUNC put   : Item # Queue -> Queue

  AXIOM
  {Q1} empty!;
       FORALL i:Item,j:Item,q:Queue,r:Queue (
  {Q2} put(i,q)!;
  {Q3} NOT put(i,q) = empty;
  {Q4} put(i,q) = put(j,r) => i = j AND q = r )

  PRED is_gen : Queue
  IND  is_gen(empty);
       FORALL i:Item,q:Queue
       ( is_gen(q) => is_gen(put(i,q)) )

  AXIOM
  {Q5} FORALL q:Queue ( is_gen(q) )

  FUNC geti : Queue -> Item
  IND  FORALL i:Item,j:Item,q:Queue
       ( geti(put(i,empty))      = i
       ; geti(put(i,put(j,q))) = geti(put(j,q))
       )

  FUNC getq : Queue -> Queue
  IND  FORALL i:Item,j:Item,q:Queue
       ( getq(put(i,empty))      = empty
       ; getq(put(i,put(j,q))) = put(i,getq(put(j,q)))
       )
```

```
    FUNC len : Queue -> Nat
    IND  len(empty) = zero;
         FORALL i:Item,q:Queue
         ( len(put(i,q)) = succ(len(q)) )

END
```

The constructor functions for queues are **empty** and **put**. The axioms Q1 ... Q5 are very similar to the axioms NAT1 ... NAT5 for natural numbers. Clearly **empty** plays a role similar to **zero** whereas put(i,...) occurs instead of succ(...).

We should check the validity, correctness, consistency and categoricity of the specification, as mentioned before. With respect to the *validity*, the reader should see if this specification corresponds with the intuition about queues. Note the fact that there are two 'get' operations, namely geti and getq. It can be argued that it is more natural to have these combined in one operation, like getq : Queue -> Item # Queue. On the other hand, the current operations are more elementary and somewhat easier to use.

With respect to the *correctness*, we should ask whether the inductive definitions are OK (in particular, the definitions of the functions geti, getq and len). Let us take the function geti as an example. We show a sequence of transformations starting with geti as a function, followed by the corresponding predicate is_geti. After that the body of this predicate definition is transformed into an equivalent Horn clause.

```
FUNC geti : Queue -> Item
IND  FORALL i:Item,j:Item,q:Queue
     ( geti(put(i,empty))      = i
     ; geti(put(i,put(j,q))) = geti(put(j,q))
     )

PRED is_geti : Queue # Item
IND  FORALL i:Item,j:Item,k:Item,q:Queue
     ( is_geti(put(i,empty),i)
     ; is_geti(put(j,q),k) => is_geti(put(i,put(j,q)),k)
     )

PRED is_geti : Queue # Item
IND  FORALL i:Item,j:Item,k:Item,q:Queue,r:Queue,s:Queue
     ( q = put(i,empty) => is_geti(q,i)
     ; put(j,q) = s AND put(i,s) = r AND is_geti(s,k)
       => is_geti(r,k)
     )
```

Finally we must check that this predicate is functional, i.e. for each queue q there must be at most one item i such that $\texttt{is\_geti}(q,i)$. Suppose that $\texttt{is\_geti}(q,i)$ and $\texttt{is\_geti}(q,j)$ both hold, then it follows from the minimality of the inductive definition of `is_geti` that at least one of the following four cases applies:

1. $q = \texttt{put}(i,\texttt{empty})$,
   $q = \texttt{put}(j,\texttt{empty})$;

2. $q = \texttt{put}(i,\texttt{empty})$,
   $\texttt{put}(n,r) = s$ AND $\texttt{put}(m,s) = q$ AND $\texttt{is\_geti}(s,j)$ (for some m,n,r,s);

3. $\texttt{put}(n,r) = s$ AND $\texttt{put}(m,s) = q$ AND $\texttt{is\_geti}(s,i)$ (for some m,n,r,s),
   $q = \texttt{put}(j,\texttt{empty})$;

4. $\texttt{put}(n,r) = s$ AND $\texttt{put}(m,s) = q$ AND $\texttt{is\_geti}(s,i)$,
   $\texttt{put}(n',r') = s'$ AND $\texttt{put}(m',s') = q$ AND $\texttt{is\_geti}(s,j)$.

Cases 2 and 3 lead to a contradiction, so only cases 1 and 4 apply. Using induction on the construction of q we can now prove that $i = j$ for all q.

Consistency can be shown as follows. We construct a model by means of sequences of the form $\langle\rangle$, $\langle i_1\rangle$, $\langle i_1, i_2\rangle$, etc. We interpret `empty` as $\langle\rangle$ and a term of the form $\texttt{put}(i,q)$ as the sequence $\langle i, i_1, \ldots, i_n\rangle$ where $\langle i_1, \ldots, i_n\rangle$ is the interpretation of q. Now it can be verified that this model makes the axioms `Q1` ... `Q5` hold. The inductive definitions cannot disturb the consistency because they define `geti`, `getq` and `len` without putting any constraints on `empty`, `put` or `is_gen`.

For *categoricity* we should ask if there should be at most one model satisfying the axioms. Since these queues are a kind of mathematical data type rather than 'real-life' systems, we feel the specification should be categorical. In order to prove this we employ the following lemma.

Lemma. Each queue can be written in a unique way as a sequence of put operations on the empty queue. In particular, let A be a model of the specification of queues as given above. Each $x \in \texttt{Queue}^A$ can be written in a unique way as a term of the form

$$\texttt{put}^A(i_1, \texttt{put}^A(i_2, \ldots\ \texttt{put}^A(i_n, \texttt{empty}^A)\ldots)) \quad (n \geq 0)$$

The proof proceeds along the same lines as for the corresponding case of natural numbers. □

Using this lemma we can prove that two models A and B of the specification of the queues are isomorphic.

It can be observed that in the above specification we employed two distinct styles, viz. an *axiomatic* style for the constructor operations **empty** and **put** whereas we used *inductive* definitions for the remaining operations. There is an alternative specification of queues which is semantically equivalent to the above specification but which is exclusively based on axioms, avoiding inductive definitions. We give this alternative below.

```
CLASS

 SORT Nat
 % ...
 SORT Item
 SORT Queue
 FUNC empty : -> Queue
 FUNC put   : Item # Queue -> Queue
 FUNC geti  : Queue -> Item
 FUNC getq  : Queue -> Queue
 FUNC len   : Queue -> Nat

 AXIOM
 {Q1} empty!;
      FORALL i:Item,j:Item,q:Queue,r:Queue (
 {Q2} put(i,q)!;
 {Q3} NOT put(i,q) = empty;
 {Q4} put(i,q) = put(j,r) => i = j AND q = r )

 PRED is_gen : Queue
 IND  is_gen(empty);
      FORALL i:Item,q:Queue
      ( is_gen(q) => is_gen(put(i,q)) )

 AXIOM
 {Q5} FORALL q:Queue ( is_gen(q) )

 AXIOM
 {Q6 } NOT geti(empty)!;
 {Q7 } NOT getq(empty)!;
       FORALL i:Item,j:Item,q:Queue (
 {Q8 } geti(put(i,empty))       = i;
 {Q9 } geti(put(i,put(j,q))) = geti(put(j,q));
 {Q10} getq(put(i,empty))       = empty;
 {Q11} getq(put(i,put(j,q))) = put(i,getq(put(j,q)));
```

```
    {Q12} len(empty)              = zero;
    {Q13} len(put(i,q))           = succ(len(q)) )

  END
```

Let us discuss this alternative specification. Its first five axioms Q1 ... Q5 are the same as before. The axioms Q6 to Q13 serve to replace the inductive definitions employed before. Some care is needed here because one cannot just copy the bodies of the earlier inductive definitions and give them the status of an axiom. The axioms Q8 ... Q13 correspond with clauses used before, but the axioms Q6 and Q7 are new. They correspond with the statement that was implicit in the IND construct, viz. the statement that the function is undefined, unless its definedness follows from the body of the definition.

Note that the axioms Q2, Q3 and Q4 are derivable from the others. A potential danger of using many axioms is that the specification becomes inconsistent. The fact that some of the axioms depend on other axioms is already an indication that it is hard to have a clear overview over this many axioms. This should be contrasted with inductive definitions that cannot give rise to inconsistencies.

2.9 Example: specification of stacks

In this section we shall give an algebraic specification of 'stacks', which are often employed as a part of program execution systems ranging from simple calculators to evaluate arithmetical expressions, up to the run-time environments for modern programming languages. Typically the stacks serve to store intermediate program results and/or return-addresses of program fragments to be resumed later. The typical property of a stack is that when retrieving items from it, the order in which these items are retrieved is the reverse of the order in which they were put onto the stack.

The example of stacks is useful for several reasons. The first reason is that it is a standard example, which has been worked out for almost every specification language. Another reason is that it will turn out to be interesting to compare the axioms of stacks with the axioms of the natural numbers: by exploiting the presence of a pop operation, only four axioms are needed instead of five (as for NAT). We must stress that the advantage of formal specification techniques is not just that they allow us to specify stacks so nicely. The advantage is that we can specify large and really complex systems to be designed and used in practice. The stack specification just serves as an example which is a small step on our way to reaching that objective.

In the formal specification we abstract away from the details of the application areas and instead we just introduce a sort of items, i.e. the things that can be put onto a stack. We need the sorts `Item` and `Stack` and we adopt the following signature:

```
SORT Item,
SORT Stack,
FUNC empty : -> Stack,
FUNC push  : Item # Stack -> Stack,
FUNC pop   : Stack -> Item # Stack
```

Fig 2.2. Signature of the specification of stacks.

The intended interpretation is as follows. `Item` is the set of items to be stored and `Stack` is the set of stacks. `empty` is the empty stack. $\texttt{push}(i, s)$ is the new stack obtained by pushing item i on stack s whereas $\texttt{pop}(s)$ denotes both the item and the new stack obtained by retrieving (popping) an element from stack s.

```
CLASS

  SORT Item
  SORT Stack
  FUNC empty : -> Stack
  FUNC push  : Item # Stack -> Stack
  FUNC pop   : Stack -> Item # Stack

  AXIOM
  {STACK1} empty!;
  {STACK2} NOT pop(empty)!;
  {STACK3} FORALL u:Item # Stack
           ( pop(push(u)) = u )

  PRED is_gen : Stack
  IND  is_gen(empty);
       FORALL i:Item,s:Stack
       ( is_gen(s) => is_gen(push(i,s)) )

  AXIOM {STACK4} FORALL s:Stack ( is_gen(s) )

END
```

The constructor functions for stacks are `empty` and `push`. If we compare this specification with the specification of natural numbers, then we can observe a certain analogy where `empty` corresponds with `zero` and `push`($i, \ldots$) corresponds with `succ`(...). In this analogy axiom `STACK1` matches axiom `NAT1`. One might wonder why the analogy does not extend to the other operations, i.e. why we do not need axioms such as:

```
AXIOM  FORALL s:Stack,t:Stack,i:Item,j:Item (
{STACK2'} push(i,s)!;
{STACK3'} NOT push(i,s) = empty;
{STACK4'} push(i,s) = push(j,t) => i = j AND s = t )
```

As it turns out, by employing the `pop` operation in the axioms, we do not need `STACK2'`, `STACK3'` and `STACK4'`. They are derivable from `STACK2` and `STACK3`. In particular, `STACK2'` follows from `STACK3` by strictness. `STACK3'` follows from `STACK2` and `STACK3`, for suppose `push(i,s) = empty`, then by `STACK3` we have that `pop(empty) = (i,s)` whence by strictness `pop(empty)!` contradicting `STACK2`. `STACK4'` states that `push` is injective, but this is expressed in an alternative way by exhibiting its inverse, which is `pop`, as can be seen from `STACK3`. We leave the validity, correctness, consistency and categoricity checks to the reader.

2.10 Example: specification of bags

In this section we shall give an algebraic specification of 'bags', which are somewhat similar to mathematical sets, but with a notion of *multiplicity* for the elements. Bags are also called multisets. An example where bags could be useful is when modelling a mail system where one and the same message can arrive several times; if the order of arrival is irrelevant but the multiplicity of the messages *is* relevant, then the mailbox should be viewed as a bag of messages. In the formal specification we abstract away from the messages, introducing a sort of items.

```
SORT Nat,
FUNC zero : -> Nat,
FUNC succ : Nat -> Nat,
-----------------------------------
SORT Item,
SORT Bag,
PRED is_in : Item # Bag,
FUNC empty : -> Bag,
FUNC ins   : Item # Bag -> Bag,
FUNC rem   : Item # Bag -> Bag,
FUNC union : Bag  # Bag -> Bag,
FUNC isect : Bag  # Bag -> Bag,
FUNC mult  : Item # Bag -> Nat
```

Fig 2.3. Signature of the specification of bags.

The intended interpretation is as follows. `Item` is the set of items to be stored and `Bag` is the set of bags (= multisets). `is_in`(i, b) means that i is contained in bag b. `empty` denotes the empty bag. `ins`(i, b) is the new bag obtained by inserting item i in bag b. `rem`(i, b) is the new bag obtained by removing item i from bag b. `union`(b, c) is the union of bags b and c. `isect`(b, c) is the intersection of bags b and c. `mult`(i, b) is the number of occurrences (the *multiplicity*) of item i in bag b.

```
CLASS

  SORT Nat
  % ...
  SORT Item
  SORT Bag
  FUNC empty : -> Bag
  FUNC ins   : Item # Bag -> Bag
  PRED is_in : Item # Bag

  AXIOM
  {BAG1} empty!;
  {BAG2} FORALL i:Item,b:Bag ( ins(i,b)! )

  AXIOM  FORALL i:Item,j:Item,b:Bag,c:Bag (
  {BAG3} NOT is_in(i,empty);
  {BAG4} is_in(i,ins(j,b)) <=> i = j OR is_in(i,b);
  {BAG5} ins(i,ins(j,b)) = ins(j,ins(i,b));
  {BAG6} ins(i,b) = ins(i,c) => b = c )
```

```
    PRED is_gen: Bag
    IND  is_gen(empty);
         FORALL i:Item,b:Bag
         ( is_gen(b) => is_gen(ins(i,b)) )

    AXIOM {BAG7} FORALL b:Bag ( is_gen(b) )

    FUNC rem : Item # Bag -> Bag
    IND  FORALL i:Item,j:Item,b:Bag
         ( rem(i,empty) = empty
         ; rem(i,ins(i,b)) = b
         ; NOT i = j => rem(i,ins(j,b)) = ins(j,rem(i,b))
         )

    FUNC union : Bag # Bag -> Bag
    IND  FORALL b:Bag
         ( union(b,empty) = b );
         FORALL i:Item,b:Bag,c:Bag
         ( union(b,ins(i,c)) = ins(i,union(b,c)) )

    FUNC isect : Bag # Bag -> Bag
    IND  FORALL i:Item,b:Bag,c:Bag
         ( isect(b,empty) = empty );
         FORALL i:Item,b:Bag,c:Bag
         ( isect(ins(i,b),ins(i,c)) = ins(i,isect(b,c))
         ; NOT is_in(i,b) => isect(b,ins(i,c)) = isect(b,c)
         )

    FUNC mult : Item # Bag -> Nat
    IND  FORALL i:Item,j:Item,b:Bag
         ( mult(i,empty) = zero
         ; mult(i,ins(i,b)) = succ(mult(i,b))
         ; NOT i = j => mult(i,ins(j,b)) = mult(i,b)
         )

  END
```

The constructor functions for bags are `empty` and `ins`. It might be tempting to think after having seen the examples of natural numbers, queues and stacks, that bags are just more of the same and that therefore the axioms could follow precisely the same pattern. One might start writing definedness axioms for `empty` and `ins` like `BAG1` and `BAG2`, which is o.k., and after that continue with axioms like

```
AXIOM FORALL b:Bag,c:Bag,i:Item,j:Item (
{BAG3'} NOT ins(i,b) = empty;
{BAG4'} ins(i,b) = ins(j,c) => i = j AND b = c )            % wrong
```

but this is not o.k. `BAG4'` does not correspond with our intuition about bags, for assume distinct items 1 and 2, then `ins(1,ins(2,empty))` must denote the same bag as `ins(2,ins(1,empty))`; this is contradicted by axiom `BAG4'`. We must reject `BAG4'` and in fact we find that the precise formulation of a suitable set of axioms for bags is a subtle matter. The axioms must involve the bag membership operation `is_in` and the right axioms `BAG3` and `BAG4` precisely describe the relationship between `is_in` and the constructor functions `empty` and `ins`, respectively. After that, two more axioms about `ins` are needed: `BAG5` and `BAG6`. Axiom `BAG5` expresses that the order of the elements is irrelevant. `BAG6` makes sure that bags do not behave as normal sets: for sets we have `ins`$(i, \emptyset)$ = `ins`$(i, \{i\})$ but $\emptyset \neq \{i\}$, so `BAG6` does not hold for sets.

Note that `BAG3'`, although not being wrong, has become a consequence of `BAG3` and `BAG4`. To see this, assume that `ins`(i, b) = `empty` for some i and b. By (`<=`) of `BAG4` we find that `is_in`$(i$,`ins`$(i, b))$ and so by substitution `is_in`$(i$,`empty`$)$, contradicting `BAG3`. Therefore `ins`$(i, b) \neq$ `empty`.

Axiom `BAG7` is a standard no-junk axiom, using the inductively defined `is_gen` predicate. In this way we obtain the right `empty`, `ins` and `is_in` operations and after that all other operations are defined inductively.

2.11 Example: specification of symbolic expressions

In this section we shall give an algebraic specification of 'symbolic expressions', which constitute an important class of terms in the programming language LISP [22].

```
SORT Sxp,
FUNC nil  : -> Sxp,
FUNC cons : Sxp # Sxp -> Sxp,
FUNC car  : Sxp -> Sxp,
FUNC cdr  : Sxp -> Sxp,
PRED atom : Sxp
```

Fig 2.4. Signature of the specification of symbolic expressions.

The intended interpretation is as follows. **Sxp** is the set of symbolic expressions, which are a kind of LISP term. They can be viewed as trees and it is customary in LISP to write them as terms with parentheses. **nil** denotes the LISP term **nil**, which is the only atomic term. **cons**(x, y) denotes the LISP term (**cons** x y) and similarly **car**(x) denotes (**car** x) and **cdr**(x) denotes (**cdr** x). The function **cons** is a kind of tree constructor whereas **car**(x) yields the left subtree of x and **cdr**(x) yields the right subtree. **atom**(x) holds precisely if x is an atomic term. The identifiers **car** and **cdr** have a historical background, originally abbreviating 'contents of address register' and 'contents of data register', referring to one of the early implementations of the language.

```
CLASS

  SORT Sxp
  FUNC nil  : -> Sxp
  FUNC cons : Sxp # Sxp -> Sxp

  AXIOM
  {SXP1} nil!;
         FORALL x:Sxp,y:Sxp,u:Sxp,v:Sxp (
  {SXP2} cons(x,y)!;
  {SXP3} NOT cons(x,y) = nil;
  {SXP4} cons(x,y) = cons(u,v) => x = u AND y = v )

  PRED is_gen : Sxp
  IND  is_gen(nil);
       FORALL x:Sxp,y:Sxp
       ( is_gen(x) AND is_gen(y) => is_gen(cons(x,y)) )

  AXIOM {SXP5} FORALL x:Sxp ( is_gen(x) )

  FUNC car : Sxp -> Sxp
  IND  FORALL x:Sxp,y:Sxp
       ( car(cons(x,y)) = x )

  FUNC cdr : Sxp -> Sxp
  IND  FORALL x:Sxp,y:Sxp
       ( cdr(cons(x,y)) = y )

  PRED atom : Sxp
  IND  atom(nil)

END
```

The constructor functions for symbolic expressions are `nil` and `cons`. The reader will certainly recognise that the axioms have the same structure as the axioms for the natural numbers. It is left as an exercise to check the validity, correctness, consistency and categoricity of the specification.

Chapter 3

Structuring algebraic specifications

3.1 Introduction

What we have seen so far were *flat specifications*, i.e., descriptions of the following form:

```
CLASS
  definitions
END
```

This is fine for small examples, but becomes prohibitive as soon as we are dealing with systems of realistic size. What we need are ways of *structuring* large specifications into independent parts and ways of *reusing* parts that have already been defined.

The situation is very similar to the situation with programming languages. Most of the earlier programming languages required their programs to be structured as a long list of type definitions, variable declarations and definitions of functions and procedures. This is for example the case in LISP and Pascal. Later it was recognised that often one wants a certain grouping, putting together type definitions and variable declarations with the definitions of the functions and procedures operating on them. In the area of programming languages this has led to the introduction of 'modules' in MODULA or 'packages' as they are called in Ada. In the area of specification languages the very same idea has become known as 'abstract data types'.

The facilities to *structure* large specifications into independent parts and to *reuse* parts already defined are provided by the *modularisation* mechanisms of COLD-K. Modular specifications in COLD-K are called *modular schemes* or just *schemes*.

We employ a two-step approach for assigning a meaning (= semantics) to the language constructs presented in this chapter. There is a procedure to reduce each scheme to a standardised form called its *normal form.* A normal form specification consists of an 'export signature' together with a flat specification and is denoted as **EXPORT** *signature* **FROM CLASS** *definitions* **END**. In the sequel we shall use the notation $\langle \Sigma, \mathcal{D} \rangle$ to denote the normal-form specification consisting of the export signature Σ and the set of definitions $\mathcal{D}$. The normal-form specification denoted by a modular scheme K will be indicated as $\langle \Sigma_K, \mathcal{D}_K \rangle$. We employ the word *denotation* for the transformation from a modular scheme to its normal-form specification. The process of assigning a denotation can be described by a term-rewriting system, yielding a unique normal-form specification for each scheme. It is the first step of our two-step approach. Then the normal-form specification can be interpreted in a model-oriented way as will be explained in Section 3.7. This is the second step. We sketch the process of determining the meaning of schemes as follows:

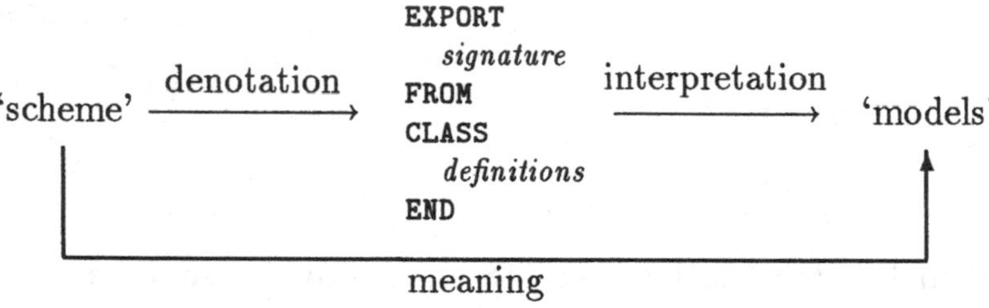

Below an overview of the various kinds of modular schemes to be introduced in this chapter is given (Table 3.1). In this table, $D_1 \ldots D_n$ are definitions, K and L are schemes, Σ is a signature, ρ is a 'renaming' and finally z is a scheme name.

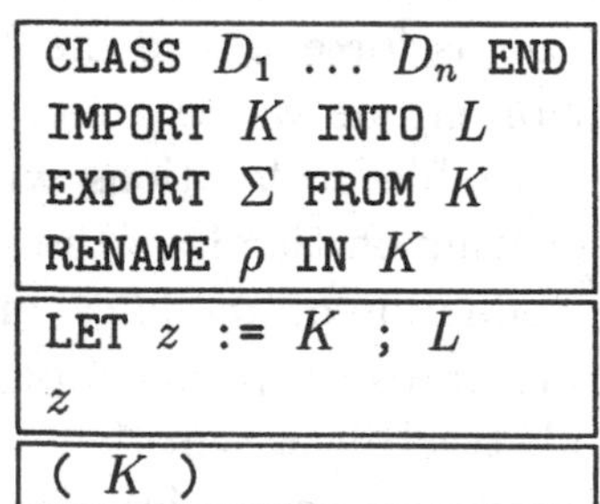

CLASS $D_1 \ldots D_n$ END
IMPORT K INTO L
EXPORT Σ FROM K
RENAME ρ IN K
LET z := K ; L
z
(K)

Table 3.1. Survey of all modular schemes.

In addition to flat schemes, export schemes, import schemes, etc. which will each be presented in a separate section, there are two rather obvious ways to construct schemes. The first way is to write down the *name* of a scheme introduced by an abbreviation scheme – obeying the scope rules. The second way is to put a modular scheme between parentheses. The definition of 'modular scheme' is meant to be *inductive* in the sense that the set of all modular schemes is the *smallest* set closed under the use of the scheme construction operators indicated in Table 3.1.

3.2 Flat schemes

The flat scheme is the simplest and most direct way of writing down a COLD-K specification. It is built by means of two keywords `CLASS` and `END` embracing a list of definitions $D_1 \ \ldots \ D_n$ of sorts, functions, predicates and axioms. Its purpose is to 'package' the definitions $D_1, \ldots, D_n$, yielding a kind of basic building block to be used for for composing more complex modular schemes. More precisely, if $D_1 \ \ldots \ D_n$ are definitions, then

`CLASS` $D_1 \ \ldots \ D_n$ `END`

is a *flat* scheme denoting the normal-form specification $\langle \Sigma_S, \mathcal{D}_S \rangle$ defined by:

Σ_S = the signature consisting of all names defined in $D_1, \ldots, D_n$,
$\mathcal{D}_S = \{D_1, \ldots, D_n\}$.

By this definition, the export signature of a flat scheme is precisely equal to the signature introduced in the $D_1 \ \ldots \ D_n$ (hence, referring to a notion of 'hiding' which will be described in the next section, we could say that a flat scheme has no hidden sorts or operations). The following is an example of a flat scheme (see Section 1.8).

```
CLASS

  SORT Switch
  FUNC on     : -> Switch
  FUNC off    : -> Switch
  FUNC toggle : Switch -> Switch

  AXIOM
  {SWITCH1} on!;
  {SWITCH2} off!;
  {SWITCH3} toggle(on)  = off;
  {SWITCH4} toggle(off) = on;
  {SWITCH5} NOT on = off;
```

```
  {SWITCH6} FORALL s:Switch ( s = on OR s = off )

END
```

3.3 Export schemes

An export scheme is essentially a modular scheme provided with an explicit export list. The purpose of this is to 'hide' certain sorts, functions and predicates in the sense that they cannot be used outside of the scheme. This can be viewed as a kind of 'information hiding'. An *export scheme* S has the following form:

EXPORT Σ FROM K

where Σ is a signature and K is an arbitrary scheme. It denotes the normal-form specification $\langle \Sigma_S, \mathcal{D}_S \rangle$ defined by:

$$\Sigma_S = \Sigma \cap \Sigma_K,$$
$$\mathcal{D}_S = \mathcal{D}_K.$$

The export signature Σ may contain names that are not defined in the scheme K; these names are simply discarded. Let us add a remark about the concrete syntax employed in COLD-K. After the keyword EXPORT a signature is given, which is a set, whose elements are separated by commas. After the keyword CLASS however, a list of definitions is given which, does not involve a separation symbol. We give an example of an export scheme and its denotation. Consider the following scheme

```
EXPORT
  SORT A,
  FUNC a : -> A,
  FUNC b : -> A
FROM
CLASS
  SORT A
  FUNC a : -> A
  FUNC c : -> A
END
```

The above scheme is equivalent to the normal-form specification:

```
EXPORT
  SORT A,
  FUNC a : -> A
FROM
CLASS
  SORT A
  FUNC a : -> A
  FUNC c : -> A
END
```

The function c is hidden. Another example of an export scheme is given below. Here the hiding mechanism provided by the export scheme is used to hide an auxiliary predicate `is_gen` in the definition of natural numbers.

```
EXPORT
  SORT Nat,
  FUNC zero : -> Nat,
  FUNC succ : Nat -> Nat
FROM
CLASS

  SORT Nat
  FUNC zero : -> Nat
  FUNC succ : Nat -> Nat

  PRED is_gen : Nat
  IND  is_gen(zero);
       FORALL n:Nat ( is_gen(n) => is_gen(succ(n)) )

  AXIOM
  {NAT1} zero!;
         FORALL m:Nat,n:Nat (
  {NAT2} succ(m)!;
  {NAT3} NOT succ(m) = zero;
  {NAT4} succ(m) = succ(n) => m = n );
  {NAT5} FORALL n:Nat ( is_gen(n) )

END
```

In this example there is one hidden predicate, viz. `is_gen`. This use of hiding is typical: `is_gen` is an auxiliary which in combination with axiom `NAT5` determines the right class of models. Yet, it hardly makes sense to invoke `is_gen` as a normal predicate. It is always `TRUE` anyhow.

3.4 Import schemes

An *import* scheme S can be used to put two schemes together. If K and L are schemes, the following is an import scheme:

IMPORT K INTO L

It denotes the normal-form specification $\langle \Sigma_S, \mathcal{D}_S \rangle$ defined by:

$$\Sigma_S = \Sigma_K \cup \Sigma_L$$
$$\mathcal{D}_S = \mathcal{D}_K \cup \mathcal{D}_L$$

In order to avoid the redefinition in L of names exported by K, all names exported by K and used in L are supposed to be implicitly defined in L. So, in order to determine the denotation of L, we first have to add to L the definitions of the names exported by K and used in L. If all names used in L are also defined in L, then the import operator is symmetric:

IMPORT K INTO L $\equiv$ IMPORT L INTO K

In the following example of an import scheme:

```
IMPORT CLASS
           SORT A
           FUNC a : -> A
         END
INTO     EXPORT
           SORT A,
           SORT B,
           FUNC f : A -> B
         FROM
         CLASS
           SORT B
           FUNC b : -> B
           FUNC f : A -> B
         END
```

the first argument of the import operator denotes the normal-form specification $\langle \{\texttt{A}, \texttt{a}\}, \{D_{\texttt{A}}, D_{\texttt{a}}\} \rangle$ with $D_{\texttt{A}}$ and $D_{\texttt{a}}$ as shown. In order to determine the denotation of the second argument (which uses the sort A but not the function a), we first have to add the definition of sort A to the text. Hence the above import scheme denotes the normal-form specification

$\langle\{\mathtt{A},\mathtt{B},\mathtt{a},\mathtt{f}\},\{D_{\mathtt{A}},D_{\mathtt{B}},D_{\mathtt{a}},D_{\mathtt{b}},D_{\mathtt{f}}\}\rangle$.

The implicit definition convention implies that the set of names defined between the brackets CLASS and END need not necessarily constitute a signature. They should constitute a signature after adding the implicit definitions provided by imports. The following is another example of an import scheme

```
IMPORT CLASS
         SORT Switch
         FUNC on     : -> Switch
         FUNC off    : -> Switch
         FUNC toggle : Switch -> Switch
         AXIOM ...
       END
INTO   CLASS
         SORT Pair
         FUNC pair  : Switch # Switch -> Pair
         FUNC first : Pair -> Switch
         FUNC last  : Pair -> Switch
         AXIOM ...
       END
```

The modularisation operators (IMPORT, EXPORT, etc.) may be combined in arbitrary ways since they can be viewed as *algebraic operations* on schemes. This approach is taken from Bergstra's Module Algebra [7].

Sometimes it is useful to consider the IMPORT operator as a kind of 'addition' of schemes, i.e. IMPORT L INTO K could just as well be written as

$$L + K$$

Such a notation makes it obvious that one can nest imports in arbitrary ways. A complex scheme such as

```
IMPORT IMPORT K INTO ( IMPORT L INTO M )  INTO N
```

is perfectly understandable as a term $(K + (L + M)) + N$. Yet, because of the fact that schemes are usually simple terms over relatively large flat schemes, the keyword-based syntax of COLD-K is probably more practical. Some care is needed concerning the order in which IMPORT and EXPORT operators are used. Just like in arithmetic where in general $\sqrt{N + I + C}$ is not the same as $N + I + \sqrt{C}$, there is a difference between:

```
EXPORT
  SORT Nat,
  SORT Item,
  SORT Queue,
  FUNC empty : -> Queue,
  FUNC put   : Item # Queue -> Queue,
  FUNC geti  : Queue -> Item,
  FUNC getq  : Queue -> Queue,
  FUNC len   : Queue -> Nat
FROM
IMPORT NAT  INTO
IMPORT ITEM INTO
CLASS ... END
```

and

```
IMPORT NAT INTO
IMPORT ITEM INTO
EXPORT
  SORT Nat,
  SORT Item,
  SORT Queue,
  FUNC empty : -> Queue,
  FUNC put   : Item # Queue -> Queue,
  FUNC geti  : Queue -> Item,
  FUNC getq  : Queue -> Queue,
  FUNC len   : Queue -> Nat
FROM
CLASS ... END
```

The difference lies in the hiding of the operations of `NAT` and `ITEM`. For instance, when `NAT` contains a `succ` function, it is hidden in the first version of `QUEUE` but is visible in the second version.

3.5 Renaming schemes

A *renaming* scheme S can be used to change names in a scheme and has the following form:

`RENAME` ρ `IN` K

where K is an arbitrary scheme and where ρ is a *renaming*, denoting a mapping from names to names. S denotes the normal-form specification $\langle \Sigma_S, \mathcal{D}_S \rangle$ defined by:

$$\Sigma_S = \rho(\Sigma_K),$$
$$\mathcal{D}_S = \rho(\mathcal{D}_K).$$

In other words, this scheme denotes the same normal-form specification as K, except that each name u in $\langle \Sigma_K, \mathcal{D}_K \rangle$ has been replaced by $\rho(u)$.

A renaming is described by a list of *pairs*, each pair consisting of a sort, predicate or function name, followed by the keyword TO and an identifier. For example, the following is a renaming:

```
SORT A            TO C,
FUNC f : A -> B TO g
```

The result of applying a renaming to a name u is determined as follows:

1. if u is a predicate or function name occurring at the left hand side of a pair, the identifier of the name is changed to the identifier at the right hand side of the pair;
2. then, all identifiers of sort names occurring at the left hand sides of pairs are changed in the name, in accordance with the corresponding right hand sides of the pairs.

In the case above, SORT A would be changed to SORT C and FUNC f : A -> B would be changed to FUNC g : C -> B, resulting in the following equivalence:

```
RENAME
  SORT A            TO C,
  FUNC f : A -> B TO g
IN
EXPORT
  SORT A,
  SORT B,
  FUNC f : A -> B
FROM
CLASS
  SORT A
  SORT B
  FUNC f : A -> B
  FUNC h : B -> A
  AXIOM FORALL a:A ( h(f(a)) = a )
END
```

is equivalent to:

```
EXPORT
  SORT C,
  SORT B,
  FUNC g : C -> B
FROM
CLASS
  SORT C
  SORT B
  FUNC g : C -> B
  FUNC h : B -> C
  AXIOM FORALL a:C ( h(g(a)) = a )
END
```

We give another example of a renaming scheme, which 'changes' the specification of switches to one of 'bits'.

```
RENAME
  SORT Switch                        TO Bit,
  FUNC on     : -> Switch            TO 1,
  FUNC off    : -> Switch            TO 0,
  FUNC toggle : Switch -> Switch TO not
IN
CLASS

  SORT Switch
  FUNC on     : -> Switch
  FUNC off    : -> Switch
  FUNC toggle : Switch -> Switch

  AXIOM ...

END
```

3.6 Abbreviation schemes

An *abbreviation* scheme can be used to give a name to a scheme. If K and L are arbitrary schemes, then the following scheme S is an abbreviation scheme:

LET x := K; L

where x is an identifier (a *scheme name*) that may be used in L. S is equivalent to the scheme L, where all occurrences of the name x in L have been replaced by K.

In other words, the name x may be used in L to denote the scheme K. Note that a scheme as such is a nameless entity. The association between the name x and the scheme K in the above abbreviated scheme is limited to the scheme L (i.e., the *scope* of x is the scheme L). For example, the following scheme:

```
LET X := CLASS SORT A END;
IMPORT X INTO
CLASS
  FUNC a : -> A
  AXIOM a!
END
```

is equivalent to:

```
IMPORT CLASS SORT A END INTO
CLASS
  FUNC a : -> A
  AXIOM a!
END
```

Below we give an example of a modular scheme where we use several abbreviation schemes.

```
LET NAT := EXPORT
             SORT Nat,
             FUNC zero : -> Nat,
             FUNC succ : Nat -> Nat
           FROM
           CLASS ... END;
LET ITEM := EXPORT SORT Item FROM CLASS ... END;
LET QUEUE := EXPORT
```

```
                    SORT Nat,
                    SORT Item,
                    SORT Queue,
                    FUNC empty : -> Queue,
                    FUNC put   : Item # Queue -> Queue,
                    FUNC geti  : Queue -> Item,
                    FUNC getq  : Queue -> Queue,
                    FUNC len   : Queue -> Nat
                  FROM
                  IMPORT NAT  INTO
                  IMPORT ITEM INTO
                  CLASS ... END;
QUEUE
```

3.7 Semantics of normal-form specifications

After normal-form reduction we are left with a normal-form specification which has the following structure:

```
EXPORT
  signature
FROM
CLASS
  definitions
END
```

Modular schemes are simply a way of writing down a normal-form specification in a more structured way. In other words, each modular scheme K is a *denotation* of a normal-form specification consisting of a signature Σ_K and a list of definitions $\mathcal{D}_K$. For a modular scheme K, the process of determining its *meaning* proceeds in two steps:

$$\mathrm{K} \xrightarrow{\text{denotation}} \begin{array}{l}\texttt{EXPORT}\\ \quad\Sigma_K\\ \texttt{FROM}\\ \texttt{CLASS}\\ \quad\mathcal{D}_K\\ \texttt{END}\end{array} \xrightarrow{\text{interpretation}} \left\{ M \mid M \text{ is a model of } \begin{array}{l}\texttt{EXPORT}\\ \quad\Sigma_K\\ \texttt{FROM}\\ \texttt{CLASS}\\ \quad\mathcal{D}_K\\ \texttt{END}\end{array} \right\}$$

Now we shall develop the notions needed to perform the second step. We need an important and fundamental operation upon algebras, which is to 'forget' certain sorts, functions and predicates.

Definition. Let $\Sigma_2 \subseteq \Sigma_1$ be signatures and A_1 a Σ_1-algebra. A Σ_2-algebra A_2 can be obtained from A_1 by removing (*forgetting*) all sorts, functions and predicates which do not occur in Σ_2. This transformation from A_1 to A_2 is called a *forgetful mapping*. □

We give an example, where we consider two given signatures Σ_1 and Σ_2 and then show how the corresponding forgetful mapping operates on a given Σ_1-algebra. Consider the following signature.

```
SORT A,
SORT B,
SORT C,
FUNC f : A -> B,
FUNC g : C -> B
```

Fig 3.1. Signature Σ_1 with sort names A, B and C.

The signature Σ_1 contains three sort names A, B and C as well as two function names f and g. Consider also the following signature, which we call Σ_2.

```
SORT A,
SORT B,
FUNC f : A -> B
```

Fig 3.2. Signature Σ_2 with sort names A and B.

The signature Σ_2 contains two sort names A, and B as well as one function name f. Note that $\Sigma_2 \subseteq \Sigma_1$. Now consider the following algebra, which we call A_1.

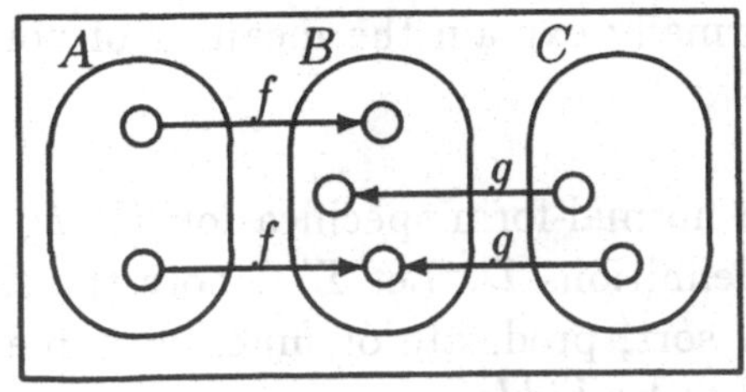

Fig 3.3. Algebra with sorts A, B and C.

The algebra of this figure has three sorts, denoted by A, B and C and clearly it is a Σ_1-algebra. Forgetting C and g reduces A_1 to the Σ_2-algebra A_2 shown below.

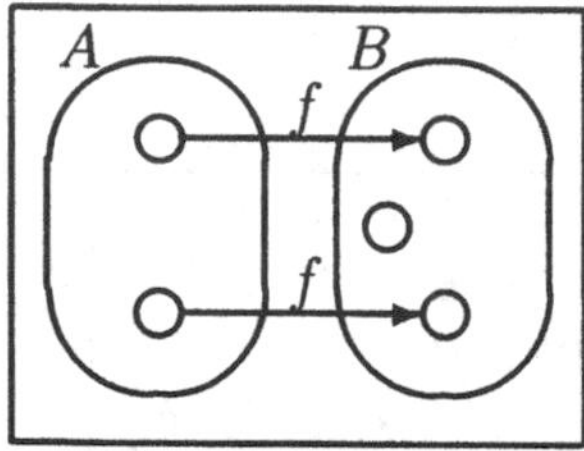

Fig 3.4. Algebra with sorts A and B.

If we write $\mathcal{F}$ to denote the forgetful mapping which forgets all sorts, predicates and functions which are not in Σ_2, we can write $\mathcal{F}(A_1) = A_2$. Alternatively, we can show the situation by means of the following 'formula'.

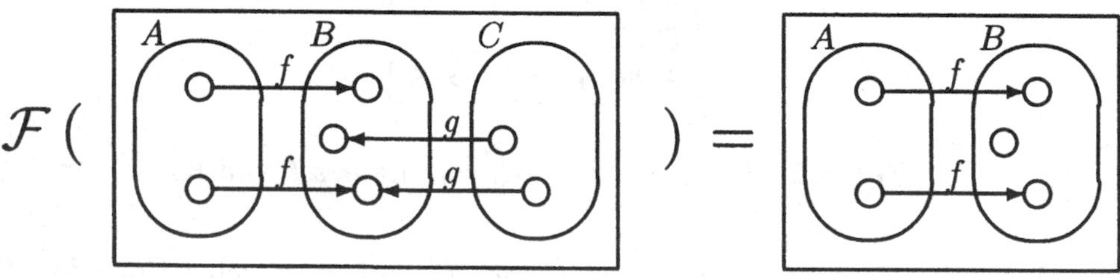

Fig 3.5. Forgetting C and g.

Now we are ready to formally explain the meaning of normal-form specifications.

Definition. Consider a normal-form specification $\langle \Sigma, \mathcal{D} \rangle$ consisting of a signature Σ and a list of definitions $\mathcal{D}$. Let Σ' denote the signature introduced by the definitions $\mathcal{D}$. A sort, predicate or function name which is in Σ' but which is not in Σ is said to be *hidden*.

Let $\mathcal{F}$ be the forgetful mapping on Σ'-algebras which forgets all sorts, predicates and functions with a hidden name. Then the *interpretation* of

$\langle \Sigma, \mathcal{D} \rangle$ is

$$\{ \mathcal{F}(A) \mid A \text{ satisfies } \mathcal{D} \}$$

which is obtained by taking the collection of all Σ'-algebras satisfying the definitions and 'forgetting' the hidden sorts, predicates and functions. □

The first step in our approach of assigning a meaning to the language constructs (normal-form reduction) is rather syntactical in nature, which can be viewed as a theoretical weakness. On the other hand, some constructs such as the abbreviation schemes and the renaming scheme are of a syntactical nature indeed and hence we feel that the approach is acceptable.

In Section 9.5 we shall have a closer look at how to do normal-form reduction, taking into account the problem of tracing back applied occurrences of names to their definitions.

3.8 Hidden names

A name is said to be *hidden* in a scheme S if it is hidden in the normal form of S; otherwise it is said to be *public.* A hidden name is created by explicitly *not* exporting it from the scheme it is defined in. The notion of being hidden is relative to a scheme, e.g., in:

```
LET X := CLASS
           SORT A
           FUNC a : -> A
         END;
LET Y := EXPORT SORT A FROM X;
LET Z := IMPORT X INTO Y;
Z
```

the function a defined in X is hidden in Y but not in X and Z. If a name must be hidden completely, it should not be exported from the flat scheme in which it is defined, as the function a in:

```
LET X := EXPORT SORT A FROM
         CLASS
           SORT A
           FUNC a : -> A
         END;
```

Now there is no way the function a can be 'accessed', no matter in what way the scheme X is used. Hidden names can be used for several purposes:

- to denote auxiliary sorts, predicates and functions that are convenient, but which could be eliminated in principle;
- to denote auxiliary predicates helpful for expressing minimality properties of sorts (cf. the is_gen predicates);
- as a means to provide a limited form of second order existential quantification;
- as a means to specify algebraic structures by means of 'representations'.

We first give an example of the third category, showing a kind of 'second order' quantification. An (arbitrary) algebra with one sort C containing a countably infinite number of objects can be specified as follows:

```
LET NAT := ...;
EXPORT
  SORT C
FROM
IMPORT NAT INTO
CLASS

  SORT C
  FUNC e : Nat -> C

  AXIOM
  {C1} FORALL n:Nat ( e(n)! );       % e is total
  {C2} FORALL m:Nat,n:Nat            % e is injective
       ( e(m) = e(n) => m = n );
  {C3} FORALL c:C EXISTS n:Nat       % e is surjective
       ( e(n) = c )

END
```

This specification specifies that there *exists* a function e enumerating all objects in the sort C.

An important application of the use of hidden sorts and operations is in specifying algebraic structures by means of *abstract representations* (the last category above), which amounts to defining one sort in terms of another. The general procedure is as follows:

1. Assume we have to define a new sort A with associated operations, to be defined in a scheme S_A.

2. Choose a sort C with associated operations, defined in a scheme S_C, as representation for the objects of sort A. Import S_C into S_A, but *do not* export the sort C and its associated operations from S_A.
3. Define a single constructor function (an *abstraction function*) mapping the 'concrete objects' of C to the 'abstract objects' of A in a surjective, but not necessarily injective way.
4. Define equality on the sort A in terms of equality on the sort C and express the surjectivity of the abstraction function ($\equiv$ the minimality of sort A) by axioms.
5. Define the remaining operations in terms of operations on the representation and make sure that the definitions are independent of the choice of representatives.

In fact, there are many different variations on this procedure, such as the use of more than one sort for the abstract representations.

An example of the use of abstract representations is the specification of sets in terms of bags. The signature of the specification is given in Figure 3.6.

```
SORT Nat,
SORT Item,
SORT Set,
PRED is_in   : Item # Set,
FUNC empty   : -> Set,
FUNC ins     : Item # Set -> Set,
FUNC rem     : Item # Set -> Set,
FUNC union   : Set # Set -> Set,
FUNC isect   : Set # Set -> Set,
FUNC diff    : Set # Set -> Set,
PRED subset  : Set # Set,
FUNC card    : Set -> Nat
```

Fig 3.6. Signature of the specification of sets.

The intended interpretation of the elements of this signature is as follows. `Nat` is the set of natural numbers, `Item` is the set of items contained in sets and `Set` is the set of finite sets of items. `is_in`(i,s) means that item i is an element of set s. If we did not adopt the restriction to ASCII-based prefix operators, we would certainly write $i \in s$ for this. `empty` is the empty set, usually written as $\emptyset$. Insertion is denoted as `ins`(i,s) which is the set s with item i inserted and similarly removal is denoted by `rem`(i,s) which is the set s with item i removed. `union`(s,t) is the union of sets s and t whereas `isect`(s,t) is the intersection of sets s and t, usually written as $s \cup t$ and $s \cap t$ respectively. `diff`(s,t) is the difference of sets s and t, usually written as $s \setminus t$. **subset**(s,t) holds if the set s is a subset of set t, usually written as $s \subseteq t$. Finally **card**(s) is the number of elements (cardinality) of set s.

The specification of sets by using bags as representations reads as follows.

```
LET NAT := ...;
LET BAG := ...;
EXPORT
  SORT Nat,
  SORT Item,
  SORT Set,
  PRED is_in  : Item # Set,
  FUNC empty  : -> Set,
  FUNC ins    : Item # Set -> Set,
  FUNC rem    : Item # Set -> Set,
  FUNC union  : Set # Set -> Set,
  FUNC isect  : Set # Set -> Set,
  FUNC diff   : Set # Set -> Set,
  PRED subset : Set # Set,
  FUNC card   : Set -> Nat
FROM
IMPORT NAT INTO
IMPORT BAG INTO
CLASS

  SORT Set
  FUNC set : Bag -> Set

  PRED is_in : Item # Set
  IND  FORALL i:Item,b:Bag
       ( is_in(i,b) => is_in(i,set(b)) )

  AXIOM  FORALL b:Bag,c:Bag (
  {SET1} set(b) = set(c) <=>
         FORALL i:Item ( is_in(i,b) <=> is_in(i,c) ) )

  PRED is_gen : Set
  IND  FORALL b:Bag ( is_gen(set(b)) )

  AXIOM
  {SET2} FORALL s:Set ( is_gen(s) )

  FUNC empty : -> Set
  IND  empty = set(empty)
```

```
FUNC ins : Item # Set -> Set
IND  FORALL i:Item,b:Bag
     ( ins(i,set(b)) = set(ins(i,b)) )

FUNC rem : Item # Set -> Set
IND  FORALL i:Item,j:Item,s:Set
     ( rem(i,empty) = empty:Set
     ; rem(i,ins(i,s)) = rem(i,s)
     ; NOT i = j => rem(i,ins(j,s)) = ins(j,rem(i,s))
     )

FUNC union : Set # Set -> Set
IND  FORALL b:Bag,c:Bag
     ( union(set(b),set(c)) = set(union(b,c)) )

FUNC isect : Set # Set -> Set
IND  FORALL b:Bag,c:Bag
     ( isect(set(b),set(c)) = set(isect(b,c)) )

FUNC diff : Set # Set -> Set
IND  FORALL s:Set
     ( diff(s,empty) = s );
     FORALL i:Item,s:Set,t:Set
     ( diff(s,ins(i,t)) = rem(i,diff(s,t)) )

PRED subset : Set # Set
IND  FORALL s:Set
     ( subset(s,s) );
     FORALL i:Item,s:Set,t:Set
     ( subset(s,t) => subset(s,ins(i,t)) )

FUNC card : Set -> Nat
IND  card(empty) = zero;
     FORALL i:Item,s:Set
     ( NOT is_in(i,s) => card(ins(i,s)) = succ(card(s)) )

END;
```

The definition of the predicate is_gen and axiom SET2 could be replaced by:

```
AXIOM {SET2} FORALL s:Set EXISTS b:Bag ( s = set(b) )
```

Let us also add some explanation concerning the double use of the identifier `empty`, a phenomenon called *overloading*. In some cases, `empty` is shorthand for the full name `FUNC empty : -> Set` and in other cases for `FUNC empty : -> Bag`. Usually the full name can be derived from the context, but when it cannot, an explicit type cast is needed to resolve the ambiguity (in COLD a type cast is *not* a type conversion). This explains why we have to write `rem(i,empty) = empty:Set` in the inductive body of the function `rem`.

Specification by representation is a powerful technique and in general it is much easier than specification by means of axioms only. The ease of use of this approach is based on the *reuse* of an existing specification. In the above example, we could reuse `BAG`. When bags are fully defined already, the only thing to be done to get sets is to formalize the idea that sets are like bags, except for the fact that the multiplicity is not relevant any more.

Very much in the same way, one could define bags in terms of sequences. If we have a specification describing finite sequences, the only thing to be done to get bags is to formalize the idea that bags are like sequences, except for the fact that the position of the elements is not relevant any more.

Clearly this technique does not make all axiomatic descriptions superfluous. After all, one needs at least a few axiomatic descriptions to get started. The technique of specification by representation has also a disadvantage, which is the fact that the resulting descriptions are less abstract; they are said to be *model-oriented*. When describing sets by means of bags, it can be argued that it is not elegant that the data type of bags plays such a dominant role.

Chapter 4

Implementing algebraic specifications

4.1 Introduction

In the previous chapters we have focused mainly on abstract specifications of data types. However, there is more to computer programming than just writing abstract specifications. It is equally important to provide efficient *implementations* of data types. In this chapter we shall discuss a number of fundamental implementation techniques using the language COLD-K. In this way we can stay within the semantical framework of one single language. This does not mean that we propose to always use COLD-K when making implementations; we only show that a number of techniques can be explained in it. One of our examples demonstrates that it is also possible to link our techniques with a common programming language like Pascal.

A key notion when discussing implementation is that of an 'algorithm'. By an *algorithm* we mean the description of a calculation that can be evaluated in a prescribed step-by-step way. One of the first issues to be addressed in this chapter is an extension of our notion of 'term' to get a richer notion called 'expression'. These expressions can be viewed as algorithms. Until now we only had terms like, for example,

```
pop(push(i,push(i,empty)))
```

In an elementary way such a term can be viewed as an algorithm: take the empty stack, push `i` onto it, then push `i` again and finally apply `pop`. Our notion of term is rather poor in the sense that we do not have a mechanism of writing such things as **if** A **then** X **else** Y. Therefore we introduce two special expressions $A?$ and $X \mid Y$. By appropriate combination of these we get a kind of if-then-else expression, viz.

```
( A ?,      X
| NOT A ?, Y
)
```

Our expressions will also include a selection and a declaration construct. In order to explain the meaning of $X \mid Y$ for arbitrary X and Y, we must adopt the viewpoint that expressions are essentially *non-deterministic.* Sections 4.2 to 4.5 are concerned with expressions. Furthermore we shall present algorithmic predicate definitions and function definitions, which are mechanisms to define predicates and functions explicitly in terms of assertions and expressions. These definition mechanisms also allow for recursion, which introduces the possibility of a functional programming style. This is the subject of Sections 4.6 and 4.7.

Using all these new language constructs, we can transform abstract specifications into algorithmic implementations. We shall present two key techniques. The first technique is a systematic approach to transform inductive definitions into algorithmic definitions. It is presented in Section 4.8. The second technique is the use of an abstraction function to establish the relationship between an abstract specification and its concrete representation. This is the subject of Sections 4.9 and 4.10.

4.2 Expressions

The notion of *expression* is a generalisation of the notion of *term*, introducing the concept of *nondeterminism*. Like terms, expressions have a *type*, which is a sequence of sorts. Unlike terms, expressions need not denote a unique value but have a set of *possible values* associated with them, which are said to be *yielded* by the expression. The values are (tuples of) objects of the type of the expression. If an expression yields no objects it is said to *fail*; otherwise it is said to *succeed.*

In Table 4.1 we show the kinds of expressions we shall employ. In this table, X and Y are expressions, A is an assertion, x is an object name and T is a type. Comparing this with the set of terms presented in Chapter 1, we see that three constructs are new: $A?$, $X \mid Y$ and SOME $x:T\ A$.

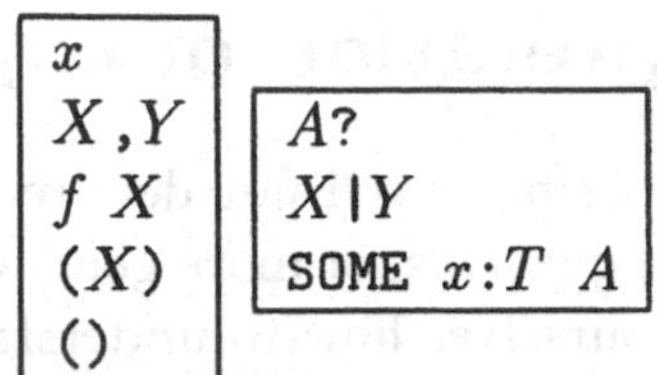

x	$A?$
X,Y	$X \mid Y$
$f\ X$	SOME $x{:}T\ A$
(X)	
$()$	

Table 4.1. Survey of all expressions.

We shall now briefly discuss the meaning and the type of each kind of expression. The notation for a *reference expression* is x. It yields the object denoted by the object name x. Its type is the type of the object name x. The notation for a *composition expression* is X,Y. It yields an object z iff z is the concatenation of an object x yielded by X and an object y yielded by Y. Its type is the concatenation of the types of X and Y. The notation for a *function application expression* is $f\ X$. It yields an object y iff there is an object x such that X yields x and $f(x) = y$. Its type is the range type of f. The notation for a *parenthesized expression* is (X). Its meaning is the same as that of X and its type is the type of X. The *empty tuple expression* is denoted as (). It yields the empty tuple of objects and its type is the empty type. The expression () is equivalent to the guard expression TRUE ?. The *guard expression* has the following notation:

$A?$

It yields the empty tuple if A holds and fails otherwise. Its type is the empty type. The *choice expression* has the following structure:

$X \mid Y$

It yields an object z iff X yields z or Y yields z. Its type is the type of X or Y, which should be the same. Finally the notation for a *selection expression* is:

SOME $x{:}T\ A$

It yields an object x if A holds for x; it fails if such an object does not exist. Its type is T. The choice and selection expressions are the only two expressions introducing nondeterminism.

4.3 Term interpretation of expressions

Because expressions (unlike terms) need not denote a unique value, we must be careful when considering equations, or more general, predicate applications. For example we should ask ourselves how to understand the assertion

```
(0|1) = (0|1)
```

We adopt the following solution: if an expression acts as an argument of a (built-in or user-defined) predicate, then the *term interpretation* of the expression should be used.

built-in predicates	*user-defined predicates*
X ! X = Y	r X

Table 4.2. Kinds of predicates.

If X is an expression, then the term interpretation of X is the *unique* tuple of objects yielded by X, if it exists, otherwise it is *undefined.* Note that the term interpretation of an expression X that is a term is identical to the previously discussed interpretation of the term X.

We give some examples. Suppose we are in a context where the scheme NAT from the standard library (see the appendix) has been imported and the following definitions have been given:

```
FUNC 0 : -> Nat
FUNC 1 : -> Nat

AXIOM 0 = zero;
      1 = succ(0)
```

Using the sort Nat and the given operations, the following assertions can be formulated, that are all true:

```
NOT (0|1) = (0|1);

FORALL n:Nat
( (n = 0 ?, 0 | NOT n = 0 ?, 1) = (n = 0 ?, 0 | NOT n = 0 ?, 1) );

FORALL n:Nat ( geq(n,0)?! );
```

```
NOT FORALL n:Nat ( gtr(n,0)?! );

NOT SOME n:Nat ( lss(n,0) )!;

NOT SOME n:Nat ( gtr(n,0) )!;

SOME n:Nat ( geq(n,0) AND leq(n,0) ) = 0
```

The equation (0|1) = (0|1) does not hold because we must use the term interpretation for the operands of the '=' construct. The term interpretation of both (0|1) and (0|1) is *undefined* and hence by strictness the equation does not hold. To see that the second assertion holds, observe that for any n we find that (n = 0 ?, 0 | NOT n = 0 ?, 1) denotes a *unique* value. To see that FORALL n:Nat (geq(n,0)?!) holds, we observe that for arbitrary n the expression geq(n,0)? is the same as TRUE?, which denotes the only value () of the empty Cartesian product. The fourth, fifth and sixth assertion are left to the reader to check. The last assertion holds because the term interpretation of the body of the selection expression yields a *unique* value for n, viz. the value 0.

It should be noted that due to the nondeterminism in expressions, the following tautology (see Section 1.7) no longer holds:

f(X)! => X!

E.g. if f(a) = c and f(b) = c, then f(a|b) = c, hence f(a|b)! but not (a|b)!. The other tautologies still hold however.

4.4 Declarations

In an assertion or expression an object can be bound to a name, which can then be used to *refer* to the object. The name should first be introduced syntactically by means of a *declaration*:

LET x:T

After this declaration we are supposed not to refer to x until a *binding* of x has been performed:

x := Y

From then on x denotes the object yielded by Y. No other bindings to x should be performed after this. Both LET x:T and x := Y yield the empty tuple – provided Y succeeds. COLD-K also provides an obvious BEGIN ... END expression which serves to restrict the scope of names introduced by means of the declarations. We give some examples. If we are in a context where the scheme NAT from the standard library has been imported, the following assertion is true:

```
LET n:Nat, n := succ(succ(zero)),
add(n,n) = mul(n,n)
```

The following expression yields $\mathtt{x}^8$ for any natural number x:

```
LET m:Nat,n:Nat,
m := mul(x,x), n := mul(m,m),
mul(n,n)
```

Simultaneous bindings are also allowed, as shown by the following example which is correct in a context where NAT is imported and where f and g are unary functions on Nat:

```
m,n := (f(zero),g(zero))
```

Declaration and binding need not follow one another immediately, and there may be more than one binding associated with a declaration (in different 'branches' of an expression), as exemplified by the following expression:

```
LET r:Queue,
( NOT len(q) = zero ?, r := getq(q)
| len(q) = zero     ?, r := empty
),
put(i,r)
```

Note that the variables introduced by LET are *logical variables* and not programming variables (in the sense of imperative programming languages). From the operational point of view they can be considered *assign-once* variables – similar to the variables in functional programming languages. So an expression such as:

```
LET n:Nat, n := 1, n := 2, n
```

makes no sense, i.e. it always fails.

4.5 Survey of assertions and expressions

We give a survey of all assertions introduced so far in Table 4.3. The first block of entries contains the logical constructs, the second block contains the constructs related to built-in predicates and user-defined predicates and the third block concerns constructs with parentheses. The last block concerns the constructs dealing with object names and their declaration.

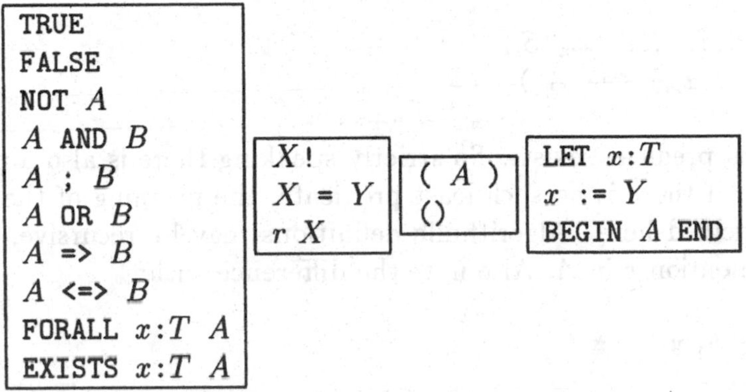

Block 1	Block 2	Block 3	Block 4
TRUE	X!	(A)	LET x:T
FALSE	X = Y	()	x := Y
NOT A	r X		BEGIN A END
A AND B			
A ; B			
A OR B			
A => B			
A <=> B			
FORALL x:T A			
EXISTS x:T A			

Table 4.3. Survey of all assertions.

We also give a survey of all expressions introduced so far in Table 4.4. The first block of entries corresponds to the terms of Chapter 1. The second and third blocks contain the constructs that are introduced in the present chapter.

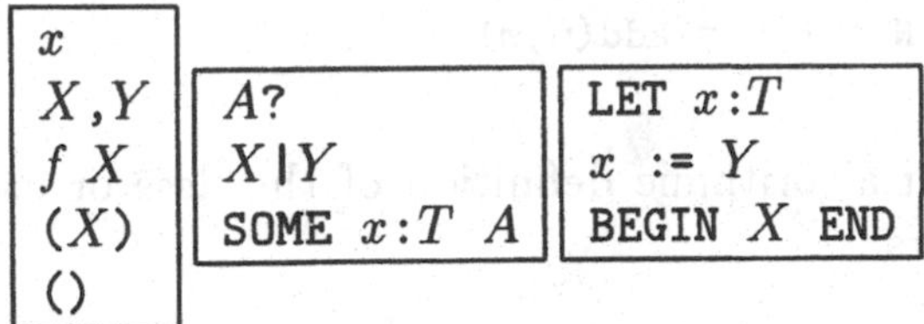

Block 1	Block 2	Block 3
x	A?	LET x:T
X,Y	X | Y	x := Y
f X	SOME x:T A	BEGIN X END
(X)		
()		

Table 4.4. Survey of all expressions.

4.6 Algorithmic predicate definitions

An algorithmic predicate definition is an explicit definition of a predicate in terms of a parameter list and a defining assertion. The general structure is as follows:

PRED r : S_1 # ... # S_m
PAR $x_1 : S_1, \ldots, x_m : S_m$
DEF A

where A is an assertion put in terms of the object names $x_1, \ldots, x_m$. It defines the least strict predicate r such that:

FORALL $x_1 : S_1, \ldots, x_m : S_m$
($r(x_1, \ldots, x_m)$ <=> A)

provided this predicate exists. So strictly speaking there is also a proof obligation here. If there is no such least predicate, the meaning of the construct is left unspecified here. Algorithmic definitions may be recursive, i.e. one is allowed to mention r in A. Also note the difference with:

PRED r : S_1 # ... # S_m
IND A

which defines the least (strict) predicate r such that A holds.

In the following example, the predicate `is_even` expresses that a natural number is even:

```
PRED is_even : Nat
PAR  n:Nat
DEF  EXISTS m:Nat ( n = add(m,m) )
```

The following is an algorithmic definition of the 'less or equal' predicate on the natural numbers:

```
PRED leq : Nat # Nat
PAR  m:Nat,n:Nat
DEF  m = n OR NOT n = zero AND leq(m,pred(n))
```

Compare this with the inductive definition:

```
PRED leq : Nat # Nat
IND  FORALL m:Nat,n:Nat
     ( leq(m,m);
       leq(m,n) => leq(m,succ(n)) )
```

4.7 Algorithmic function definitions

An algorithmic function definition is an explicit definition of a function in terms of a parameter list and a defining expression. The general structure is:

FUNC f : S_1 # ... # S_m -> V_1 # ... # V_n
PAR $x_1 : S_1, \ldots, x_m : S_m$
DEF X

where X is an expression put in terms of the object names $x_1, \ldots, x_m$. It defines the least (strict) function f such that:

FORALL $x_1 : S_1, \ldots, x_m : S_m$, $y : V_1$ # ... # V_n
($f(x_1, \ldots, x_m)$ = y <=> X = y)

provided this function exists. The above definition implies that the value of $f(x_1, \ldots, x_m)$ is equal to the *term interpretation* of X. Furthermore one should note the difference with:

FUNC f : S_1 # ... # S_m -> V_1 # ... # V_n
IND A

which defines the least (strict) function f such that A holds.

The function sqr of the following example defines the square of a natural number:

```
FUNC sqr : Nat -> Nat
PAR  n:Nat
DEF  mul(n,n)
```

The following is an algorithmic definition of the addition function on the natural numbers:

```
FUNC add : Nat # Nat -> Nat
PAR  m:Nat,n:Nat
DEF  ( n = zero     ?; m
```

```
    | NOT n = zero ?; succ(add(m,pred(n)))
    )
```

Compare this with the inductive definition:

```
FUNC add : Nat # Nat -> Nat
IND  FORALL m:Nat,n:Nat
     ( add(m,zero) = m;
       add(m,succ(n)) = succ(add(m,n)) )
```

As illustrated by the examples of algorithmic definitions, recursion in algorithmic definitions is allowed (even mutual recursion in algorithmic *and* inductive definitions).

4.8 From inductive to algorithmic definitions

An inductive predicate definition can be turned into an algorithmic definition in a systematic way. As an example we take the `leq` predicate on the natural numbers:

```
PRED leq : Nat # Nat
IND  FORALL m:Nat,n:Nat
     ( leq(m,m);
       leq(m,n) => leq(m,succ(n)) )
```

defining the least (strict) predicate `leq` satisfying the assertion:

```
FORALL m:Nat,n:Nat
( leq(m,m);
  leq(m,n) => leq(m,succ(n)) )
```

The kernel of our approach is a transformation, consisting of five steps, which is applied to the body of this inductive definition.

Step 1: first rewrite the assertion into strict Horn clause form and take care that all the right-hand sides of the implications are identical (to `leq(m,i)` in this case):

```
FORALL m:Nat,n:Nat,i:Nat
( m = i => leq(m,i);
  leq(m,n) AND i = succ(n) => leq(m,i) )
```

Step 2: turn the conjunction of the implications into a single implication by taking the disjunction of the left-hand sides of the implications:

```
FORALL m:Nat,n:Nat,i:Nat
( m = i OR (leq(m,n) AND i = succ(n)) => leq(m,i) )
```

Step 3: move the universal quantifiers binding the object names not occurring in the right-hand side of the implication into the left-hand side, turning them into existential quantifiers. I.e., use the fact that $\forall x(A \Rightarrow B)$ is equivalent to $\exists x(A) \Rightarrow B$ if x does not occur free in B:

```
FORALL m:Nat,i:Nat
( EXISTS n:Nat (m = i OR (leq(m,n) AND i = succ(n)))
  => leq(m,i) )
```

Step 4: distribute the existential quantifiers over the disjunction and eliminate them where possible:

```
FORALL m:Nat,i:Nat
( m = i OR EXISTS n:Nat (leq(m,n) AND i = succ(n))
  => leq(m,i) )
```

Step 5: use the fact that the predicate is the least predicate satisfying the assertion to turn the implication into an equivalence:

```
FORALL m:Nat,i:Nat
( leq(m,i) <=>
  ( m = i OR EXISTS n:Nat (leq(m,n) AND i = succ(n)) ) )
```

This concludes the five step transformation. So, `leq` is the least predicate satisfying the above assertion which, by definition, is the same as the predicate defined by:

```
PRED leq  : Nat # Nat
PAR  m:Nat,i:Nat
DEF  m = i OR EXISTS n:Nat (leq(m,n) AND i = succ(n))
```

Using the pred function the existential quantifier can be removed from this definition, turning it into the equivalent definition:

```
PRED leq : Nat # Nat
PAR  m:Nat,i:Nat
DEF  m = i OR leq(m,pred(i))
```

which is equivalent to the more 'operational' definition:

```
PRED leq : Nat # Nat
PAR  m:Nat,i:Nat
DEF  m = i OR NOT i = zero AND leq(m,pred(i))
```

This concludes the transformation process for predicates. We shall present a similar approach for *functions*. An inductive function definition can be turned into an algorithmic definition in very much the same way as an inductive predicate definition. As an example we take the add function on the natural numbers:

```
FUNC add : Nat # Nat -> Nat
IND  FORALL m:Nat,n:Nat
     ( add(m,zero) = m;
       add(m,succ(n)) = succ(add(m,n)) )
```

defining the least (strict) function add satisfying the assertion:

```
FORALL m:Nat,n:Nat
( add(m,zero) = m;
  add(m,succ(n)) = succ(add(m,n)) )
```

We give the sequence of transformed assertions below.

Step 1: first rewrite this assertion into Horn clause form and take care that all the right hand sides of the implications are identical (to add(m,i) = k in this case):

```
FORALL m:Nat,n:Nat,i:Nat,j:Nat,k:Nat
( i = zero AND k = m => add(m,i) = k;
  i = succ(n) AND j = add(m,n) AND k = succ(j) => add(m,i) = k )
```

Step 2: turn the conjunction of the implications into a single implication by taking the disjunction of the left-hand sides of the implications:

```
FORALL m:Nat,n:Nat,i:Nat,j:Nat,k:Nat
( (i = zero AND k = m ) OR
  (i = succ(n) AND j = add(m,n) AND k = succ(j))
  => add(m,i) = k )
```

Step 3: move the universal quantifiers binding the object names not occurring in the right-hand side of the implication into the left-hand side, turning them into existential quantifiers.

```
FORALL m:Nat,i:Nat,k:Nat
( EXISTS n:Nat,j:Nat
  ( (i = zero AND k = m) OR
    (i = succ(n) AND j = add(m,n) AND k = succ(j)) )
  => add(m,i) = k )
```

Step 4: distribute the existential quantifiers over the disjunction and eliminate them where possible:

```
FORALL m:Nat,i:Nat,k:Nat
( (i = zero AND k = m) OR
  EXISTS n:Nat,j:Nat (i = succ(n) AND j = add(m,n) AND k = succ(j))
  => add(m,i) = k )
```

Step 5: use the fact that the function is the least function satisfying the assertion to turn the implication into an equivalence:

```
FORALL m:Nat,i:Nat,k:Nat
( add(m,i) = k <=>
  (i = zero AND k = m) OR
  EXISTS n:Nat,j:Nat
  ( i = succ(n) AND j = add(m,n) AND k = succ(j) ) )
```

So, add is the least function satisfying the above assertion, which is the same as the function defined by:

```
FUNC add : Nat # Nat -> Nat
PAR  m:Nat,i:Nat
```

```
DEF  SOME k:Nat
     ( (i = zero AND k = m) OR
       EXISTS n:Nat,j:Nat
       ( i = succ(n) AND j = add(m,n) AND k = succ(j) ) )
```

This may not look very algorithmic yet, but it can be changed, first of all, by eliminating the `SOME` construct. First note that for all pairs `(m,i)` we find that the `SOME` construct has a defined value (referred to as `k`). If the first clause in the body of the `SOME` construct applies (`i = zero`), the value of `k` is just `m`. Otherwise the second clause applies and the value of `k` is `succ(j)`. So we eliminate the `SOME` construct, and express directly that `add(m,i)` yields `m` or `succ(j)`, depending on a case-analysis.

```
FUNC add : Nat # Nat -> Nat
PAR  m:Nat,i:Nat
DEF  ( i = zero ?, m
     | EXISTS n:Nat,j:Nat
       ( i = succ(n) AND j = add(m,n) ) ?, succ(j)
     )
```

Next, the existential quantification can be simplified to:

```
FUNC add : Nat # Nat -> Nat
PAR  m:Nat,i:Nat
DEF  ( i = zero ?, m
     | EXISTS n:Nat ( i = succ(n) ) ?,  succ(add(m,n))
     )
```

(using a so-called scope extension, details of which are given in Section 10.2) which is equivalent to:

```
FUNC add : Nat # Nat -> Nat
PAR  m:Nat,i:Nat
DEF  ( i = zero     ?, m
     | NOT i = zero ?, succ(add(m,pred(i)))
     )
```

4.9 Implementing an algebraic specification

By *implementing* an algebraic specification we mean the construction of a model of the specification in some programming language. We describe this by giving a procedure to transform a specification in a 'correctness-preserving' way to another specification put in terms of primitives implemented in the programming language. The latter specification can then be mapped directly to the programming language.

By a *correctness-preserving transformation* on a specification S we mean a modification of S that transforms S to a specification S' such that S' is an implementation of S and the signature of S' is the same as that of S. This implies that each model of S' is also a model of S. We propose the following general procedure.

Suppose that we want to implement the sort A with associated operations, as specified algebraically in a scheme S_A by means of constructor functions for the sort A and inductive definitions for the non-constructor operations associated with A. The procedure consists of three main steps, followed by a translation to the programming language.

1. Introduction of a concrete sort with concrete operations and an abstraction function relating them to A. There are several substeps:

   (a) Choose a sort C with associated operations, defined in a scheme S_C, in terms of which A and its associated operations are to be implemented. The sort C and its associated operations should correspond with a data type already implemented in the programming language. Import S_C into S_A, but *do not* export the sort C and its associated operations from S_A.
   (b) Define an *abstraction function* f mapping the 'concrete objects' of C to the 'abstract objects' of A in a surjective, but not necessarily injective way.
   (c) Define a predicate `equal` on the sort C with the intended interpretation that `equal`(x,y) iff $f(x) = f(y)$.
   (d) For each operation associated with A (including the constructor functions) inductively define a corresponding operation on C.
   (e) Prove that the abstraction function f is surjective and that the corresponding operations on A and C behave in the same way with respect to f ('homomorphically').

2. Elimination of old definitions related to A. There are two substeps:

   (a) Add the surjectivity and the homomorphic properties of f as axioms to the specification. These axioms specify the operations on A directly in terms of the operations on C (using f) and uniquely characterize f.

(b) Remove the now redundant bodies of the definitions of the operations on A and the body of the definition of f.

3. Transformation of the inductive definitions of the operations on C to algorithmic form.

The entire procedure can be followed by the translation of the specification to the programming language. This is done by representing objects of sort A as objects of sort C and interpreting the abstraction function f as the identity function.

The main aim of the above steps is to obtain a 'simulation of A', which is realised using C and its operations. There are many different variations on this procedure, such as the use of more than one sort C for implementing the objects of sort A. Another variation occurs when the abstraction function f is partial; in that case its domain of definedness should be characterised by a predicate called the *representation invariant*.

4.10 Example: implementation of sets

In this section we shall present a fairly large example of the technique proposed in Section 4.9. Suppose we want to implement the specification `SET` of finite sets from the standard library (see the appendix) in terms of the data type of 'lists', as available through a number of Pascal[23] type definitions and routines described by a formal specification `LIST`, whose signature is given in Figure 4.1 below.

```
SORT Item,
SORT List,
FUNC nil  : -> List,
FUNC cons : Item # List -> List,
FUNC hd   : List -> Item,
FUNC tl   : List -> List
```

Fig 4.1. Signature of the specification of lists.

The interpretation of this signature is that `Item` is the set of items to be contained in lists and `List` is the set of finite lists of objects of type `Item`. `nil` is an atomic value, which can be viewed as the empty list. `cons` is the list constructor in the sense that `cons`(i, s) is the list s with i appended at the head of s. `hd` serves to take the first element (the 'head') of a list and `tl`(s) yields the tail of s, that is s with its head removed.

```
LET LIST :=
EXPORT
  SORT Item,
  SORT List,
  FUNC nil  : -> List,
  FUNC cons : Item # List -> List,
  FUNC hd   : List -> Item,
  FUNC tl   : List -> List
FROM
CLASS

  SORT Item
  SORT List

  FUNC nil  : -> List
  FUNC cons : Item # List -> List

  PRED is_gen : List
  IND  is_gen(nil);
       FORALL i:Item,s:List
       ( is_gen(s) => is_gen(cons(i,s)) )

  AXIOM
  {LIST1} nil!;
          FORALL i:Item,j:Item,s:List,t:List  (
  {LIST2} cons(i,s)!;
  {LIST3} NOT cons(i,s) = nil;
  {LIST4} cons(i,s) = cons(j,t) => i = j AND s = t );
  {LIST5} FORALL s:List ( is_gen(s) )

  FUNC hd : List -> Item
  IND  FORALL i:Item,s:List
       ( hd(cons(i,s)) = i )

  FUNC tl : List -> List
  IND  FORALL i:Item,s:List
       ( tl(cons(i,s)) = s )

END;
```

The specifications SET_IMPL1, SET_IMPL2 and SET_IMPL3 presented below reflect the results of the steps with the corresponding number from the implementation procedure. The Pascal program SET_IMPL4 presented below is obtained as a translation of SET_IMPL3.

We begin with the specification SET_IMPL1 given below.

```
LET SET_IMPL1 :=
EXPORT
  SORT Item,
  SORT Nat,
  SORT Set,
  PRED is_in  : Item # Set,
  FUNC empty  : -> Set,
  FUNC ins    : Item # Set -> Set,
  FUNC rem    : Item # Set -> Set,
  FUNC union  : Set # Set -> Set,
  FUNC isect  : Set # Set -> Set,
  FUNC diff   : Set # Set -> Set,
  PRED subset : Set # Set,
  FUNC card   : Set -> Nat
FROM
IMPORT NAT INTO
IMPORT LIST INTO
CLASS

  SORT Set

  FUNC set : List -> Set
  IND  set(nil) = empty;
       FORALL i:Item,s:List
       ( set(cons(i,s)) = ins(i,set(s)) )

  PRED equal : List # List
  IND  FORALL s:List,t:List
       ( subset(s,t) AND subset(t,s) => equal(s,t) )

  PRED is_in : Item # Set

  PRED is_in : Item # List
  IND  FORALL i:Item,j:Item,s:List
       ( is_in(i,cons(i,s));
         is_in(i,s) => is_in(i,cons(j,s)) )

  FUNC empty : -> Set

  FUNC empty : -> List
  IND  empty = nil
```

```
FUNC ins : Item # Set -> Set

FUNC ins : Item # List -> List
IND  FORALL i:Item,s:List
   ( ins(i,s) = cons(i,s) )

PRED is_gen : Set
IND  is_gen(empty);
     FORALL i:Item,s:Set
     ( is_gen(s) => is_gen(ins(i,s)) )

AXIOM
{SET1} empty:Set!;
       FORALL i:Item,j:Item,s:Set (
{SET2} ins(i,s)!;
{SET3} NOT is_in(i,empty:Set);
{SET4} is_in(i,ins(j,s)) <=> i = j OR is_in(i,s);
{SET5} ins(i,ins(j,s)) = ins(j,ins(i,s));
{SET6} ins(i,ins(i,s)) = ins(i,s) );
{SET7} FORALL s:Set ( is_gen(s) )

FUNC rem : Item # Set -> Set
IND  FORALL i:Item,j:Item,s:Set
     ( rem(i,empty:Set) = empty;
       rem(i,ins(i,s)) = rem(i,s);
       NOT i = j => rem(i,ins(j,s)) = ins(j,rem(i,s)) )

FUNC rem : Item # List -> List
IND  FORALL i:Item,j:Item,s:List
     ( rem(i,nil) = nil;
       rem(i,cons(i,s)) = rem(i,s);
       NOT i = j => rem(i,cons(j,s)) = cons(j,rem(i,s)) )

FUNC union : Set # Set -> Set
IND  FORALL s:Set
     ( union(s,empty) = s );
     FORALL i:Item,s:Set,t:Set
     ( union(s,ins(i,t)) = ins(i,union(s,t)) )

FUNC union : List # List -> List
IND  FORALL s:List
     ( union(s,nil) = s );
     FORALL i:Item,s:List,t:List
     ( union(s,cons(i,t)) = cons(i,union(s,t)) )
```

```
FUNC isect : Set # Set -> Set
IND  FORALL s:Set
     ( isect(s,empty) = empty );
     FORALL i:Item,s:Set,t:Set
     ( is_in(i,s) => isect(s,ins(i,t)) = ins(i,isect(s,t));
       NOT is_in(i,s) => isect(s,ins(i,t)) = isect(s,t) )

FUNC isect : List # List -> List
IND  FORALL s:List
     ( isect(s,nil) = nil );
     FORALL i:Item,s:List,t:List
     ( is_in(i,s) => isect(s,cons(i,t)) = cons(i,isect(s,t));
       NOT is_in(i,s) => isect(s,cons(i,t)) = isect(s,t) )

FUNC diff : Set # Set -> Set
IND  FORALL s:Set
     ( diff(s,empty) = s );
     FORALL i:Item,s:Set,t:Set
     ( diff(s,ins(i,t)) = rem(i,diff(s,t)) )

FUNC diff : List # List -> List
IND  FORALL s:List
     ( diff(s,nil) = s );
     FORALL i:Item,s:List,t:List
     ( diff(s,cons(i,t)) = rem(i,diff(s,t)) )

PRED subset : Set # Set
IND  FORALL s:Set
     ( subset(s,s) );
     FORALL i:Item,s:Set,t:Set
     ( subset(s,t) => subset(s,ins(i,t)) )

PRED subset : List # List
IND  FORALL s:List
     ( subset(nil,s) );
     FORALL i:Item,s:List,t:List
     ( subset(s,t) AND is_in(i,t) => subset(cons(i,s),t) )

FUNC card : Set -> Nat
IND  card(empty:Set) = zero;
     FORALL i:Item,s:Set
     ( NOT is_in(i,s) => card(ins(i,s)) = succ(card(s)) )

FUNC card : List -> Nat
```

```
    IND  card(nil) = zero;
         FORALL i:Item,s:List
         ( is_in(i,s) => card(cons(i,s)) = card(s);
           NOT is_in(i,s) => card(cons(i,s)) = succ(card(s)) )

END;
```

Recall that we are in the process of implementing the sort Set and its operations, as specified algebraically in a scheme SET. We want to employ the sort List with its operations, as given by the scheme LIST. We assume that the sort List and its operations have already been implemented in Pascal. We have imported LIST into SET_IMPL1 without exporting the sort List and its operations.

The function set plays the role of the abstraction function (which was called f in Section 4.9), mapping the concrete list objects to the abstract set objects. Note that set is surjective, that is

```
FORALL s:Set EXISTS t:List ( s = set(t) )
```

because each set can be written as ins(i_1, ins(i_2,... ins(i_n, empty)...)), which is equal to set(cons(i_1, cons(i_2,... cons(i_n, nil)...))). Also note that set is not injective: cons(i,empty) and cons(i,cons(i,empty)) are both mapped to ins(i, empty).

For each set operation we have introduced an inductively defined operation on lists. E.g., for the set operation ins: Item # Set -> Set, whose behaviour was described by the axioms SET2 ... SET6, we have introduced a function ins : Item # List -> List defined by an IND clause. Furthermore we have introduced an equality predicate. Now corresponding operations on Set and List behave homomorphically with respect to the function set, i.e.

```
FORALL i:Item,s:List,t:List
( set(s) = set(t)        <=> equal(s,t)
; is_in(i,set(s))        <=> is_in(i,s)
; empty                   =  set(empty)
; ins(i,set(s))           =  set(ins(i,s))
... etc.
)
```

After this we proceed with SET_IMPL2.

```
LET SET_IMPL2 :=
```

```
EXPORT
  SORT Item,
  SORT Nat,
  SORT Set,
  PRED is_in  : Item # Set,
  FUNC empty  : -> Set,
  FUNC ins    : Item # Set -> Set,
  FUNC rem    : Item # Set -> Set,
  FUNC union  : Set # Set -> Set,
  FUNC isect  : Set # Set -> Set,
  FUNC diff   : Set # Set -> Set,
  PRED subset : Set # Set,
  FUNC card   : Set -> Nat
FROM
IMPORT NAT INTO
IMPORT LIST INTO
CLASS

  SORT Set
  FUNC set    : List -> Set
  PRED is_in  : Item # Set
  FUNC empty  : -> Set
  FUNC ins    : Item # Set -> Set
  FUNC rem    : Item # Set -> Set
  FUNC union  : Set # Set -> Set
  FUNC isect  : Set # Set -> Set
  FUNC diff   : Set # Set -> Set
  PRED subset : Set # Set
  FUNC card   : Set -> Nat

  AXIOM
  {SET'1} FORALL s:Set EXISTS t:List ( s = set(t) );
  {SET'2} FORALL i:Item,s:List,t:List
          ( set(s) = set(t)         <=> equal(s,t)
          ; is_in(i,set(s))         <=> is_in(i,s)
          ; empty                    =  set(empty)
          ; ins(i,set(s))            =  set(ins(i,s))
          ; rem(i,set(s))            =  set(rem(i,s))
          ; union(set(s),set(t))     =  set(union(s,t))
          ; isect(set(s),set(t))     =  set(isect(s,t))
          ; diff(set(s),set(t))      =  set(diff(s,t))
          ; subset(set(s),set(t))   <=> subset(s,t)
          ; card(set(s))             =  card(s)
          )
```

```
PRED equal : List # List
IND  FORALL s:List,t:List
     ( subset(s,t) AND subset(t,s) => equal(s,t) )

PRED is_in : Item # List
IND  FORALL i:Item,j:Item,s:List
     ( is_in(i,cons(i,s));
       is_in(i,s) => is_in(i,cons(j,s)) )

FUNC empty : -> List
IND  empty = nil

FUNC ins : Item # List -> List
IND  FORALL i:Item,s:List
     ( ins(i,s) = cons(i,s) )

FUNC rem : Item # List -> List
IND  FORALL i:Item,j:Item,s:List
     ( rem(i,nil) = nil;
       rem(i,cons(i,s)) = rem(i,s);
       NOT i = j => rem(i,cons(j,s)) = cons(j,rem(i,s)) )

FUNC union : List # List -> List
IND  FORALL s:List
     ( union(s,nil) = s );
     FORALL i:Item,s:List,t:List
     ( union(s,cons(i,t)) = cons(i,union(s,t)) )

FUNC isect : List # List -> List
IND  FORALL s:List
     ( isect(s,nil) = nil );
     FORALL i:Item,s:List,t:List
     ( is_in(i,s) => isect(s,cons(i,t)) = cons(i,isect(s,t));
       NOT is_in(i,s) => isect(s,cons(i,t)) = isect(s,t) )

FUNC diff : List # List -> List
IND  FORALL s:List
     ( diff(s,nil) = s );
     FORALL i:Item,s:List,t:List
     ( diff(s,cons(i,t)) = rem(i,diff(s,t)) )

PRED subset : List # List
IND  FORALL s:List
     ( subset(nil,s) );
     FORALL i:Item,s:List,t:List
```

```
        ( subset(s,t) AND is_in(i,t) => subset(cons(i,s),t) )

    FUNC card : List -> Nat
    IND  card(nil) = zero;
         FORALL i:Item,s:List
         ( is_in(i,s) => card(cons(i,s)) = card(s);
           NOT is_in(i,s) => card(cons(i,s)) = succ(card(s)) )

  END;
```

We have added the surjectivity and the homomorphic properties of `set` as the axioms SET'1 and SET'2 and we have removed the bodies of the set operations and of the function `set`, which have become redundant. The above specification now consists of two parts. The first part mainly contains signature information of set operations. Furthermore it shows a way of interpreting lists as sets – as described by the axioms SET'1 and SET'2. The second part starts with the definition of `equal` and it contains explicit definitions of set-oriented list operations. For example we have `empty`, `ins`, `rem`, `union` etc. on lists. Next we proceed with SET_IMPL3 (step 3 of the implementation process).

```
  LET SET_IMPL3 :=
  EXPORT
    SORT Item,
    SORT Nat,
    SORT Set,
    PRED is_in  : Item # Set,
    FUNC empty  : -> Set,
    FUNC ins    : Item # Set -> Set,
    FUNC rem    : Item # Set -> Set,
    FUNC union  : Set # Set -> Set,
    FUNC isect  : Set # Set -> Set,
    FUNC diff   : Set # Set -> Set,
    PRED subset : Set # Set,
    FUNC card   : Set -> Nat
  FROM
  IMPORT NAT INTO
  IMPORT LIST INTO
  CLASS

    SORT Set
    FUNC set    : List -> Set
    PRED is_in  : Item # Set
    FUNC empty  : -> Set
```

```
FUNC ins    : Item # Set -> Set
FUNC rem    : Item # Set -> Set
FUNC union  : Set # Set -> Set
FUNC isect  : Set # Set -> Set
FUNC diff   : Set # Set -> Set
PRED subset : Set # Set
FUNC card   : Set -> Nat

AXIOM
{SET'1} FORALL s:Set EXISTS t:List ( s = set(t) );
{SET'2} FORALL i:Item,s:List,t:List
        ( set(s) = set(t)          <=> equal(s,t)
        ; is_in(i,set(s))          <=> is_in(i,s)
        ; empty                     =  set(empty)
        ; ins(i,set(s))             =  set(ins(i,s))
        ; rem(i,set(s))             =  set(rem(i,s))
        ; union(set(s),set(t))      =  set(union(s,t))
        ; isect(set(s),set(t))      =  set(isect(s,t))
        ; diff(set(s),set(t))       =  set(diff(s,t))
        ; subset(set(s),set(t)) <=> subset(s,t)
        ; card(set(s))              =  card(s)
        )

% PRED equal : List # List
% IND  FORALL s:List,t:List
%      ( subset(s,t) AND subset(t,s) => equal(s,t) )

  PRED equal : List # List
  PAR  s:List,t:List
  DEF  subset(s,t) AND subset(t,s)

% PRED is_in : Item # List
% IND  FORALL i:Item,j:Item,s:List
%      ( is_in(i,cons(i,s));
%        is_in(i,s) => is_in(i,cons(j,s)) )

  PRED is_in : Item # List
  PAR  i:Item,s:List
  DEF  NOT s = nil;
       hd(s) = i OR is_in(i,tl(s))

% FUNC empty : -> List
% IND  empty = nil

  FUNC empty : -> List
```

```
  DEF  nil

% FUNC ins : Item # List -> List
% IND  FORALL i:Item,s:List
%      ( ins(i,s) = cons(i,s) )

  FUNC ins : Item # List -> List
  PAR  i:Item,s:List
  DEF  cons(i,s)

% FUNC rem : Item # List -> List
% IND  FORALL i:Item,j:Item,s:List
%      ( rem(i,nil) = nil;
%        rem(i,cons(i,s)) = rem(i,s);
%        NOT i = j => rem(i,cons(j,s)) = cons(j,rem(i,s)) )

  FUNC rem : Item # List -> List
  PAR  i:Item,s:List
  DEF  ( s = nil      ?, nil
       | NOT s = nil ?,
         ( hd(s) = i      ?, rem(i,tl(s))
         | NOT hd(s) = i ?, cons(hd(s),rem(i,tl(s)))
         )
       )

% FUNC union : List # List -> List
% IND  FORALL s:List
%      ( union(s,nil) = s );
%      FORALL i:Item,s:List,t:List
%      ( union(s,cons(i,t)) = cons(i,union(s,t)) )

  FUNC union : List # List -> List
  PAR  s:List,t:List
  DEF  ( t = nil     ?, s
       | NOT t = nil ?, cons(hd(t),union(s,tl(t)))
       )

% FUNC isect : List # List -> List
% IND  FORALL s:List
%      ( isect(s,nil) = nil );
%      FORALL i:Item,s:List,t:List
%      ( is_in(i,s) => isect(s,cons(i,t)) = cons(i,isect(s,t));
%        NOT is_in(i,s) => isect(s,cons(i,t)) = isect(s,t) )

  FUNC isect : List # List -> List
```

```
  PAR  s:List,t:List
  DEF  ( t = nil     ?, nil
       | NOT t = nil ?,
         ( is_in(hd(t),s)     ?, cons(hd(t),isect(s,tl(t)))
         | NOT is_in(hd(t),s) ?, isect(s,tl(t))
         )
       )

% FUNC diff : List # List -> List
% IND  FORALL s:List
%      ( diff(s,nil) = s );
%      FORALL i:Item,s:List,t:List
%      ( diff(s,cons(i,t)) = rem(i,diff(s,t)) )

  FUNC diff : List # List -> List
  PAR  s:List,t:List
  DEF  ( t = nil     ?, s
       | NOT t = nil ?, rem(hd(t),diff(s,tl(t)))
       )

% PRED subset : List # List
% IND  FORALL s:List
%      ( subset(nil,s) );
%      FORALL i:Item,s:List,t:List
%      ( subset(s,t) AND is_in(i,t) => subset(cons(i,s),t) )

  PRED subset : List # List
  PAR  s:List,t:List
  DEF  s = nil OR
       NOT s = nil AND is_in(hd(s),t) AND subset(tl(s),t)

% FUNC card : List -> Nat
% IND  card(nil) = zero;
%      FORALL i:Item,s:List
%      ( is_in(i,s) => card(cons(i,s)) = card(s);
%        NOT is_in(i,s) => card(cons(i,s)) = succ(card(s)) )

  FUNC card : List -> Nat
  PAR  s:List
  DEF  ( s = nil     ?, zero
       | NOT s = nil ?,
         ( is_in(hd(s),tl(s))     ?, card(tl(s))
         | NOT is_in(hd(s),tl(s)) ?, succ(card(tl(s)))
         )
       )
```

```
END;
```

SET_IMPL3 is the result of transforming the inductive definitions of the set-oriented operations on List to algorithmic form. The old definitions are still present – as a comment. Finally we can translate everything to Pascal and add a standard implementation of the data type of lists. It is based on the representation of lists as chains of cells, where each cell is a record, consisting of an item and a pointer. This is sketched in Figure 4.2. which shows the representation of a list with two items i_1 and i_2.

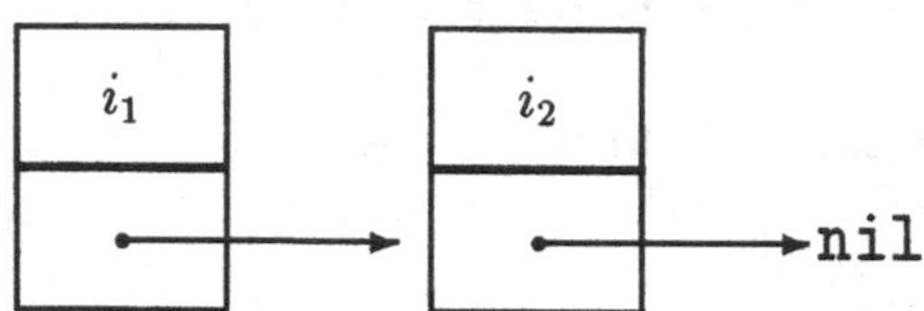

Fig 4.2. Implementation of lists.

We give the resulting complete Pascal program SET_IMPL4 below.

```
program SET_IMPL4;

type Bool  = boolean;
     Nat   = integer;
     Item  = Nat;
     List  = ^RList;
     RList = record
               head : Item;
               tail : List
             end;

function cons(i:Item;s:List) : List;
var t:List;
begin
  new(t);
  t^.head := i;
  t^.tail := s;
  cons := t
end;
```

```
function hd(s:List) : Item;
begin
  hd := s^.head
end;

function tl(s:List) : List;
begin
  tl := s^.tail
end;

type Set = List;

function is_in(i:Item;s:Set) : Bool;
begin
  if not (s = nil)
  then if hd(s) = i
       then is_in := true
       else is_in := is_in(i,tl(s))
  else is_in := false
end;

function empty : Set;
begin
  empty := nil
end;

function ins(i:Item;s:Set) : Set;
begin
  ins := cons(i,s)
end;

function rem(i:Item;s:Set) : Set;
begin
  if s = nil
  then rem := nil
  else if hd(s) = i
       then rem := rem(i,tl(s))
       else rem := cons(hd(s),rem(i,tl(s)))
end;

function union(s,t:Set) : Set;
begin
  if t = nil
  then union := s
  else union := cons(hd(t),union(s,tl(t)))
```

```
end;

function isect(s,t:Set) : Set;
begin
  if t = nil
  then isect := nil
  else if is_in(hd(t),s)
       then isect := cons(hd(t),isect(s,tl(t)))
       else isect := isect(s,tl(t))
end;

function diff(s,t:Set) : Set;
begin
  if t = nil
  then diff := s
  else diff := rem(hd(t),diff(s,tl(t)))
end;

function subset(s,t:Set) : Bool;
begin
  if s = nil
  then subset := true
  else subset := is_in(hd(s),t) and subset(tl(s),t)
end;

function card(s:Set) : Nat;
begin
  if s = nil
  then card := 0
  else if is_in(hd(s),tl(s))
       then card := card(tl(s))
       else card := card(tl(s)) + 1
end;

function equal(s,t:Set) : Bool;
begin
  equal := subset(s,t) and subset(t,s)
end;

begin
end.
```

We add some explanation about the relationship between SET_IMPL3 and SET_IMPL4 for the operation is_in. The conjunction (';' connective) is treated as a 'McCarthy AND' or 'conditional AND'. The value of the first conjunct is tested first and if this yields already FALSE, the second clause is not evaluated any more. In the same way the disjunction ('OR' connective) is treated as a 'conditional OR'. The main reason for doing this is related to the fact that Pascal does not have the same built-in strictness principles as COLD: care is needed not to dereference `nil` pointers. A similar remark applies to `subset`.

This concludes our example. Although we employed the imperative programming language Pascal, we only did so at the very end of our transformation process. This should not be considered as the only way of approaching the phenomenon of imperative programming. On the contrary, the concepts of 'state' and 'state modification' are very fundamental and they deserve a study in their own right, rather than serving as a kind of target language only. The second part of this text is entirely devoted to state-based specification – and again of course implementation. This will require the introduction of several new COLD-K constructs and using these, we can present another rich collection of specification and implementation techniques.

Part II

State-based specification

Chapter 5

From algebras to states

5.1 Introduction

Part I introduced a collection of notations and techniques for *algebraic specifications.* These notations and techniques are relatively close to usual mathematics. As already shown by the examples of Part I, algebraic specifications suffice to describe a wide range of data types (Booleans, numbers, sets, bags, sequences, tuples, maps, stacks, queues, etc.) and they can even be used to describe syntax and semantics of languages, to describe rules and strategies of games and to describe many more non-trivial aspects of complex systems. Of course there are some differences between the notations and techniques of Part I and usual mathematics, like the restriction to first-order predicate logic with inductive definitions, the special way of treating partial functions and undefinedness and, most of all, the modularisation constructs. The latter difference reveals that COLD-K has its roots in software engineering and systems engineering, rather than in general purpose mathematics.

There is one more phenomenon which is characteristic for many branches of software engineering and systems engineering: special provisions for describing state-based systems. These special provisions include programming variables and operations with side-effects, giving rise to a style of programming called *imperative programming.* There are also special provisions for specification and reasoning purposes, and these lead to specifications based on concepts like preconditions, postconditions, invariants, etc.

Part II is about these special provisions for describing state-based systems. It extends and completes the notations and techniques of Part I such that a wide range of programs and systems can be described at various levels of abstraction in a natural way, while staying close to the tradition of software engineering and systems engineering.

During the first two decades of computer programming there was hardly any style of programming other than imperative programming. One of the reasons for this was the Von Neumann computer architecture which can be understood as a state-based machine where a central processing unit affects the state of a few registers and of a large memory in a step-by-step manner (most computers today are based on the Von Neumann architecture). In 1959 the advent of the LISP language introduced an alternative style, called functional programming and around 1977 the advent of PROLOG provided logic programming as another alternative. Still, the majority of the software products is being written in the imperative style, using languages like FORTRAN, Pascal, C, Ada and C++. It can be expected that the imperative style will remain important for many more years and this is one of the main motivations for having special provisions for describing state-based systems in COLD-K and for presenting them in this text. Functional programming and logic programming are very valuable as well, but here it suffices to point out that these are covered to a certain extent by the notations and techniques of Part I. In particular, functional programs are covered to a certain extent by recursive functions, except that functions are not treated as 'objects' in COLD-K (the language COLD-K does not support higher-order functions). Logical programming boils down to writing inductive definitions.

There is another important reason for having special provisions to describe state-based systems, which is the fact that such provisions enable a very *natural* way of dealing with certain systems. Examples of systems where algebraic specifications tend to be unnatural are file-systems and data-base systems. When using a UNIX file system, one can enter commands, changing the state of the file system, although the state itself does not become explicit as an argument of the commands: the command `cd ..` modifies the 'current working directory' such that it moves one position upwards in the tree structure of directories and after that the command `lpr prog.c`, say, takes the file `prog.c` from the *new* current working directory. The fact that (state) arguments of operations are implicit is typical in many descriptions of state-based systems.

5.2 What is a state-based specification?

Floyd [24] was one of the first to introduce specifications and a system of reasoning for imperative programs, using annotated flow charts. Starting from Floyd's technique, Hoare [25] introduced specifications and a system of reasoning for imperative programs based on textual representations. This system has become known as Hoare logic. It involves triples (called asserted programs)

$$\{P\}s\{Q\}$$

where P is a precondition, s is a program and Q is a postcondition. By now, Hoare logic has been incorporated into the field of mathematical logic, where its generalisations are known as *algorithmic logic* or *dynamic logic* [8]. Using algorithmic/dynamic logic, one writes

$$P \Rightarrow [s]Q$$

to denote that if P holds, then for all states reachable by executing s, we find that Q holds. The notation of dynamic logic has been incorporated in COLD-K. In order to formulate preconditions and postconditions, first-order predicate logic still plays an important role. A typical example of a postcondition could be that some (variable) array a with domain Index is sorted. The state itself remains implicit and to express this property we would have to write a formula like:

```
FORALL i:Index, j:Index ( leq(i,j) => leq(a(i),a(j)) )
```

The specification of data types and the specification of state-based systems are often considered as two completely separate issues. Data types are often specified using equational logic whereas in Hoare logic, one usually adopts a *fixed* data sort (i.e. not user-defined in equational logic), Nat for instance. To specify a division algorithm s as a Hoare triple, one writes

```
{NOT y = 0} s {x = add(mul(q,y),r) AND lss(r,y)}
```

where it must be understood that x, y, q and r are programming variables and that s cannot modify x and y. To specify the same using dynamic logic one writes

```
NOT y = 0 => [ s ] x = add(mul(q,y),r) AND lss(r,y)
```

The full range of notations and techniques presented in Part I can be used to introduce arbitrary data types instead of a fixed number of data types. In the COLD-K approach presented in this text, specification of data types and specification of state-based systems are considered in combination and below we shall introduce a *unified view*.

In classical programming languages one uses programming variables, arrays and pointer structures (and similar structures) as the (variable) components of states. The approach adopted in COLD-K is that certain functions and predicates will be 'variable'. Indicating that a function or predicate is variable in COLD-K is done by the keyword VAR. It is also possible to have variable predicates, which is plausible because predicates are close to (but not the same as) Boolean functions. When a function is variable this means that it corresponds to a mathematical function which may vary from state to state. Procedures are the operations to perform state transitions.

To give a first impression, we show a very simple specification which introduces a variable function `mem` together with a procedure `upd`. We assume that `CHAR` provides for the sort `Char` of ASCII characters. The variable `mem` can be viewed as an infinite memory bank and `upd` as an assignment procedure. The first axiom is about the definedness of `mem`. The clause `MOD mem` indicates that `upd` has 'modification access' to `mem`. The second and the third axiom are just assertions in dynamic logic – which is available in COLD-K. The second axiom specifies the effect of $\mathtt{upd}(n, c)$ for address n. The third axiom specifies the effect of $\mathtt{upd}(n, c)$ for addresses n' with $n' \neq n$, for which $\mathtt{mem}(n')$ keeps its *previous* value.

```
LET MEMORY :=
EXPORT
  SORT Nat,
  SORT Char,
  FUNC mem : Nat -> Char,
  PROC upd : Nat # Char ->
FROM
IMPORT NAT INTO
IMPORT CHAR INTO
CLASS

  FUNC mem : Nat -> Char VAR

  AXIOM FORALL n:Nat ( mem(n)! )

  PROC upd : Nat # Char  ->  MOD mem

  AXIOM FORALL n:Nat, c:Char (
        < upd(n,c) > TRUE;
        [ upd(n,c) ] mem(n) = c )

  AXIOM FORALL n:Nat, n':Nat, c:Char (
        NOT n = n' => [ upd(n,c) ] mem(n') = PREV mem(n') )

END
```

5.3 Procedure names and class signatures

In COLD-K the special operations that perform state transitions are called *procedures*. Procedures can be introduced using the keyword `PROC` and they have a domain type as part of their name (just like functions, which also have a domain type, as explained in Section 1.3).

Definition. A *procedure name* consists of:

- an identifier p,
- a type S_1 # ... # S_m, called the *domain type* of the procedure name.

The notation for this is

PROC p : S_1 # ... # S_m -> □

The same conventions concerning equality of names and omission of type information apply as for functions. In particular, in an applied occurrence of a name we only write the identifier of the name and it should be possible to reconstruct the other components of a name from the context.

Functions serve as named and parameterised abstractions of static expressions; likewise, procedures serve as named and parameterised abstractions of state-based algorithms. In particular, procedures can have side-effects and may be nondeterministic. In fact the language COLD-K allows for a more general notion of procedure name where also a range type is included (similar to 'functions' in Pascal or C), but this is considered outside the scope of Part II (see Section 10.9).

We need another kind of signatures which may also contain procedure names. These will be called *class signatures.* Procedures look similar to functions, in the sense that they can have parameters, but at the semantic level they are different.

Definition. A *class signature* Γ is a set of sort, predicate, function and procedure names such that each sort occurring in a name in Γ is also a member of Γ. □

By way of example we give a class signature below.

```
SORT V,
SORT W,
FUNC x : -> V,
FUNC f : V -> W,
PROC p : ->
```

Fig 5.1. Class signature with sorts, functions and a procedure.

Since we generalised certain concepts from Part I and added procedures, we must extend the notion of 'model' of a specification to include the concepts associated with state-transformations. At the semantic level, the unified view turns into what might be called the *states as algebras* approach, which is the subject of the next section.

5.4 States as algebras

Recall that a signature Σ is a set of sort, predicate and function names such that each sort occurring in a name in Σ is also a member of Σ. Recall also that a Σ-algebra A is an indexed family of sets, predicates and partial functions. When u is an element of Σ, where for example u is `SORT V`, there is a set $\mathtt{V}^A$ in this algebra A. The elements of signatures are names, which are syntactic entities and in a Σ-algebra these have semantic counterparts viz. a (mathematical) set for each sort name, a relation for each predicate name and a partial function for each function name. By way of example, let us consider the signature Σ given by:

```
SORT V,
SORT W,
FUNC x : -> V,
FUNC f : V -> W
```

Fig 5.2. Signature Σ with two sorts and two functions.

It equals the signature of Figure 5.1., except that the procedure `p` has been removed. Any Σ-algebra with Σ as above should have two collections of objects, one for `V` and one for `W`. Below we show such a Σ-algebra where the set of objects of sort `V` has two elements and the set of objects of sort `W` has three elements. The partial function corresponding to the syntactic `FUNC x : -> V` yields the object denoted by the arrow labelled x whereas the function corresponding to `FUNC f : V -> W` is undefined for the object denoted by x.

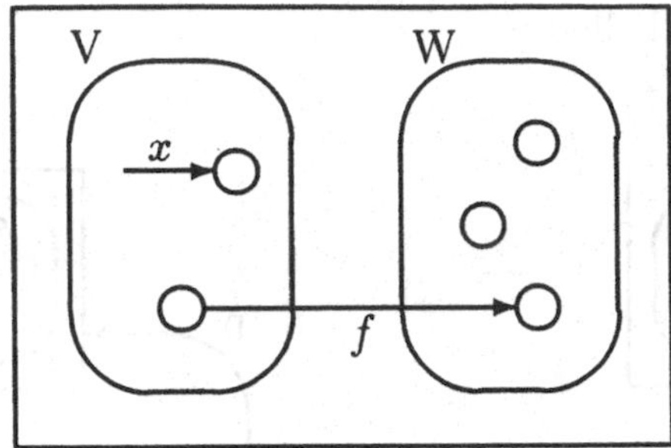

Fig 5.3. Σ-algebra with sorts V and W.

For algebraic specifications the notion of Σ-algebra can serve as a semantic counterpart for the syntax presented in Part I. When discussing variables and state transformations, it cannot. We need a richer notion called a *class*. The intuition behind it is a state machine where algebras are associated with the states. Each state of a class has a Σ-algebra associated with it, where Σ is fixed for all states of the class. In addition to the collection of states, a class has zero or more transition relations associated with it. One state is marked as the initial state.

Since each state has its own algebra associated with it, it is possible to have variable sorts, predicates and functions. When a sort is variable this means that it has different collections of objects in different states. In the present chapter and throughout Part II we shall not exploit the options for variable sorts. To simplify the presentation, the sorts are kept constant and the only variables are functions and predicates. The more general approach will be presented in Section 10.9 and further.

Below we show an example of a class which has five states. One state has been labelled s_0 and is supposed to be the initial state. For each state we show two ovals indicating the two sets of objects corresponding with sorts V and W as well as a few function arrows. There is one transition relation and its transitions have been labelled p.

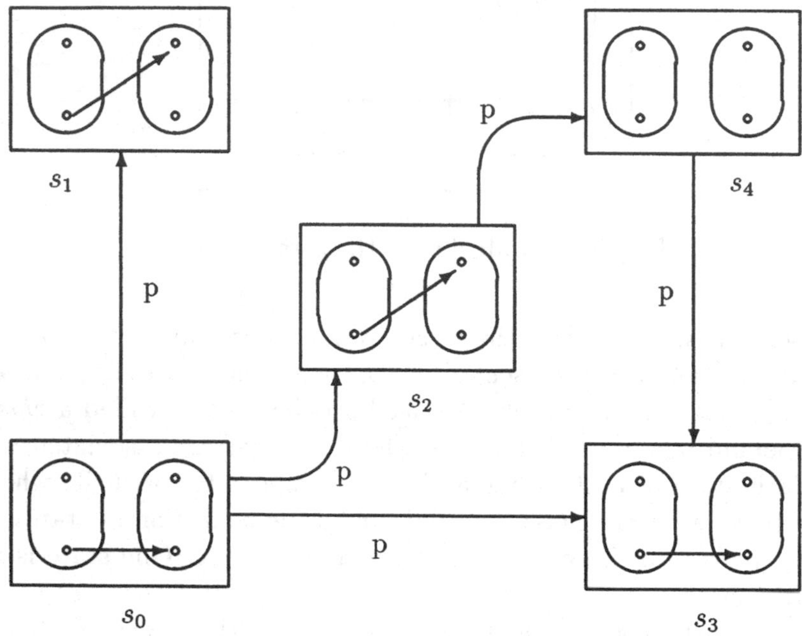

Fig 5.4. Class with five states.

5.5 Classes

After the preparations of introducing class signatures and the informal presentation of a 'class' in the previous section, we can define the class concept precisely. The complete definition of a class below extends over three definitions; the first definition is concerned with 'transitions' and 'transition relations'. The second definition explicitly introduces a 'class' as consisting of three parts, namely a collection of states, an initial state and a collection of transition relations. Finally the third definition introduces a restriction called 'constant sorts'.

We shall consider an arbitrary collection **State** of objects called 'states', where each state has a Σ-algebra associated with it. Procedure names will be interpreted as transition relations.

Definition (Transition relation). Consider a signature Σ and a collection of *states* **State** together with a mapping from states to algebras such that a Σ-algebra $A(s)$ is associated with each state s.

For a procedure name p with domain S_1 # ... # S_m -> , a *transition relation* for p is an $m+2$-ary relation $\mathcal{T}_p$ consisting of tuples of the following form:

$$(s, x_1, \ldots, x_m, t)$$

where $s, t \in$ **State** and $x_i \in S_i^{A(s)}$ for $i = 1, \ldots, m$. A tuple $(s, x_1, \ldots, x_m, t)$ is called a *transition* and often is denoted as $(s, x_1, \ldots, x_m \rightarrow t)$. □

Very often the intuition behind a transition $(s, x_1, \ldots, x_m \rightarrow t)$ is that some procedure is invoked with $x_1, \ldots, x_m$ as actual parameter values and causes a system to go from state s to state t. We use the above definition to define the notion of a Γ-class.

Definition. (Γ-class). Consider a class signature Γ and let Σ be the signature that is equal to Γ with all procedure names removed. We define a Γ-*class* as a triple consisting of:

- a non-empty collection of *states* **State** and a mapping from states to Σ-algebras;
- a distinguished state $s_0 \in$ **State**, called the *initial state*;
- a collection of transition relations $\mathcal{T}_p$, one for each procedure name $p \in \Gamma$.

□

The transition relations $\mathcal{T}_p$ serve as the interpretations of the procedures p. In particular if the transition $(s, x_1, \ldots, x_n \rightarrow t)$ is in $\mathcal{T}_p$, this means that procedure p when invoked in state s with parameters $x_1, \ldots, x_n$ can lead to the new state t. Note that procedures can be non-deterministic with respect to the result states. The following definition introduces a particularly simple kind of class.

Definition. (Constant sorts). Consider a Γ-*class* with collection of *states* **State** where an algebra $A(s)$ is associated with each state s.

Then we say that this class has *constant sorts* if for each sort name S, the corresponding carrier set is the same in each state. More precisely, we require

$$S^{A(s)} = S^{A(t)}$$

for all sort names $S \in \Gamma$ and for all $s \in$ **State** and $t \in$ **State**. □

Throughout this text we shall only use classes with constant sorts, except for Section 10.9, where we shall consider other classes as well. For convenience, we often just write 'class' instead of 'class having constant sorts'.

We shall give an example of a Γ-class below where we assume that Γ is the following class signature:

```
SORT Bool,
FUNC bit : -> Bool,
PROC set : -> ,
PROC reset : ->
```

Fig 5.5. Class signature with procedures `set` and `reset`.

Note that according to the definition of the class concept, there must be a Σ-algebra associated with each state, where Σ is Γ with all procedure names removed. This Σ is given in the figure below.

```
SORT Bool,
FUNC bit : -> Bool
```

Fig 5.6. Signature with one sort and one function.

The Γ-class below has two states where the collection of objects of sort `Bool` is constant, and where the function `bit` is modified by both transition relations, labelled `set` and `reset`.

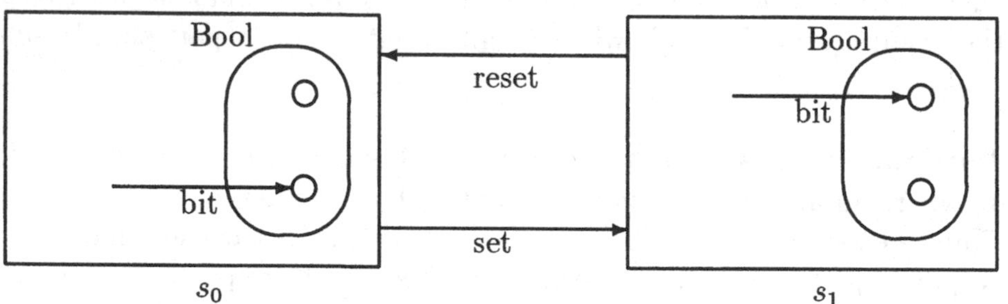

Fig 5.7. Class with procedures `set` and `reset`.

From this example we see that it is important *not* to identify algebras which happen to be isomorphic. Although both s_0 and the other state have isomorphic algebras, they cannot be identified because the modification of the bit function is relevant.

Of course this is not the only possible Γ-class. In fact the collection of all Γ-classes is enormous and it is certainly appropriate to view it as a 'class' rather than a set. We show one more Γ-class for the same Γ below.

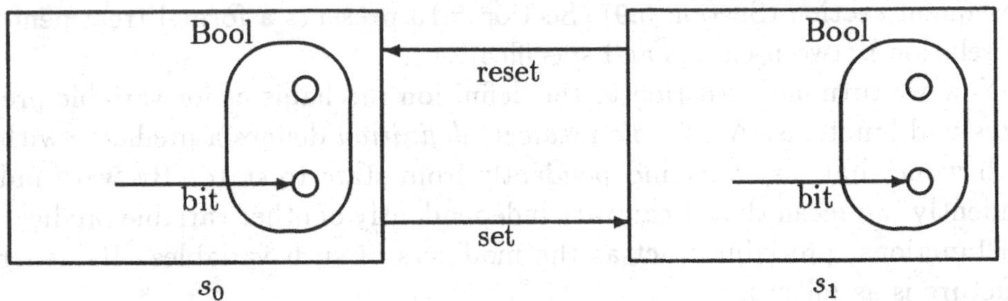

Fig 5.8. Class with procedures **set** and **reset**.

Distinct states can have the same algebra associated with them – as shown by the example. In other words, states are not *extensional*. Also classes with infinitely many states are allowed.

Although in the current section we distinguished clearly between syntactic constructs and the corresponding semantical objects associated with classes, it is often cumbersome to stick meticulously to this distinction. Instead we shall often use an informal style of discussing COLD-K texts where we do not make the distinction: if a name is introduced by the keyword FUNC we just call it a function – even though stricly speaking this is not the case. We do not expect this to cause any problems for a reader who has become familiar with the COLD-K class concept and the 'states as algebras' approach

5.6 Introducing variables

The COLD-K language offers a rich collection of notations and mechanisms to introduce class signatures and to impose various constraints on the states and state transformations. Writing a formal specification in COLD-K means specifying classes. There are several mechanisms for constraining the possible states and state transformations of a class. We distinguish the following kinds of constraints:

- constraints which can be indicated in the definition of sorts, functions, predicates and procedures themselves;
- constraints specified by means of axioms, requiring an extension of the assertion language for dealing with the dynamic aspects.

There are a number of ways to define sorts, functions, predicates and procedures, each introducing constraints on the possible states and state transformations.

In this section we shall discuss the definition of *variable* predicates and functions. In Section 5.7 the definition mechanisms for procedures are presented. The constraints imposed by means of axioms will be addressed in a subsequent section (Section 5.9). Section 5.10 presents a formal treatment of the relation between classes and specifications.

Now we turn our attention to the definition mechanisms for variable predicates and functions. A *variable predicate definition* defines a predicate with a truth value that may vary independently from state to state. By 'vary independently' we mean that it can vary independently of other variable predicates and functions; procedures act as the modifiers of such variables. Its general structure is as follows.

PRED r : S_1 # ... # S_m VAR

We give a small example concerning a sort `Atom`. In a situation where it is conceivable that certain atoms are 'valid' whereas others are not and where it is furthermore the case that the notion of being 'valid' is dynamic, one could employ the following variable predicate definition:

```
SORT Atom
PRED valid : Atom VAR
```

One can add axioms, such as the axiom that in each state at least one atom must be valid: `AXIOM EXISTS a:Atom ( valid(a) )`.

The typical applications include those of classical programming variables. Often the elements of complex data structures have various kinds of 'tag-bits' associated with them. These can be quite well described by variable predicates. In the small example below there is a sort of 'nodes' and two properties of nodes, called `is_leaf` and `is_root`. These are modelled as dynamic properties because adding a subtree might convert a leaf node into a non-leaf node and a root node into a non-root node.

```
SORT Node
PRED is_leaf : Node VAR
PRED is_root : Node VAR
```

A *variable function definition* defines a function with a value that may vary independently from state to state. Its general structure is as follows:

FUNC f : S_1 # ... # S_m -> V_1 # ... # V_n VAR

The typical applications include those of classical simple programming variables, variable arrays and complex data structures built up using pointers. In the following example we have the sort of 'indices', modelled by the sort `Index` and associated with each index there is some value, of sort `Nat`, say. The association of natural numbers with indices is assumed to be dynamic and this situation is modelled by the function `array` which maps indices to natural numbers. This function is made 'variable' as indicated by the keyword `VAR`. To access the cell with index i the usual notation `array`(i) for function application is used.

```
SORT Index
SORT Nat
FUNC array : Index -> Nat VAR
```

The procedures to modify such variable functions will be presented in Section 5.7. In the table below we summarise the various ways of defining predicates and functions, indicating the corresponding keywords. The last block in the table contains the newly added definition mechanism.

body	*keyword*
empty	
inductive	IND
algorithmic	DEF
variable	VAR

Table 5.1. Survey of predicate and function definitions.

5.7 Procedure definitions

The notation for a procedure definition is as follows.

PROC p : S_1 # ... # S_m -> *body*

We consider two ways of introducing procedures: 'constrained procedures' and 'algorithmic procedures'. A constrained procedure definition is a coarse mechanism for restricting the possible state transitions of the procedure. In general it should be complemented by suitable axioms. An algorithmic procedure definition characterises a procedure completely; when adding axioms making statements about the procedure, care is needed not to introduce inconsistencies.

A *constrained procedure definition* introduces a transition relation with specific constraints indicated by the MOD and USE clauses. The notation for it is:

PROC p : S_1 # ... # S_m ->
MOD $V_1, \ldots, V_k$ USE $p_1, \ldots, p_l$

where $V_1, \ldots, V_k$ are names of variables and $p_1, \ldots, p_l$ are names of procedures. The meaning of this definition is as follows. Only those state transitions are possible for p which can be reached by successive state transitions consisting of either

- modification of the variables mentioned in the list of *modification rights*, by which we mean the variables mentioned after the MOD keyword; or
- state transitions corresponding with procedures mentioned in the list of *use rights*, by which we mean the procedures mentioned after the USE keyword.

As before axioms can be added. In the following example we show a variable function array and a procedure upd which has modification rights with respect to this variable, assuming the sorts Index and Nat.

```
FUNC array : Index -> Nat VAR
PROC upd : Index # Nat ->  MOD array
```

It is important to have provisions like our MOD clauses for indicating how procedures may or may not affect variables. In Hoare logic these modification rights are often treated somewhat implicitly. For example when we mentioned the Hoare triple

{NOT y = 0} s {x = add(mul(q,y),r) AND lss(r,y)}

specifying the division algorithm s, it had to be understood that x, y, q and r are programming variables and that s cannot modify x and y. In COLD-K, s could be modelled as a procedure changing the variables q and r such that they contain the quotient and the remainder of the division when s has terminated, as indicated below.

```
FUNC x : -> Nat  VAR
FUNC y : -> Nat  VAR
FUNC q : -> Nat  VAR
FUNC r : -> Nat  VAR

PROC s : ->
MOD  q,r

AXIOM NOT y = 0 => [ s ] x = add(mul(q,y),r) AND lss(r,y)
```

An *algorithmic procedure* introduces a transition relation which is given by a special kind of expression (a statement). The notation for an algorithmic procedure definition is as follows.

PROC p : S_1 # ... # S_m ->
PAR $x_1 : S_1, \ldots, x_m : S_m$
DEF X

where X is a *statement*. The free variables of X must be in $\{x_1, \ldots, x_m\}$. It introduces the transition relation $\mathcal{T}_p$ as described by X. $\mathcal{T}_p$ contains a transition $(s, x_1, \ldots, x_m \rightarrow t)$ if the interpretation of $X(x_1, \ldots, x_m)$ contains the transition $(s \rightarrow t)$. Statements may have side-effects and in Chapter 8 we shall introduce these statements in detail – and come back to the topic of algorithmic procedure definitions in Section 8.3.

Now we give a survey of the definition mechanisms for procedures. The two ways of defining procedures have been put together with the corresponding keywords in the following table.

body	*keyword*
constrained	MOD USE
algorithmic	DEF

Table 5.2. Survey of procedure definitions.

5.8 Comparison with imperative programs

In classical imperative programming languages one encounters various kinds of variable 'data structures'. The most elementary data structure is a *simple programming variable* – the kind of thing declared as VAR x:Nat in Pascal or

`Nat x` in C. This is a peculiar and non-trivial concept: a programming variable is quite unlike a logical variable – as introduced by the `LET`, `FORALL`, `EXISTS`, `SOME` and `PAR` constructs in COLD-K. A simple programming variable behaves like a storage cell, which can have different values in different states.

More complicated data structures can be built using pointers. A *pointer* is a data object to which a special look-up operation called 'dereferencing' can be applied. The third concept we mention is the *array*. An n-dimensional array is a structured collection of simple programming variables (cells); to access a particular cell in an n-dimensional array one needs to provide n index values. Using COLD-K, these concepts can be approached as follows:

- a simple programming variable is viewed as a variable 0-ary function;
- a pointer is an object and pointer dereferencing is viewed as a 1-ary variable function on pointers;
- an n-dimensional array is viewed as a variable n-ary function.

For each of the three concepts of simple programming variable, pointer and array, let us compare a simple example in Pascal and the corresponding COLD-K text. Assuming the type `Nat`, defined by `TYPE Nat = integer` in Pascal, the following declaration introduces a simple programming variable which in each state contains precisely *one* value of sort `Nat`.

```
VAR x:Nat;                                                    (Pascal)
```

This should be compared with the situation in COLD-K where we assume that the sort `Nat` is introduced by `SORT Nat` and that it has been provided with the usual axioms. Since a simple programming variable is viewed as a variable 0-ary function, the following definition in COLD-K introduces a variable function which in each state contains at most *one* value of sort `Nat`.

```
FUNC x : -> Nat  VAR
```

In Pascal there is a type constructor to make pointer-types. Assuming again a type `Nat` as before, the following Pascal definition introduces the type `NatPtr` containing pointers to `Nat` values.

```
TYPE NatPtr = ^Nat;                                           (Pascal)
```

The postfix dereferencing operation `^` can be applied to each `p` of type `NatPtr` and then the expression `p^` yields an object of type `Nat`. Let us compare this with the situation in COLD-K where a pointer is just an object and dereferencing is viewed as a unary variable function on pointers.

```
SORT NatPtr
FUNC deref : NatPtr -> Nat VAR
```

If `p` is of type `NatPtr`, then the expression `deref(p)` yields an object of type `Nat`.

Now we turn our attention to n-ary arrays and for the example we take $n = 2$. Assuming an index domain `Index`, defined by `TYPE Index = 0..31` in Pascal, the following declaration introduces a two-dimensional array containing precisely 32×32 values of sort `Nat`, in each state. To access the cell with indices 2,3 one writes `a[2,3]`.

```
VAR a : ARRAY[Index,Index] OF Nat;                    (Pascal)
```

In COLD-K an n-dimensional array is viewed as a variable n-ary function. Assuming an index domain `Index`, e.g. defined by `SORT Index`, omitting the further details of `Index`, the following COLD-K definition introduces a variable function on $\{0..31\} \times \{0..31\}$.

```
FUNC a : Index # Index -> Nat VAR
```

To access the cell with indices (2,3) the usual notation for function application is employed, writing `a(2,3)`.

We conclude this section by mentioning some of the advantages of the COLD-K approach, where the concepts of simple programming variables, pointers and n-dimensional arrays are unified with generalisations of the concepts of 0-ary functions, 1-ary functions and n-ary functions, respectively:

- no restriction to predefined data types;
- minimalisation of the number of concepts needed (e.g. array look-up is viewed as function application);
- reduction of implementation bias in a specification (uniform notation for look-up);
- there is a clear distinction between the static ingredients of states (sorts, functions, predicates) and the mechanisms that describe state transformations.

5.9 From predicate logic to dynamic logic

The assertions presented in Part I apply to individual states. In order to talk about the essential aspect of procedures viz. the state transformations, we must extend the set of assertions. There are a number of options:

- talking about states explicitly,
- using Hoare logic [25],
- using Dijkstra's *wp* calculus [26],
- using Algorithmic Logic [27], [28], better known as Harel's dynamic logic [8].

The first option is in conflict with the tradition of imperative programming, where the state always remains implicit. Hoare logic and the *wp* calculus are valuable approaches which have received much attention in the scientific and methodological literature. Both are closely related to the fourth option, dynamic logic, which however is somewhat more general. The option chosen in COLD-K is dynamic logic. Four constructs are added to the assertion language; of these the 'always assertion' and the 'sometimes assertion' are taken from dynamic logic.

- initially assertion,
- always assertion,
- sometimes assertion,
- previously assertion.

The syntactic form of an *initially assertion* is simply as follows.

```
INIT
```

The interpretation is that the assertion holds in the initial state s_0 only. Recall that in every class there is precisely one initial state. The initially assertion is very useful for describing various kinds of initialisation conditions. Furthermore it frequently occurs in assertions about invariants.

We give a typical example of an initialisation condition. It is again about a variable function `array` which maps indices to natural numbers. The axiom states that in the initial state s_0 all cells of the array contain `zero` values.

```
FUNC array : Index -> Nat VAR
AXIOM INIT => FORALL i:Index ( array(i) = zero )
```

Next we introduce two mechanisms for making statements about state transitions called 'always assertion' and 'sometimes assertion'. In order to explain their meaning we must use a notion of 'history' which plays a role because sometimes it is convenient to mention the 'previous state' (keyword `PREV`) in a postcondition. A *history* is a finite sequence of states.

The notation for an *always assertion* is as follows.

$[\ X\ ]\ A$

The interpretation is that, whenever execution of X succeeds, A holds. It is called an 'always assertion' because it can be read as *always after X we find that A holds*. More precisely, [X] A holds in state s with history $(s_1, ..., s_n)$ if for all t such that X transforms s to t we find that A holds in t with history $(s_1, ..., s_n, s)$. Note that [X] A does not involve the subsequent future states. Its implications are restricted to the state immediately after the execution of X. The construction

AXIOM [X] A

means that [X] A holds for all $s \in$ **State**, taking the empty sequence of states () as history. The always assertion [X] A adds one state to the history in which A is interpreted. When A does not contain any occurrence of the PREV operation, the histories are completely irrelevant. The *history length* is a static notion. For example, in

AXIOM [X] [Y] A

the assertion A is in a context where the history length is 2.

The 'sometimes assertion' is the counterpart of the 'always assertion' very much in the same way the existentially quantified assertion (keyword EXISTS) is the counterpart of the universally quantified assertion (keyword FORALL). The notation for a *sometimes assertion* is as follows.

< X > A

The interpretation is that < X > A holds in state s with history $(s_1, ..., s_n)$ if there exists a state t such that X transforms s to t and A holds in t with history $(s_1, ..., s_n, s)$. Always assertions and sometimes assertions can be 'nested' and it is allowed to write e.g. AXIOM [X] < Y > A, although in practice this is not needed often.

We give a small example which is again about the variable function `array` which maps indices to natural numbers. The procedure `clear` is introduced by means of a constrained procedure definition. It has `array` in its modification rights and in addition to that it is specified by an axiom. The axiom formally states that in every state obtained by executing `clear` the assertion `FORALL i:Index ( array(i) = zero )` holds.

```
SORT Index
SORT Nat
FUNC array : Index -> Nat VAR
```

```
PROC clear : -> MOD array
AXIOM [ clear ] FORALL i:Index ( array(i) = zero )
```

This axiom does not guarantee that `clear` terminates. Indeed, an implementation of `clear` which aborts or enters an infinite loop, still satisfies the axiom. We could avoid this using a sometimes assertion.

```
AXIOM < clear > FORALL i:Index ( array(i) = zero )
```

although the latter axiom by itself does not guarantee that *all* result states satisfy `FORALL i:Index ( array(i) = zero )`. If `clear` is known to be deterministic, then the latter axiom says that it terminates and together with the determinism of `clear`, it implies the total correctness of `clear`.

In typical applications the always assertion occurs as the conclusion of an implication assertion, as in the following example:

```
PRED  ok : VAR

AXIOM ok => [ clear ] FORALL i:Index ( array(i) = zero )
AXIOM ok => < clear > TRUE
```

There is a variable predicate called `ok` with the intuition that it indicates whether it is allowed to invoke `clear`. It acts as a precondition. Then a sometimes assertion is used to make sure that `clear` has at least one possible result state.

In COLD-K the full power of dynamic logic can be used to specify procedures. This provides us with an expressive power and flexibility which goes beyond the usual pre- and postcondition pairs (as in VDM). Although many examples do not need this generality, it sometimes is very convenient. The example below is taken from [8] and it is concerned with a procedure `f` which must 'undo' the effect of another procedure `g`, in a sense to be made precise below. We use the repetition statement, denoted by the postfix operator `*`, although this will not be introduced formally until Chapter 8.

```
LET GENERALISED_UNDO :=
EXPORT
   SORT Nat,
   FUNC y : -> Nat,
   PROC f : -> ,
   PROC g : ->
FROM
```

```
IMPORT NAT INTO
CLASS

   FUNC y : -> Nat VAR

   PROC g : ->  MOD y

   AXIOM FORALL z : Nat
         ( < g > TRUE;
           y = z => [ g ] y = mul(4,z) )

   PROC f : ->  MOD y

   AXIOM FORALL z : Nat
         ( y = z => [ g* ] < f* > y = z )

END
```

In the above example we see first of all a simple programming variable y and the procedure g. This procedure has the effect of quadrupling the value of y for those states where y is defined. The first axiom is a straightforward specification of g. But now note the use of [ ] and < > in the second axiom. The latter axiom asserts that f 'undoes' g in the sense that any computation of applying g some number of times to y can be backtracked to its original value by applying f some number of times to the result. The specification of f leaves room for many different implementations of f, such as setting y to y − 1 or setting y to y / 2.

Let us also give another example which is not easily done with a pre- and postcondition pair. The example below specifies a procedure select which selects a natural number, leaving the result in a variable n.

```
LET SELECT :=
EXPORT
   SORT Nat,
   FUNC n : -> Nat,
   PROC select : ->
FROM
IMPORT NAT INTO
CLASS

   FUNC n : -> Nat VAR

   PROC select : ->  MOD n
```

```
    AXIOM FORALL z : Nat
          ( < select > n = z )

END
```

Here n is a simple programming variable and the procedure select has the effect of assigning an arbitrary natural number to n. The axiom requires select to have result states for every possible value of n. For example an implementation of select which always selects 0 would be wrong. In every state s and for every natural number z there must be a state t such that the transition $(s \rightarrow t)$ is in the transition relation $\mathcal{T}_{\mathtt{select}}$ and such that in state t the variable n has the value z. It depends a bit on the operational interpretation of procedures whether this means that select is just non-deterministic or that its implementation is based on backtracking.

This concludes the examples and we proceed with describing the fourth construct to be added to the assertion language.

The notation for a *previously assertion* is as follows.

PREV A

It states that A holds in the 'previous state'. More precisely, PREV A holds in state s with history $(s_1, ..., s_n)$ if A holds in state s_n with history $(s_1, ..., s_{n-1})$. It can only be used within an 'always assertion' or a 'sometimes' assertion. This guarantees that there *is* a previous state. If in [X] A there is an occurrence of PREV in A, then this PREV refers to the state immediately before execution of X. This corresponds with a precise point in the text, viz. the point immediately before the [...] construct. In the same way, if in < X > A there is an occurrence of PREV in A, then it refers to the state just before execution of X. We can nest PREVs provided they occur in a context with a sufficiently large history length. For example

AXIOM [X] [Y] PREV PREV A

is all right, provided A contains no further PREVs. The following example is about a seat reservation system for aeroplanes. Seats are coded as natural numbers and there is a simple storage system modelled by the variable predicate is_free and two assignment procedures called free and lock. The clause MOD is_free indicates that free and lock have 'modification access' to is_free. The first axiom explains the effect of free(n) and lock(n) for address n. The second axiom describes what happens with addresses n' with $n' \neq n$, which is that is_free(n') keeps its previous status. We freely use the import and export constructs, postponing the discussion on their meaning and role for state-based specifications until section 5.10.

```
LET RESERVATION :=
EXPORT
  SORT Nat,
  PRED is_free : Nat,
  PROC free : Nat  -> ,
  PROC lock : Nat  ->
FROM
IMPORT NAT INTO
CLASS

  PRED is_free : Nat  VAR
  PROC free : Nat  ->  MOD is_free
  PROC lock : Nat  ->  MOD is_free

  AXIOM FORALL n:Nat (
        < free(n) > TRUE;
        [ free(n) ] is_free(n);
        < lock(n) > TRUE;
        [ lock(n) ] NOT is_free(n) )

  AXIOM FORALL n:Nat, n':Nat ( NOT n = n' => (
        [ free(n) ] is_free(n') <=> PREV is_free(n') ;
        [ lock(n) ] is_free(n') <=> PREV is_free(n') ) )

END
```

The PREV operator of COLD-K is related to Jones' *hooking* operator employed in VDM [2] (though it is somewhat more general). Indeed, hooking is a useful notation and sometimes it is very convenient to write $\overleftarrow{\texttt{a!}}$ as a shorthand for PREV a! and $\overleftarrow{\texttt{NOT a!}}$ as a shorthand for PREV NOT a! etc.

Since we have added four new kinds of assertions, it seems useful to give a survey of all assertions.

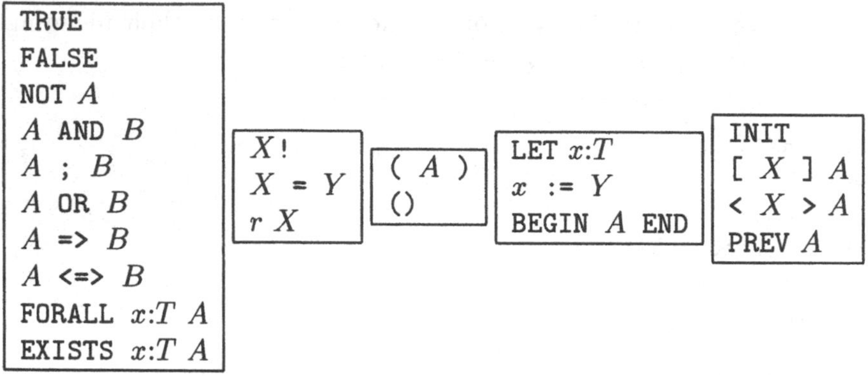

TRUE FALSE NOT A A AND B A ; B A OR B A => B A <=> B FORALL $x{:}T$ A EXISTS $x{:}T$ A	X! X = Y r X	(A) ()	LET $x{:}T$ x := Y BEGIN A END	INIT [X] A < X > A PREV A

Table 5.3. Survey of all assertions.

Analogous to the previously assertion, there is a *previously expression.* It is meant for use in postconditions and the notation for it is as follows

PREV X

Its interpretation is the interpretation of X in the previous state. The type of PREV X is the type of X. Since PREV refers to a previous state, it may only be used in the scope of an 'always assertion' or a 'sometimes' assertion, i.e. after a [...] or a < ... > construct. This guarantees that the notion of 'previous state' is meaningful. length is determined statically. The previously expression in [X] ... PREV Y ... refers to a state just before execution of X. This corresponds with a precise point in the text, viz. the point immediately before the [...] construct. Formally, we need the same notion of 'history' as for the previously assertion. Again, the hooking notation is useful.

The following example demonstrates the use of the previously expression. It is about the same seat reservation system as above. Again a seat can be 'free' or 'not free'. We employ BOOL from the standard library as given in Appendix B, providing for the sort Bool and its operations.

```
LET RESERVATION' :=
EXPORT
  SORT Nat,
  SORT Bool,
  FUNC is_free : Nat -> Bool,
  PROC free : Nat  -> ,
  PROC lock : Nat  ->
FROM
IMPORT NAT INTO
IMPORT BOOL INTO
```

```
CLASS

   FUNC is_free : Nat -> Bool VAR

   AXIOM FORALL n:Nat ( is_free(n)! )

   PROC free : Nat  ->  MOD is_free
   PROC lock : Nat  ->  MOD is_free

   AXIOM FORALL n:Nat (
         < free(n) > TRUE;
         [ free(n) ] is_free(n) = true;
         < lock(n) > TRUE;
         [ lock(n) ] is_free(n) = false )

   AXIOM FORALL n:Nat, n':Nat ( NOT n = n' => (
         [ free(n) ] is_free(n') = PREV is_free(n') ;
         [ lock(n) ] is_free(n') = PREV is_free(n') ) )

END
```

We give a survey of the resulting set of expressions, where we added PREV X in a last box.

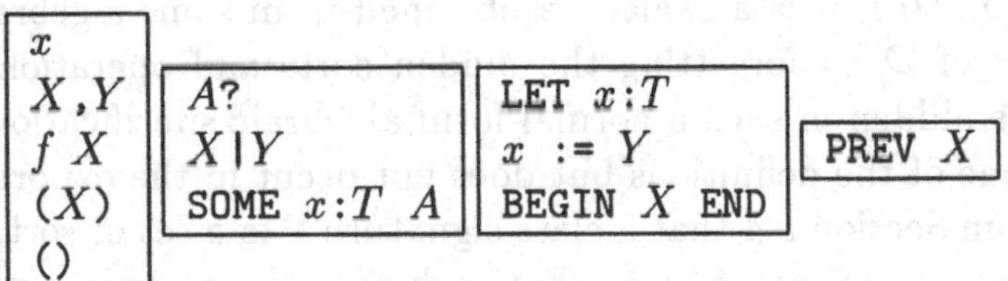

Table 5.4. Survey of all expressions.

After the introductions in Sections 5.1 to 5.3, we introduced the class concept in Sections 5.4 and 5.5. We introduced a class as a special kind of state machine based on the *states as algebras* approach. In Sections 5.6 to 5.9 we introduced the syntactic constructs needed to specify classes and for each individual construct we gave its interpretation in terms of ingredients of classes or constraints on them. In the next section we shall have a more formal look at the notion of 'model' of a specification and we shall define what is meant when we say that a class is a model of a specification.

5.10 Classes and specifications

In this section we shall have a rather formal discussion about the relation between classes which are semantic entities and specifications which are syntactic entities. The reader who wants to focus on the practical aspects of writing formal specifications might want to skip this section on first reading of the text.

A state-based specification is said to be *in normal form* if it is of the form `EXPORT` Γ `FROM CLASS` $\mathcal{D}$ `END` where Γ is a class signature containing only names introduced in $\mathcal{D}$. By means of normal form reduction every state-based specification can be brought into that form. We view such a normal-form state-based specification as a pair $(\Gamma, \mathcal{D})$. Exactly the same process of normal-form reduction used for algebraic specifications applies to state-based specifications. For the details of this reduction we refer to Chapter 3. Therefore the process of determining the meaning of (state-based) schemes is as follows:

$$\text{`scheme'} \xrightarrow{\text{denotation}} \begin{array}{l}\texttt{EXPORT} \\ \quad \textit{class signature} \\ \texttt{FROM} \\ \texttt{CLASS} \\ \quad \textit{definitions} \\ \texttt{END}\end{array} \xrightarrow{\text{interpretation}} \text{`classes'}$$

Recall from Part I that an algebra A is a model of a normal-form algebraic specification $(\Sigma, \mathcal{D})$ if it is a Σ-algebra obtained from some algebra satisfying the definitions of $\mathcal{D}$ by forgetting the hidden sorts and operations. We say that a name is hidden in such a normal-form algebraic specification if it is introduced by one of the definitions but does not occur in the export signature. Recall also from Section 5.4 that a class signature Γ is a set of sort, predicate, function and procedure names such that each sort occurring in a name in Γ is also a member of it.

Definition. A *normal-form state-based specification* is a pair $(\Gamma, \mathcal{D})$ where Γ is a class signature which contains only names introduced in $\mathcal{D}$. $\mathcal{D}$ may contain definitions of variable or dependent functions and predicates as well as procedures and sorts. A Γ'-class C' *satisfies the definitions of* $\mathcal{D}$ iff the following hold:

1. Γ' equals the class signature of $\mathcal{D}$ in the sense that it contains precisely the names introduced by the definitions of $\mathcal{D}$;
2. all states of C' satisfy the constraints introduced by $\mathcal{D}$. □

Note that signatures are a special case of class signatures and that algebraic specifications are a special case of state-based specifications.

Definition. A Γ-class C *is a model of* a normal-form state-based specification $(\Gamma, \mathcal{D})$ if it is a Γ-class obtained from some Γ′-class satisfying the definitions of $\mathcal{D}$ by forgetting

1. the transition relations $\mathcal{T}_p$ for all hidden procedures p;
2. the hidden sorts, functions and predicates of each state. □

This concludes the definition of a class being a model of a state-based specification. It is worthwhile to review the mechanism of forgetting hiddens in more detail. Let Σ' be Γ' without its procedures and similarly let Σ be Γ without its procedures. If Γ' is the class signature of $\mathcal{D}$ and Γ acts as the export signature, then forgetting the hidden sorts, functions and predicates introduces a mapping $\mathcal{F}$: Σ'-algebras $\rightarrow$ Σ-algebras which we call a *forgetful mapping*. This deals with the hiding problem at the level of algebras and the obvious next step is to 'lift' $\mathcal{F}$ to the level of classes. A class with

1. a set of states **State** where each state s has algebra $A(s)$ associated with it,
2. an initial state s_0 and
3. the transition relations $\mathcal{T}_p$ for the procedure names p in Γ',

is mapped to the class defined by

1. the set of states **State** where each state s has algebra $\mathcal{F}(A(s))$,
2. the initial state s_0 and
3. the transition relations $\mathcal{T}_p$ for the procedure names p in Γ.

We illustrate these definitions by an example dealing with the Booleans and a variable function `bit: -> Bool`. There is a hidden procedure `reset` for modifying `bit` and there is one more procedure modifying `bit`, called `set`.

```
EXPORT
  SORT Bool,
  FUNC bit : -> Bool,
  PROC set : ->
FROM
IMPORT BOOL INTO
CLASS

  FUNC bit : -> Bool VAR
  PROC set   : -> MOD bit
  PROC reset : -> MOD bit
```

```
    AXIOM  < set > TRUE;
           [ set ] bit = true;
           < reset > TRUE;
           [ reset ] bit = false

END
```

The above state-based specification has infinitely many models; we show only one particularly simple model amongst these, which is a class with precisely two states. In the picture below we show how this model is obtained as the result of the forgetful mapping $\mathcal{F}$ applied to the two-state class shown in the upper part of the picture. The latter class satisfies the definitions of `BOOL` and the definitions concerning `bit`, `set` and `reset`. To keep the picture simple, only three functions from `BOOL` are shown, whereas `and`, `or`, etc. are not shown.

Note that the procedure `reset` is no longer present in the resulting class anymore and furthermore that each state in the result has an algebra associated with it, which does not contain the functions `true`, `false`, `not`, etc. The fact that these are no longer present is due to the effect of hiding everything except `Bool`, `bit` and `set`.

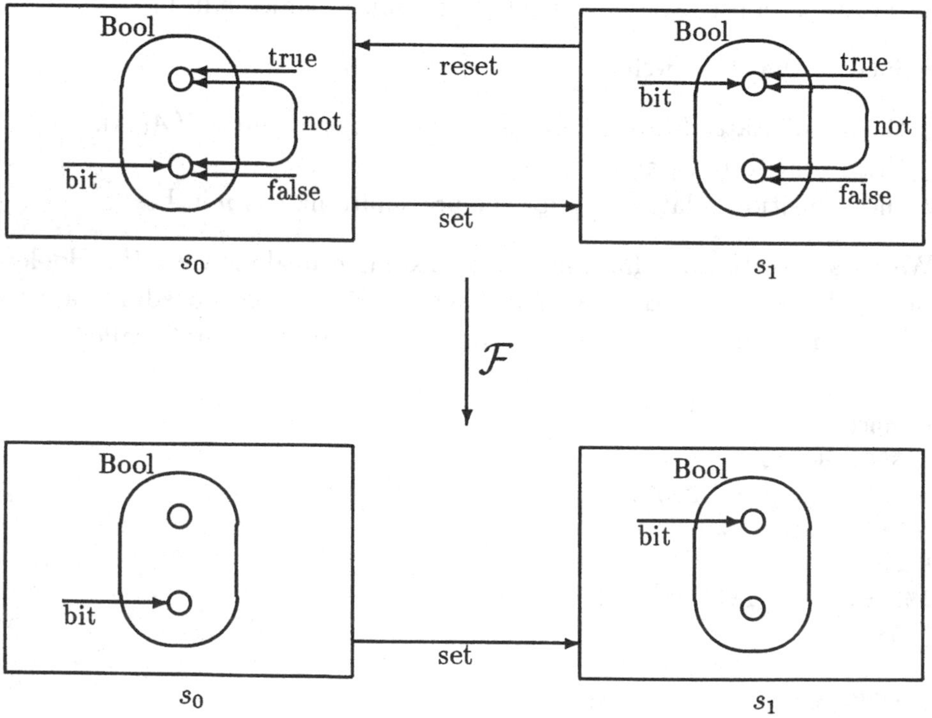

Fig 5.9. Class with procedure `set` obtained by hiding.

In Part I there was a notion of 'model', relating algebras and algebraic specifications, whereas here in Part II we introduced a new notion of 'model', relating classes and state-based specifications. In Section 9.6 we shall compare these notions. There it will be shown that the new notion is an extension of the old notion.

Looking back, this chapter introduced a lot of machinery to describe classes, which are state machines of a special kind, based on the *states as algebras* approach. It is now time to leave these definitions and to turn our attention to the more practical and methodological aspects of *using* this machinery. This is the subject of the next chapter.

Chapter 6

Setting up state-based specifications

6.1 Kinds of axioms

In Chapter 2 a number of techniques for setting up algebraic specifications were given. Now we want to do the same for state-based specifications. Recall that a state-based specification serves to describe a system whose model is a 'class'. A class is a kind of state-machine where each state has an algebra associated with it. Because each such algebra can be viewed as a static world model, classes with their state transitions can be viewed to model *dynamic systems*. Special language constructs to specify these systems were introduced, such as procedures and the operators of dynamic logic. It is typical for these language constructs that they leave the sort of states implicit.

Therefore the techniques of Chapter 2 are mostly useful for describing the static aspects of states, whereas we need complementary guidelines for dealing with the dynamic aspects of a system. This is the main topic of this chapter. Key notions are that of precondition, postcondition and invariant.

In practice it turns out that there are certain patterns that occur quite often in state-based specifications, providing methodological guidelines for systematically setting up state-based specifications. In this chapter we shall do this, focusing on the *axioms*, and we adopt a classification distinguishing four distinct roles an axiom can play. These roles correspond to typical syntactic patterns. We shall refer to these by saying that there are four *kinds* of axioms:

1. properties of all states;
2. invariance properties;
3. properties of the initial state;
4. properties of state transitions including pre- and postcondition axioms and termination axioms.

The properties of all states correspond to the axioms as treated in Part I whereas the other kinds of axioms are new; they deal with the state-based aspects of a system. A property for all states takes the shape

AXIOM A

An invariance axiom takes the shape

AXIOM INIT => I; I => [p] I.

It states the invariance of the assertion I with respect to p. An initial state axiom takes the shape

AXIOM INIT => A.

Properties of state transitions can be described by pre- and postcondition axioms which have the shape AXIOM *pre* => [p] *post* for assertions *pre* and *post*. Properties of state transitions also include termination properties which have the shape AXIOM *pre* => < p > TRUE.

Most of this chapter is devoted to various examples of state-based specifications. There are examples concerning traffic lights, attributes, buffers and finally there is an example dealing with a simple display device. While doing the examples, we shall use them to introduce methodological concepts and discuss alternatives: e.g. in Section 6.2 we use the traffic light system as a stepping-stone to discuss the notion of invariance. Section 6.3 presents the example concerning attributes, but at the same time it presents an important kind of syntactic sugar. Section 6.4 presents the example concerning buffers which is a nice occasion to reconsider the style of specification employed and to discuss the alternatives.

Section 6.5 is a large example. Section 6.6 provides a methodological checklist whereas Section 6.7 is a discussion section.

6.2 Example: specification of traffic lights

We shall present a very simple example in which all four kinds of axioms are used. We consider a road crossing with traffic lights. The formal specification only covers the modelling of the state and state transitions but does not cover aspects of timing. In that sense the traffic light example is not very realistic, and also it has very little to do with software specification, but it serves quite well to illustrate the four kinds of axioms. The picture below sketches a simple road crossing with two streets called `east_street` and `north_street`. The `east_street` carries the traffic moving from west to east or vice versa whereas the north_street carries the traffic moving in directions from south to north or vice versa.

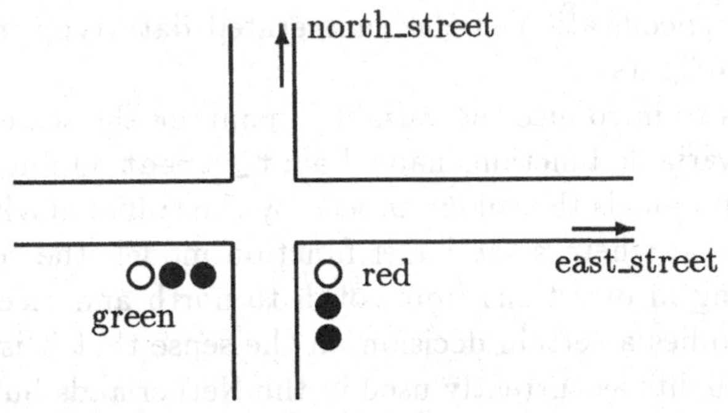

Fig 6.1. Road crossing with traffic lights.

6.2.1 Properties of all states

Recall that the meaning of an axiom is that it holds in *all* states, and so indeed pure algebraic specifications serve to express properties of all states. In practice all state-based specifications begin with an algebraic specification fragment and this is also the case for the traffic light example. The first specification fragment is concerned with the various colours which the traffic lights can take. We introduce the sort Colour which is nothing but an enumerated data type with values **green**, **yellow** and **red**. Although it is possible to take such enumerated data types from a library, we include its definitions directly as part of the state-based specification of the traffic lights. The sort Colour is described by three axioms where the first axiom is about definedness, the second axiom is about 'no confusion' and the third axiom is about 'no junk'. Note that you only give the definitions (omitting CLASS, END, etc.).

```
SORT Colour
FUNC green  : -> Colour
FUNC yellow : -> Colour
FUNC red    : -> Colour

AXIOM green! AND yellow! AND red!

AXIOM NOT green = yellow;
      NOT green = red;
```

```
        NOT yellow = red

    AXIOM FORALL c:Colour (c = green OR c = yellow OR c = red)
```

This concludes the specification of the enumerated data type modelling the colours of the traffic lights.

The next step is to introduce the variables spanning the state space of the traffic lights using variable functions named **east_street** and **north_street**. The former function models the colour as seen by the traffic moving from west to east and vice versa, whereas the latter function models the colour as seen by the traffic moving in directions from south to north and vice versa. This choice already embodies a certain decision, in the sense that it is adequate to describe the traffic lights as currently used in the Netherlands but it is useless to describe the traffic lights employed in e.g. the Federal Republic of Germany, or GB, where the red and yellow lights may be active simultaneously so as to indicate that the green light is about to be activated.

```
FUNC east_street  : -> Colour VAR
FUNC north_street : -> Colour VAR
```

Also for classes, there are properties which should hold in all states, including all intermediate states. We show two axioms stating the properties of all states below. The first axiom is about the definedness of the two variables **east_street** and **north_street**. The second axiom uses an auxiliary predicate named **enabled** and serves to avoid both directions being enabled simultaneously, which would lead to accidents. The latter property of both directions not being enabled simultaneously should hold in *all* states, because we assume that even an intermediate state of short duration not having this property is too serious a violation of safety conditions.

```
AXIOM east_street! AND north_street!

PRED enabled : Colour
PAR  c:Colour
DEF  c = green OR c = yellow

AXIOM NOT ( enabled(east_street) AND enabled(north_street) )
```

6.2.2 Invariance properties

When a class offers several procedures, there might be an assertion which should hold *before* and *after* execution of any of these procedures. In intermediate states, the assertion may (temporarily) be violated. Such an assertion is called an *invariant*. This notion of invariant is an important concept, not only as a specification technique but also as an implementation technique. It occurs in many variations and in many roles – probably the role of loop invariants being known best. As it turns out, there is not just a single notion of invariant; the notion is always 'with respect to' an initial state and a collection of state transition relations. For example, a loop invariant is an invariant with respect to the loop initialisation and the loop body. We shall focus on invariants as a specification technique and our notion of invariant will most often be 'with respect to' the initial state characterised by INIT and some collection of procedures.

In the example we introduce two procedures called **enable_north** and **enable_east**. The procedure **enable_north** serves to model the transition from a state where the **east_street** is enabled (traffic can move from west to east and vice versa) to a state where the **north_street** is enabled. Clearly **enable_north** can be viewed as the sequential composition of two or more intermediate steps but we postpone the discussion of such intermediate steps for a while. There is an invariant with respect to the initial state (characterised by INIT) and the collection of procedures { **enable_north**, **enable_east** }. In a slightly more sloppy style we shall refer to this situation by saying that it is an invariant with respect to **enable_north** and **enable_east**.

```
PROC enable_north : ->
MOD  east_street, north_street

PROC enable_east : ->
MOD  east_street, north_street
```

We introduce the invariant as a predicate. Although it is optional to write the invariant 'in situ' in the axioms, it is in general a good idea to have a name for it. In this case its name is TLI – for Traffic Light Invariant. When TLI holds, the traffic flow is enabled in at least one direction, so as to avoid a complete traffic jam.

```
PRED TLI :
DEF  (east_street = green) OR (north_street = green)
```

We should take care, because the invariant TLI should not contradict the 'properties of all states'. In particular it may not contradict the properties stated by the axiom `east_street! AND north_street!` and the axiom `NOT (enabled(east_street) AND enabled(north_street))`. As usual, the absence of contradictions is shown by constructing a model and in this case it suffices to consider a state where `east_street = green` and `north_street = red`. This takes care of the consistency and the next step concerns preparations for stating the invariance of `TLI`. We introduce an auxiliary procedure: especially if there are many procedures, this is a useful technique for keeping the invariance axiom readable.

```
PROC enable : ->
DEF  ( enable_north
     | enable_east
     )
```

In the definition of `enable` we used the | operator denoting *choice*; the proper definition of the choice operator is postponed until Section 8.2. Here it suffices to know that the meaning of `enable`, which is a relation on State × State, is the union of the relations of `enable_north` and `enable_east`.

If we follow the above hint of adopting an auxiliary procedure, the invariance axiom can always be of the same shape. We put it as a comment for reasons which will become clear soon.

```
% AXIOM INIT => TLI;
%       TLI => [ enable ] TLI
```

When dealing with invariants there are two alternative options, depending on the logical status of the invariance axiom:

1. `TLI` and the invariance axiom are just an aid in setting-up the state-based specification. In a later phase, the invariance with respect to the collection of procedures $\{p_1, \ldots, p_k\}$ say, must be derivable from the definitions or the pre- and postconditions of $p_1, \ldots, p_k$.

2. `TLI` and the invariance axiom are an essential part of a state-based specification; they are not derivable.

In the majority of cases the first option is taken; in this text we shall always use the first option except for one example in Section 8.7.4. When adopting the first option the invariance axiom is best treated as a comment – to distinguish it from a property with a true axiomatic status. We advise explicitly choosing one of these options when formulating an invariant and the invariance axiom;

the first option gives rise to proof obligations offering a systematic approach to writing initialisation conditions and pre- and postconditions. The second option leads to weaker obligations: 'only' the absence of contradictions must be taken care of. In the traffic light example we choose the first option – which is the reason for treating the above axiom as a comment.

6.2.3 Properties of the initial state

Recall that each class has precisely one initial state. We employ the special assertion `INIT` which holds in this initial state only.

```
AXIOM INIT => east_street = green AND north_street = red
```

We have the proof obligation that the axiomatically stated property of the initial state must imply the invariant `TLI`. Indeed, from `east_street = green` it follows that `TLI` holds.

6.2.4 Properties of state transitions

Now we turn our attention to the fourth and last kind of axiom, viz. the state transition properties including pre- and postcondition axioms and termination axioms. In typical applications, there is one pre- and postcondition axiom for each procedure *p*, by which we mean an axiom with a conditional 'always assertion' of the form `AXIOM` *pre* `=> [` *p* `]` *post*. We show the axioms for `enable_east`.

```
PRED pre_east :
DEF  TRUE

PRED post_east :
DEF  east_street = green AND north_street = red

AXIOM pre_east => [ enable_east ] post_east
```

Again we have a proof obligation. We have chosen the first option (see previous section) for the role of the invariant where `TLI` is an aid in setting-up the state-based specification. Therefore we must show that `TLI => [ enable_east ] TLI` which is easy because `TLI` is equivalent with `east_street = green OR north_street = green`, so `post_east => TLI`.

A 'termination' axiom may be added for each procedure, by which we mean an axiom using a sometimes assertion as follows:

```
AXIOM pre_east => < enable_east > TRUE
```

In view of the fact that COLD-K procedures have a *relation* as their meaning, rather than an execution sequence, such a termination axiom refers to a rather weak notion of termination. Whether a given algorithmic procedure will terminate or not depends on the adopted execution model, which is left open in COLD-K. Next, we specify the procedure `enable_north`, which is of course analogous to the specification of `enable_east`.

```
PRED pre_north :
DEF  TRUE

PRED post_north :
DEF  north_street = green AND east_street = red

AXIOM pre_north => [ enable_north ] post_north

AXIOM pre_north => < enable_north > TRUE
```

The picture below shows a state transition established by `enable_north`. At the left-hand side of the picture we see a state with `east_street = green` and `north_street = red` whereas at the right-hand side of the picture we see a state with `north_street = green` and `east_street = red`.

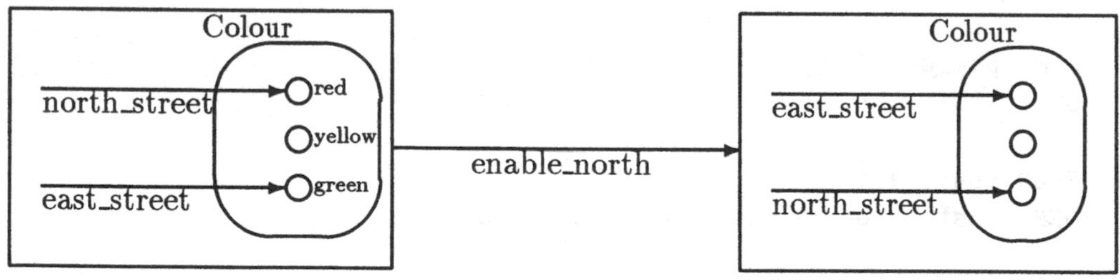

Fig 6.2. State transition.

The specification so far does not exclude that intermediate states arise during the execution of `enable_north` and `enable_east`. In particular, the Dutch traffic light system has at least one intermediate state where the yellow light is activated. It serves to make the road crossing free of cars, which of course takes some time. An actual sequence of state transitions involved in

enable_north could be as shown by the following picture.

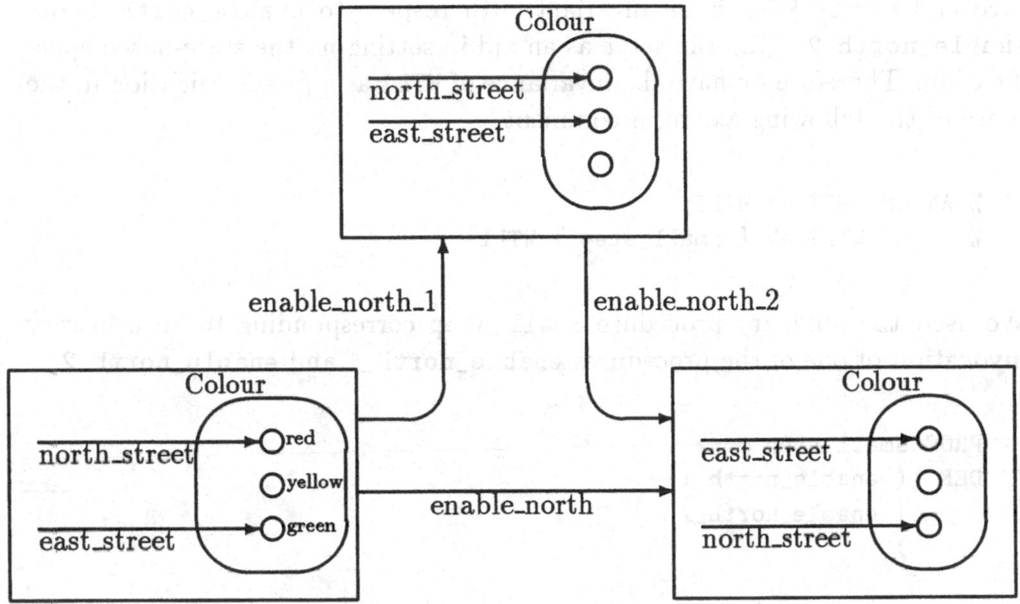

Fig 6.3. State transition with intermediate state.

The above gives a nice opportunity to show that the notion of 'invariant' is a *relative* notion. Suppose that the two small steps of the state transition from Figure 6.3 correspond to two procedures **enable_north_1** and **enable_north_2**, then we see that **TLI** is *not* an invariant with respect to { **enable_north_1**, **enable_north_2** }. At the same time we see that there is another property, which is weaker than **TLI** and which we could call **WTLI**, for Weak Traffic Light Invariant. It is defined as the assertion that both directions do not have a red light at the same time.

```
PROC enable_north_1 : ->
MOD  east_street

PROC enable_north_2 : ->
MOD  east_street, north_street

PRED WTLI :
DEF  NOT((east_street = red) AND (north_street = red))
```

It is not hard to give pre- and postconditions of the procedure `enable_north_1` and `enable_north_2` as suggested by means of the above mentioned picture and clearly `WTLI` is an invariant with respect to `enable_north_1` and `enable_north_2`. `WTLI` can serve as an aid in setting-up the state-based specification. Therefore we have the invariance of `WTLI` as a proof obligation in the sense of the following axiom in comment.

```
% AXIOM INIT => WTLI;
%       WTLI => [ small_step ] WTLI
```

We used the auxiliary procedure `small_step` corresponding to an arbitrary invocation of one of the procedures `enable_north_1` and `enable_north_2`.

```
PROC small_step : ->
DEF  ( enable_north_1
     | enable_north_2
     )
```

For each of the small step procedures there is a pre- and postcondition axiom as well as a termination axiom. We only show the axioms for `enable_north_1` and `enable_north_2` and it is a straightforward extension to add the procedures `enable_east_1` and `enable_east_2` along the same lines.

```
PRED pre_north_1 :
DEF  north_street = red

PRED post_north_1 :
DEF  east_street = yellow

AXIOM pre_north_1 => [ enable_north_1 ] post_north_1

AXIOM pre_north_1 => < enable_north_1 > TRUE

PRED pre_north_2 :
DEF  TRUE

PRED post_north_2 :
DEF  north_street = green AND east_street = red

AXIOM pre_north_2 => [ enable_north_2 ] post_north_2

AXIOM pre_north_2 => < enable_north_2 > TRUE
```

It is a routine matter to check the invariance of **WTLI** with respect to the procedures **enable_north_1** and **enable_north_2** and in fact with respect to *all* procedures of the example.

This concludes the traffic light example which served to explain the four kinds of axioms mentioned at the beginning of this chapter. In the next sections we shall give some more examples of small but useful state-based specifications.

6.3 Example: specification of attributes

In this section we shall specify *attributes* and reduce them to a simple mechanism for associating values with instances. The specification below is a state-based specification, because the attributes can be modified – like a classical programming variable. There is a function **attr** which yields the value of the attribute for a given instance. There is a procedure **set_attr** for assigning a value to the attribute of a given instance. This procedure has the effect of modifying the function **attr**. Again we shall build the specification in an incremental manner, mixing formal and informal texts and beginning with a naive version. We will then introduce more subtle aspects of the specification.

```
LET ATTR :=
EXPORT
  SORT Inst,
  SORT Item,
  FUNC attr     : Inst        -> Item,
  PROC set_attr : Inst # Item ->
FROM
CLASS

  SORT Inst
  SORT Item

  FUNC attr : Inst -> Item  VAR

  PROC set_attr : Inst # Item ->  MOD attr

  AXIOM {ATTR1} FORALL i:Inst,v:Item ( < set_attr(i,v) > TRUE )

  AXIOM {ATTR2} FORALL i:Inst,v:Item
                ( [ set_attr(i,v) ] ( attr(i) = v ) )

END
```

The problem with the above version of axiom ATTR2 is that it is too weak because it allows the attribute values of *all* instances to be modified. Therefore we propose a correction to the postcondition of set_attr, stating explicitly that after execution of set_attr(i,v), the value of attr(j) for every *other* instance j remains as before.

```
% correction (1)

AXIOM   FORALL i:Inst,v:Item (
{ATTR2} [ set_attr(i,v) ]
        ( attr(i) = v AND
          FORALL j:Inst
          ( NOT j = i => ( attr(j) = PREV attr(j) ) ) ) )
```

Still we should not be satisfied with the above axiom: because of the strictness of '=', the postcondition is too strong. To see this, recall that equality is *strict*, by which we mean that $X = Y$ implies that X! and Y!. In this case PREV attr(j) occurs as the right-hand side of an equation and so this equation implies (PREV attr(j))!. So when the sort Inst has at least two objects, the postcondition in the above version of ATTR2 makes a statement about the definedness of the attr function in the state *before* execution of set_attr(i,v). Therefore we propose the following final version of axiom ATTR2.

```
% correction (2)

AXIOM   FORALL i:Inst,v:Item (
{ATTR2} [ set_attr(i,v) ]
        ( attr(i) = v AND
          FORALL j:Inst, w:Item
          ( NOT j = i => ( w = attr(j) <=> w = PREV attr(j) ) ) ) )
```

Let us explain this final version of ATTR2. Consider some instance j (where j $\neq$ i) for which in the previous state (before set_attr(i,v)) the 'attribute' value was already defined and had value w, say. Then we can read the bi-implication in the postcondition from right to left (<=) and then the conclusion w = attr(j) shows that attr(j) still has its old value w. Next consider some instance j (where j $\neq$ i) for which in the previous state the attribute was *not* defined. So there is no w such that PREV attr(j) equals w (use strictness of '='). Now suppose attr(j) would have some value w; then we read the bi-implication from left to right (=>) with conclusion that PREV attr(j) equals w *which however was not the case*. Therefore we conclude that attr(j) does not have some value w, in other words: if attr(j) was undefined in the previous state, then it remains undefined. Finally we mention a subtle syntactic detail of ATTR2: we have arranged the layout of the bi-implication and its equations such that the PREV operator comes last. In this way we easily restrict the scope of the PREV operator without using brackets (PREV has relatively low priority). Summarising, we can read ATTR2 as follows: set_attr(i,v) sets the value of attr(i) to v and all other instances (j) keep their attribute value – if they have one. If their attr value was undefined, then it remains undefined.

When we compare this example with the classification of axioms into four kinds proposed in the beginning of this chapter, it can be seen that we only used the fourth category of 'properties of state transitions'.

Let us add a remark about syntactic sugar which could be useful in view of the elaborate postcondition needed to state that *the value of* attr(j) *for every other instance* j *remains as before*. By way of syntactic sugar one could write

```
% syntactic sugar

  PROC set_attr : Inst # Item ->
  PAR  i,v
  MOD  attr(i)
  POST attr(i) = v
```

to capture the definition of set_attr and the axioms ATTR1 and ATTR2 at once. This idea has been worked out in the language COLD-1 [29].

This concludes the example concerning attributes. In the next section we shall give an example concerning buffers.

6.4 Example: specification of buffers

In this section we shall specify a sort of *buffers* with put and get operations. The buffers serve to store values of sort Item which are treated in a FIFO (first in first out) manner. The following picture sketches a buffer in which three items i_0, i_1 and i_2 have been entered (in that order).

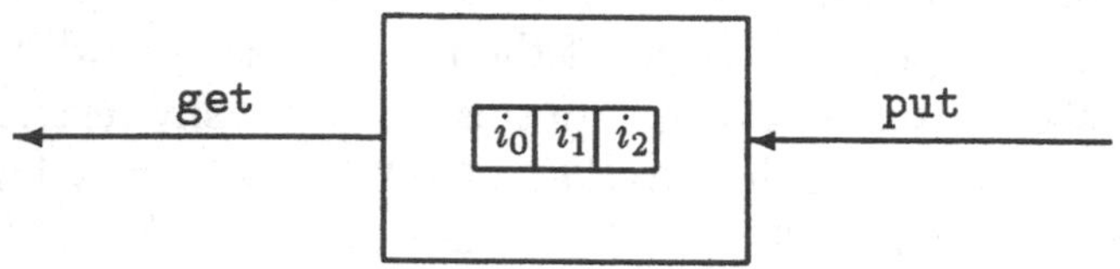

Fig 6.4. Buffer containing three items.

We shall construct the specification in an incremental manner, as before. The example builds upon the standard class descriptions NAT and SEQ which are assumed to be taken from the standard library (see B.2 and B.7 in the appendix). NAT is concerned with natural numbers as discussed in Chapters 1 and 2. SEQ is concerned with finite sequences and since these have not been discussed yet, we show the export signature here as well.

```
LET SEQ :=
EXPORT
  SORT Item,
  SORT Nat,
  SORT Seq,
  FUNC empty :              -> Seq,
  FUNC cons  : Item # Seq -> Seq,
  FUNC hd    : Seq          -> Item,
  FUNC tl    : Seq          -> Seq,
  FUNC len   : Seq          -> Nat,
  FUNC sel   : Seq # Nat  -> Item,
  FUNC cat   : Seq # Seq  -> Seq,
  FUNC rev   : Seq          -> Seq
FROM
IMPORT NAT INTO
CLASS
  % ...
END;
```

There are three operations exported by BUFFER, with the following intended interpretation. For an item i and a buffer b, put(i, b) means to add i to the contents of buffer b. Similarly get(b) removes one item from the buffer b, making the result available in out. The function out thus records the last item obtained by get.

```
LET BUFFER :=
EXPORT
  SORT Seq,
  SORT Item,
  SORT Buffer,
  PROC put : Item # Buffer -> ,
  PROC get : Buffer        -> ,
  FUNC out :               -> Item
FROM
IMPORT NAT INTO
IMPORT SEQ INTO
CLASS

  SORT Buffer

  FUNC cont : Buffer -> Seq  VAR

  FUNC len : Buffer -> Nat
  PAR  b:Buffer
  DEF  len(cont(b))
```

An alternative would have been to use the queues as specified in Part I, but here we simply start from scratch, using `SEQ`. We shall refer to `cont`(b) as the *contents* of b. There is an invariant named `BI` for Buffer Invariant, which asserts that `cont`(b) is defined for all buffers b. The invariant is mainly an aid in setting up the state-based specification. This gives rise to a proof obligation for the initial state and for the state transitions of the procedures `put` and `get`. We postulate the truth of the invariant in the initial state.

```
PRED BI :
DEF  FORALL b:Buffer ( cont(b)! )

AXIOM {BUF1} INIT => BI

% AXIOM BI => [ buffer_op ] BI

PROC buffer_op : ->
DEF  ( put(SOME i:Item (), SOME b:Buffer ())
     | get(SOME b:Buffer(gtr(len(b),zero)))
     )
```

The above `buffer_op` is an auxiliary procedure, corresponding to the invocation of an 'arbitrary' buffer operation (with a restriction on the parameter of **get**). We proceed with the **put** operation.

```
FUNC add : Seq # Item -> Seq
PAR  s:Seq,i:Item
DEF  cat(s,cons(i,empty))

PROC put : Item # Buffer -> MOD cont

AXIOM  FORALL i:Item,b:Buffer
{BUF2} ( cont(b)! => < put(i,b) > TRUE )

AXIOM  FORALL i:Item,b:Buffer
{BUF3} ( cont(b)! => [ put(i,b) ]
         ( cont(b) = add(PREV cont(b),i);
           FORALL c:Buffer,s:Seq
           ( NOT c = b => (s = cont(c) <=> s = PREV cont(c))) )
```

The first clause in the postcondition of put(i,b) in axiom BUF3 uses the add function – which is auxiliary. The definition of add employs the *concatenation* operation cat on sequences which comes from SEQ. After execution of put(i,b) the new contents of the buffer is add(PREV cont(b),i) which can only be the case if cont(b) was already defined. This explains that the definedness of cont(b) is a precondition. For an explanation of the bi-implication construct used in BUF3 we refer to the explanation of ATTR2 in section 6.3, which is a very similar case. The next operation is get which is very similar to the put operation. We use a dedicated variable out to pass the result of get. Although COLD-K provides for result passing of procedures, we consider this construct as outside the scope of Part II; hence we use the somewhat clumsy approach with out.

```
PROC get : Buffer -> MOD cont, out

FUNC out : -> Item VAR

AXIOM  FORALL b:Buffer
{BUF4} ( gtr(len(b),zero) => < get(b) > TRUE )

AXIOM  FORALL b:Buffer
{BUF5} ( gtr(len(b),zero) => [ get(b) ]
         ( cons(out,cont(b)) = PREV cont(b);
           FORALL c:Buffer,s:Seq
           ( NOT c = b => (s = cont(c) <=> s = PREV cont(c))) )
```

```
END
```

We mention the axioms used in the buffer example according to our standard classification.

1. properties of all states: the axioms of NAT and SEQ;
2. invariance properties: BI (which is derivable);
3. properties of the initial state: BUF1;
4. properties of state transitions: BUF2 ... BUF5.

Before going to the next example we should discuss the particular style used here and we should mention an alternative style. The style used applies to most other state-based specifications, but BUFFER is a nice occasion to discuss it. The style used is to treat the invariants *explicitly*, which gives rise to *implementation freedom*. For example, a programmer wanting to implement BUFFERS can choose algorithms for put and get which proceed in two or more steps where in the intermediate states the invariant need not hold. This is very typical for the way such algorithms work: first they change the data structures involved to achieve the main effect of put or get. After that there is a cleaning-up step where the invariant is established again. Let us compare this with a different style where we would give BI the status of an axiom, which is essentially the same as writing `AXIOM FORALL b:Buffer ( cont(b)! )`. If we take this axiom seriously in the sense that it applies to the implementation directly, then this prohibits intermediate states where cont(b) is temporarily undefined. From the viewpoint of the COLD-K writer the latter style is easier, because the proof obligations and some of the preconditions simply vanish. To make this style usable in connection with practical implementations however requires a certain liberal view on the relation between a specification and its implementation (a notion called the *implementation relation*, to be addressed in Section 8.8). In this liberal style one assumes a certain implicit abstraction step built-in to this implementation relation. Throughout this text we shall stick to the first style (the *explicit style*).

In addition to this fundamental issue of *explicit* or *implicit* treatment of implementation freedom, there are many variations on BUFFERS with respect to minor details. We mention a few variations. For example one could strengthen the precondition of put(i, b), which now is cont(b)!, to become BI. This is a valid option which has the consequence that it allows for a slightly larger class of implementations. When the precondition is cont(b)!, the put operation must work, even if the data structures of some other buffers are messed up. When the precondition is BI, the put operation need only work when at a 'global' level *all* data structures dealing with buffers are in correct form. As a second variation one could decide to add a `peep` operation which is like `get` but which has no side-effect. And so on.

This concludes the example concerning buffers. In the next section we shall give an example concerning a display device.

6.5 Example: specification of a display

The example is a simplified version of a description of a VDU-like display device. The simplification lies in the fact that the display is *one-dimensional* – as contrasted with real VDU displays which are two-dimensional. The simplification only serves to keep the example small enough for the purposes of this text. We begin with algebraic specifications of characters and strings and we use `NAT` from the library. The specification of `CHAR` makes explicit that `Char` is a kind of subset of `Nat` by means of the function `ord`, which is an embedding; `chr` is its inverse. At the same time `ord` and `chr` act as a kind of conversion functions. The predicate `dom` characterises the domain of `chr`. We adopt specific details of the ASCII character set.

```
LET CHAR :=
EXPORT
  SORT Char,
  SORT Nat,
  FUNC chr : Nat  -> Char,
  FUNC ord : Char -> Nat,
  FUNC minchar :  -> Char,
  FUNC maxchar :  -> Char,
  FUNC blank :    -> Char,
  FUNC tilde :    -> Char
FROM
IMPORT NAT INTO
CLASS

   SORT Char
   FUNC min : -> Nat
   FUNC max : -> Nat

   FUNC chr : Nat -> Char
   FUNC ord : Char -> Nat

   PRED dom : Nat
   PAR  m:Nat
   DEF  leq(min,m) AND leq(m,max)
```

```
  AXIOM
  {CHAR1} min = 0 AND max = 127;
          FORALL m:Nat (
  {CHAR2} chr(m)! <=> dom(m);
  {CHAR3} dom(m) => ord(chr(m)) = m )

  PRED is_gen : Char
  IND  FORALL m:Nat ( dom(m) => is_gen(chr(m)) )

  AXIOM {CHAR4} FORALL c:Char ( is_gen(c) )

  FUNC minchar : -> Char DEF chr(min)
  FUNC maxchar : -> Char DEF chr(max)

  FUNC blank : -> Char
  DEF  chr(32)

  FUNC tilde : -> Char
  DEF  chr(126)

END;
```

A version of CHAR has been adopted as a part of the standard library (see the appendix). Strings are nothing but sequences of characters and we re-use SEQ from the standard library. The instantiation of schemes from the standard library is somewhat clumsy, which is mainly caused by the fact that the treatment of 'parameterised schemes' is delayed until part III. In Section 10.4 an alternative will be treated.

```
LET STRING :=
EXPORT
  SORT Char,
  SORT Nat,
  SORT String,
  FUNC empty :                      -> String,
  FUNC cons  : Char # String        -> String,
  FUNC hd    : String               -> Char,
  FUNC tl    : String               -> String,
  FUNC len   : String               -> Nat,
  FUNC sel   : String # Nat         -> Char,
  FUNC cat   : String # String      -> String,
  FUNC rev   : String               -> String
FROM
IMPORT NAT INTO
```

```
IMPORT CHAR INTO
CLASS

  % ... as SEQ
  % (with Seq replaced by String and Item by Char)
END;
```

The following picture sketches the display as a one-dimensional screen with eight positions that can contain characters (A, B, C, white space etc.) and one distinguished position which corresponds to the cursor.

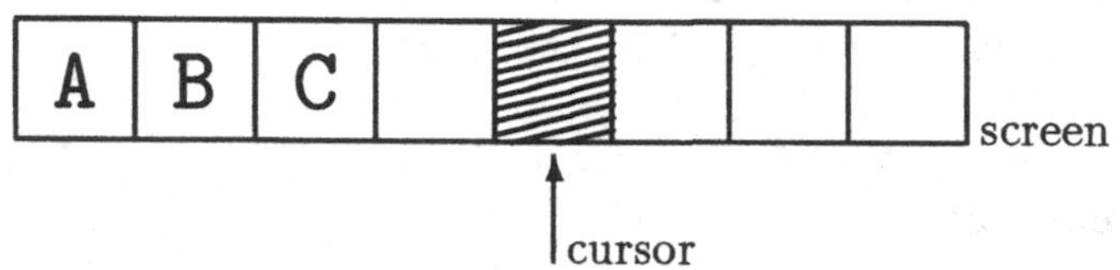

Fig 6.5. Display device with cursor and screen.

The DISPLAY specification below starts with giving the signature of the class and the intended interpretation of the predicates, functions and procedures in its signature – in comment.

```
LET DISPLAY :=
EXPORT
  SORT Nat,
  SORT Char,
  SORT String,
  FUNC screen : -> String,
  FUNC cursor : -> Nat,
  FUNC po : -> Nat ,   % "number of positions"
  PROC cr : ->     ,   % "carriage return"
  PROC bc : ->     ,   % "backwards cursor"
  PROC ce : ->     ,   % "clear to end of line"
  PROC cl : ->     ,   % "clear display"
  PROC nd : ->     ,   % "next datum"
  PROC cm : Nat -> ,   % "cursor motion"
  PROC pr : Char ->    % "print character"
FROM
```

We introduce a constant po for number of *po*sitions. In order not to allow the display example to be completely trivial we assume that po > 1 which will be expressed by means of an axiom later.

The next step is to import algebraic specifications of the relevant data types, in particular natural numbers, characters and strings. After that we introduce the variables spanning the state space – which is an important decision – and in this case we choose two variables. Next we elaborate upon the remaining `CLASS ... END` part of `DISPLAY`.

```
IMPORT NAT    INTO
IMPORT CHAR   INTO
IMPORT STRING INTO

CLASS

  FUNC screen : -> String  VAR
  FUNC cursor : -> Nat     VAR
```

Not all value-pairs for `screen` and `cursor` correspond to acceptable states. Therefore we formulate an invariant named `DI` for Display Invariant. In order to keep the invariant readable we introduce auxiliary predicates. We employ an auxiliary predicate `printable` where we make use of the adopted specific details from the ASCII character set.

```
FUNC po : -> Nat

AXIOM gtr(po,1)

PRED printable : Char
PAR  c:Char
DEF  leq(ord(blank),ord(c)) AND leq(ord(c),ord(tilde))

PRED DI1 :
DEF  len(screen) = po

PRED DI2 :
DEF  lss(cursor,po)

PRED DI3 :
DEF  FORALL i:Nat ( lss(i,po) => printable(sel(screen,i)) )

PRED DI :
DEF  DI1 AND DI2 AND DI3
```

We must make up our minds about the role of the invariant and as usual we choose again to let DI and its invariance serve as an aid in setting up the state-based class description. This gives rise to proof obligations offering a systematic approach to writing an initialisation condition and pre- and post conditions. The following procedure is auxiliary. It corresponds to an invocation of an *arbitrary* operation of DISPLAY (with the proper restrictions on parameters).

```
PROC display_op : ->
DEF  ( cr
     | bc
     | ce
     | cl
     | nd
     | cm(SOME i:Nat (lss(i,po)))
     | pr(SOME c:Char (printable(c)))
     )
```

Here is the invariance axiom; we treat it as a comment because it should be derivable. We also give the initialisation, split over three assertions labelled INI1, INI2 and INI3.

```
% AXIOM INIT => DI;
%       DI => [ display_op ] DI

AXIOM  INIT => (
{INI1} len(screen) = po;
{INI2} cursor = 0;
{INI3} FORALL i:Nat ( lss(i,po) => sel(screen,i) = blank ) )
```

By way of proof obligation we must show that INIT => DI. Therefore we assume INIT and then show DI1, DI2 and DI3 respectively.

1. DI1 is INI1;
2. DI2 follows from INI2 because cursor $= 0 < 1 <$ po;
3. DI3 follows from INI3 because blanks are printable.

Now we turn our attention to the description of the operations. Our first operation is called cr for *c*arriage *r*eturn and it serves to bring the cursor back to its leftmost position.

```
PROC cr : -> MOD cursor
```

```
AXIOM < cr > TRUE

AXIOM [ cr ] cursor = 0
```

The proof obligation is to show that DI => [cr] DI. So we assume a state where DI holds and then we consider a state obtained by executing cr. For the latter state we must show that DI1, DI2 and DI3 hold.

1. DI1 holds because it only depends on screen;
2. DI2 holds because cursor $= 0 < 1 <$ po;
3. DI3 holds because it only depends on screen.

Now we turn our attention to the next operation called bc for *b*ackwards *c*ursor. This operation moves the cursor one position backwards (if possible). Clearly it only needs modification rights with respect to cursor and not to screen.

```
PRED pre_bc :
DEF  cursor!

PROC bc : -> MOD cursor

AXIOM pre_bc => < bc > TRUE

AXIOM pre_bc => [ bc ]
        ( LET cursor':Nat; cursor' := PREV cursor;
          cursor' = 0 => cursor = 0;
          gtr(cursor',0) => cursor = pred(cursor') )
```

Note that the behaviour of bc is not specified for states where NOT cursor!, which means that this specification allows for 'GIGO' implementations of bc (Garbage In $\Rightarrow$ Garbage Out). The proof obligation is DI => [bc] DI. Therefore, assuming DI and considering a state obtained by executing bc, we show DI1, DI2 and DI3.

1. DI1 holds because it only depends on screen;
2. DI2 holds because there are two cases: (a) if PREV cursor $= 0$ then cursor is not modified, hence DI2 is not affected; the second case (b) is when PREV cursor > 0 and then we use that cursor $=$ cursor'$-1 <$ po because cursor' $<$ po;
3. DI3 holds because it only depends on screen.

Now we turn our attention to ce, for *c*lear to *e*nd of line. ce clears everything from the cursor to the end of the screen. It does not move the cursor. We need a non-trivial precondition for which we introduce a special precondition predicate. Throughout this display device example we choose to only introduce such predicates when they are non-trivial; we omit them when they would be TRUE – as for cr.

```
PROC ce : -> MOD screen

PRED pre_ce :
DEF  lss(cursor,len(screen))

AXIOM pre_ce => < ce > TRUE

AXIOM pre_ce => [ ce ]
                ( len(screen) = len(PREV screen);
                  FORALL i:Nat ( lss(i,cursor) =>
                     sel(screen,i) = sel((PREV screen),i) );
                  FORALL i:Nat ( leq(cursor,i) AND lss(i,po) =>
                     sel(screen,i) = blank ) )
```

Note that if we adopt TRUE as a precondition for ce, the postcondition of ce would be too strong, implying the definedness of screen and cursor $<$ len(screen). Note that in practice the precondition does not require special care, because it is a logical consequence of DI.

We have the obligation of showing that DI => [ce] DI. So we assume a state where DI holds and then we consider a state obtained by executing ce. For the latter state we must show that DI1, DI2 and DI3 respectively hold again.

1. DI1 holds because it holds in the previous state and len(screen) keeps its value;
2. DI2 holds because it only depends on cursor;
3. DI3 holds because for each position either (a) its character remains the same, or (b) a blank is written – which is printable.

The next operation is called cl, for *cl*ear display. It serves to move the cursor to the leftmost position (0) and to clear the screen.

```
PROC cl : -> MOD screen, cursor

FUNC  blanks : -> String
DEF   SOME s:String
```

```
    ( len(s) = po;
      FORALL i:Nat ( lss(i,po) => sel(s,i) = blank ) )

AXIOM < cl > TRUE

AXIOM [ cl ] screen = blanks AND cursor = 0
```

To deal with the proof obligation DI => [cl] DI, assume DI and consider a state after execution of cl.

1. DI1 holds because len(blanks) = po;
2. DI2 holds because cursor $= 0 < 1 <$ po;
3. DI3 holds because blanks are printable.

The next operation is nd, a name which probably comes from *n*ext *d*atum (the names of the operations have been kept compatible with the UNIX termcap facility). It moves the cursor one position forwards (if possible).

```
PRED pre_nd :
DEF  cursor!

PROC nd : -> MOD cursor

AXIOM pre_nd => < nd > TRUE

AXIOM pre_nd => [ nd ]
       ( LET cursor':Nat; cursor' := PREV cursor;
         lss(cursor',pred(po)) => cursor = succ(cursor');
         cursor' = pred(po) => cursor = cursor' )
```

Let us verify our proof obligation DI => [nd] DI – as before. Assume DI and consider a state after nd.

1. DI1 holds because it only depends on screen;
2. DI2 holds because there are two cases: (a) if cursor' $<$ po $- 1$ then the increment of cursor preserves DI2; the second case (b) is when cursor' $=$ po $- 1$ in which case the cursor stays at the same position;
3. DI3 holds because it only depends on screen.

Next comes the operation cm for *c*ursor *m*otion (or *c*ursor *m*ovement). This operation serves for moving the cursor to an arbitrary position and it is specified as follows.

```
PROC cm : Nat -> MOD cursor

AXIOM FORALL i:Nat ( lss(i,po) => < cm(i) > TRUE )

AXIOM FORALL i:Nat ( lss(i,po) => [ cm(i) ] cursor = i )
```

We have the proof obligation `DI => [ cm(SOME i:Nat (lss(i,po))) ] DI`. Therefore we assume a state where `DI` holds and consider a state obtained by executing `cm(i)` for some `i` $<$ `po`. `DI1`, `DI2` and `DI3` must hold again.

1. `DI1` holds because it only depends on `screen`;
2. `DI2` follows from `cursor = i` and `lss(i,po)`;
3. `DI3` holds because it only depends on `screen`.

Finally we arrive at `pr` for *pr*int. It sends characters to the display to be printed. The character is put at the position of the cursor. The cursor and the subsequent text move one position forwards (if possible). Therefore it has modification rights with respect to both `screen` and `cursor`.

```
PROC pr : Char -> MOD screen, cursor

PRED pre_pr :
DEF  lss(cursor,len(screen))

AXIOM FORALL c:Char ( pre_pr AND printable(c) => < pr(c) > TRUE )

AXIOM FORALL c:Char ( pre_pr AND printable(c) => [ pr(c) ]

        ( LET cursor':Nat; cursor' := PREV cursor;
          LET screen':String; screen' := PREV screen;

          len(screen) = len(screen');
          sel(screen,cursor') = c;

          lss(cursor',pred(po)) => cursor = succ(cursor');
          cursor' = pred(po) => cursor = cursor';

          FORALL i:Nat ( lss(i,cursor') =>
              sel(screen,i) = sel(screen',i) );

          FORALL i:Nat ( gtr(i,cursor') AND lss(i,po) =>
              sel(screen,i) = sel(screen',pred(i)) ) ) )
```

```
END
```

Note that it is not sufficient just to say that the screen is updated at the position of the old cursor (clause `sel(screen,cursor') = c` above). We must also say that the other screen positions keep their old value (or shift) and that the cursor goes one position to the right, except when the old cursor value is $po - 1$, in which case the cursor does not move. Since the postcondition makes equality statements involving `PREV` values, we need a non-trivial precondition and we introduce a special precondition predicate named `pre_pr`. Again in practice this `pre_pr` does not require special care because of the fact that `DI` implies `pre_pr`.

We must show that `DI => [ pr(SOME c:Char (printable(c))) ] DI`. So we assume `DI` and then we consider a state after `pr(c)` for some printable c. Again we must show the three constituents of the invariant.

1. `DI1` holds because it holds in the previous state and `len(screen)` keeps its value;
2. `DI2` follows from the case analysis of the postcondition where the case `cursor' = po - 1` is treated explicitly: the cursor does not move in that case;
3. `DI3` holds because all characters (but one) of the screen were already on the screen in the previous state; furthermore c is known to be printable.

6.6 How to set up an axiomatic state-based class description

In this section we shall formulate some methodological guidelines on setting up axiomatic state-based class descriptions. Most of these have been illustrated already by the examples of the previous sections. Although the list below does not work as a recipe, it might help as a checklist.

1. Give the signature of the class and the intended interpretation (intuition) of the sorts, predicates, functions and procedures in the signature.
2. Import algebraic specifications of relevant data types.
3. Choose the variables which span the state space. The choice should be guided by intuition and also by the goal of minimising the number of additional constraints and invariants needed. Too many variables tend to make the specification confusing; however, if there is just one variable, then the possibilities of the modification rights are poorly exploited.
4. Assign modification rights to the procedures. No procedure should have modification rights with respect to variables which it need not modify.

5. Formulate invariants: as a 'redundant' help for specifying the effect of the procedures, or expressing additional constraints on the state space (an example of the latter will be given in Section 8.7.4).
6. Where needed, introduce auxiliaries, such as functions and predicates that depend on the variables, auxiliary procedures for keeping the invariance axioms readable and auxiliary predicates serving as invariants, preconditions and postconditions.
7. Give axioms, according to the four categories: (1) properties of all states; (2) invariance properties; (3) properties of the initial state and (4) properties of state transitions. In the latter category, there are typically a pre- and postcondition axiom and a termination axiom for each procedure.

6.7 Discussion

The checklist of the previous section and the styles employed and advised throughout the examples of this chapter should not be taken as a rigid standard (not allowing any deviations). The language COLD-K offers many constructs which can be used in many ways and it would be wrong to be prescriptive. In fact, the careful reader may notice that throughout the various examples slightly different alternative solutions and layout styles have been used for similar problems. Moreover, this chapter has focused on *axiomatic* state-based specifications, but surely *algorithmic* state-based specifications are equally useful. In this text we shall only consider algorithmic descriptions when we discuss implementation of state-based specifications, but in fact an algorithmic state-based specification is absolutely valid in the role of specification as well.

Let us also pause a moment to look back to the specification of `DISPLAY` which is somewhat larger than the earlier examples and also more realistic than the traffic light example. The amount of work in writing this specification is almost proportional to the number of procedures N. There is a constant part, which introduces the algebraic data types, spans the state space, formulates the invariant and states a suitable property of the initial state. Then for each procedure there is a similar piece of work, viz. to introduce the procedure with its `MOD` clause, to give the properties of state transitions and to verify that that the procedure preserves the invariant `DI`. Moreover, the specification of one procedure does not interfere with the specification of another procedure. So we could say that the amount of work W to set up a state-based specification with N procedures requires a certain 'constant' C plus some work w for each procedure, as described by the following formula:

$$W = C + w.N$$

Of course, this formula should only be viewed as a heuristic.

Chapter 7

Structuring state-based specifications

7.1 Introduction

When constructing large state-based specifications, the modularisation facilities offered by COLD-K make it possible to split up a large specification into many smaller ones: essentially the same modularisation mechanisms which are available for algebraic specifications are also available for state-based specifications. In Section 5.10 the meaning of these structuring mechanisms was explained using a two-step approach: the first step is a process of normal form reduction and the second step is to interpret normal forms in terms of 'classes'.

Recall that the modularisation mechanisms include flat class descriptions of the form `CLASS ... END`, and import, export and abbreviation, which are denoted using the keywords `IMPORT` and `INTO`, `EXPORT` and `FROM` and `LET`. Typically a large state-based specification is constructed in a bottom-up fashion, beginning with the introduction of relevant algebraic data types and after that the introduction of one or more state-machines, possibly combined to form a more complex machine and possibly provided with a user interface layer. The introduction of relevant data types can often be viewed as a formalisation or modelling of the application domain. We summarise this in Table 7.1, which can be viewed as a methodological guideline.

phase	*activity*
application domain modelling	introduction of algebraic data types
system description	introduction of state-machines

Table 7.1. Bottom-up construction of a large state-based specification.

Although modularisation helps in mastering the complexity of a system, there is hardly any possibility for information hiding: when one is reading or writing part of the last top-level class description of a large structured specification, it is hard to avoid an understanding of most of the preceding class descriptions. The first important step in mastering the complexity of a large specification is to reuse well-established and familiar existing class descriptions, and of course the standard library offers opportunities for that form of reuse. Secondly, the use of invariants as an aid in setting up state-based specifications can also help in mastering the complexity. Furthermore there are many techniques, coming from the field of language definition and denotational semantics, which can be used successfully. As a fourth point we mention the use of automated tools, which can be of help too: a syntax and typechecker can be of great help to eliminate many small mistakes and the use of tools generating overview pictures to keep a clear view of the module structure can be of help as well.

We mentioned four issues concerning mastering complexity, each of its own particular nature. Reuse of class descriptions is a kind of macro-technique in the sense that it applies to entire modules. Using invariants and techniques from denotational semantics etc. are a kind of micro-technique because they apply to the internal details of the modules. The last point is concerned with tool-support rather than with mental tools.

There is no such thing as a standard recipe for setting up *large* state-based specifications and we feel that the best thing we can do here is to give a non-trivial example. The example is not a really big specification, but it might provide some useful insights and it certainly shows an interesting combination of various techniques. In particular, most of this chapter consists of a state-based specification concerning an INGRES-like database system. An earlier version of this specification was worked out in cooperation with J.H.A. Gelissen and W.E. Baats, see [30]. The example serves to illustrate a number of techniques:

1. The use of the standard library to get started quickly.
2. Sharing of state-based descriptions. By sharing we mean that one description is imported into (= shared by) more than one higher-level description.
3. Constructor functions and inductive definitions for modelling the syntax of a language. In this case we shall be concerned with fragments of a simple query language.
4. Inductive definitions to define the well-formedness of the language. This well-formedness will depend on the state but nevertheless, as it turns out, it can be described by means of purely algebraic techniques.
5. Interpreting elements of a language where bound variables play a role.

The technique is to have meaning functions taking an additional argument, i.e. a mapping from names to tuples.

6. Using simple set-theoretical constructs for giving the semantics of queries.

7.2 Example: specification of a database

7.2.1 Tuples and relations

The first step in setting up a large specification is to introduce the *application-domain specific* concepts. In so doing we shall use NAT, CHAR, SET, SEQ and MAP from the standard library as given class descriptions. Our INGRES-like database system is a *relational* database system and obviously the application-domain specific concepts include *relations* and also tuples, strings, etc. We shall adopt a lot of simplifications in order to let the specification fit within the scope and size of this book; one of the first simplifications is that we restrict the kind of values that can be stored in the database to *strings*, thereby excluding other useful data types such as numbers. Therefore, the data type String is a starting point and although the internal structure of the strings is irrelevant, we define strings as sequences of characters. Even stronger, the theory of normal forms suggests that we do not make any use of the internal structure of strings, for the first of Codd's normal forms [31] requires the values stored in the database to be *atomic*. After that we immediately proceed with *tuples*, but here we must be careful because there is a possibility of confusion. In the standard library we have things called tuples in TUP2 and these are in fact pairs, which have a fixed length. Along the same lines we could construct TUP3, etc.

```
LET STRING :=
EXPORT
  SORT Char,
  SORT Nat,
  SORT String,
  FUNC empty :                   -> String,
  FUNC cons  : Char # String     -> String,
  FUNC hd    : String            -> Char,
  FUNC tl    : String            -> String,
  FUNC len   : String            -> Nat,
  FUNC sel   : String # Nat      -> Char,
  FUNC cat   : String # String   -> String,
  FUNC rev   : String            -> String
FROM
IMPORT NAT INTO
```

```
IMPORT CHAR INTO
CLASS

  % ... as SEQ (see appendix)
  % (with Seq replaced by String and Item by Char)
END;
```

In database terminology 'tuples' are sequences of arbitrary length, although the tuples that are in one and the same relation should all have the same length. Therefore we shall not use TUP2, TUP3, etc. but instead take a suitable instantiation of SEQ, renaming Seq to Tuple.

```
LET TUPLE :=
EXPORT
  SORT String,
  SORT Nat,
  SORT Tuple,
  FUNC empty :                -> Tuple,
  FUNC cons  : String # Tuple -> Tuple,
  FUNC hd    : Tuple          -> String,
  FUNC tl    : Tuple          -> Tuple,
  FUNC len   : Tuple          -> Nat,
  FUNC sel   : Tuple # Nat    -> String,
  FUNC cat   : Tuple # Tuple  -> Tuple,
  FUNC rev   : Tuple          -> Tuple
FROM
IMPORT NAT INTO
IMPORT STRING INTO
CLASS

  % ... as SEQ (see appendix)
  % (with Seq replaced by Tuple and Item by String)
END;
```

A *relation* in database terminology is a set of tuples where all tuples have the same length. The fact that all tuples of a relation should have the same length will be dealt with by a kind of *dynamic typing* mechanism to be worked out in Section 7.2.2, rather than by the *static typing* mechanism as provided by the language COLD-K. The dynamic aspect lies in the fact that the user can dynamically introduce relation names, which get a type as soon as they are introduced. The type associated with a relation name indicates the length of all tuples in any relation of that name. Below we introduce the sort Relation whose objects are arbitrary sets of tuples.

```
LET RELATION :=
EXPORT
  SORT Tuple,
  SORT Nat,
  SORT Relation,
  PRED is_in : Tuple # Relation,
  FUNC empty :                        -> Relation,
  FUNC ins   : Tuple # Relation       -> Relation,
  FUNC rem   : Tuple # Relation       -> Relation,
  FUNC union : Relation  # Relation -> Relation,
  FUNC isect : Relation  # Relation -> Relation,
  FUNC diff  : Relation  # Relation -> Relation,
  PRED subset: Relation  # Relation,
  FUNC card  : Relation               -> Nat
FROM
IMPORT NAT INTO
IMPORT TUPLE INTO
CLASS
  % ... as SET (see appendix)
  % (with Set replaced by Relation and Item by Tuple)
END;
```

We introduce *relation names* as the objects of a sort RName. Relation names could be defined as strings as well, but their structure is irrelevant here.

```
LET RNAME :=
CLASS
  SORT RName
END;
```

7.2.2 Database schemas

Until now we have not mentioned anything really specific about the INGRES-like database system: the above definitions introduce the basic data types which play a role in *any* relational database system. Furthermore: we have not discussed any system at all; instead we have only introduced objects of a purely mathematical nature. The next step is to introduce the dynamic typing mechanism, as already mentioned, and a true system aspect: the fact that relation types can be associated with relation names. This association is variable and it corresponds to the ability of the database system to store a database schema. The distinction between *database schema* and *database contents* is of fundamental importance. A database schema tells you how many relations can be stored, how they are named and what the type is of each relation. For example, a database schema could specify that there is one variable relation named **employee** whose type is sketched by the following template.

field 0	*field 1*

Fig 7.1. Template of relation with two fields.

The database contents provide the named relations themselves, which are collections of tuples, probably corresponding to facts in the real world. For example the database contents could consist of the relation named **employee**, given by the following database picture.

field 0	*field 1*
'Hans'	'Stiphout'
'Loe'	'Geldrop'
'Reinder'	'Eindhoven'

Fig 7.2. Relation with two fields.

By way of simplification we assume that the type of a relation is simply a natural number – the length of all of its tuples. In more realistic database systems, it could be a sequence of field types which could be either *string* or *integer*; in that case a relation having type (*integer*, *string*) would mean that its elements are tuples of length 2 where the first field is an integer and the second is a string. One could even go one step further, introducing field names – which again we do not. Because of this, we refer to fields by their positions 0, 1, etc. and we shall come back to this field selection mechanism later when we specify the retrieval operations of the database system.

The class description TYPING below consists of two parts. The first part introduces the notion of type correctness for relations. The second part of the class description TYPING introduces a variable mapping from relation names to relation types.

```
LET TYPING :=
EXPORT
```

```
    SORT Nat,
    SORT RName,
    SORT Relation,
    PRED uniform : Relation,
    FUNC type    : Relation         -> Nat,
    PRED check   : Relation # Nat,
    FUNC type    : RName            -> Nat,
    PROC type_it : RName # Nat      ->
  FROM
  IMPORT NAT      INTO
  IMPORT RNAME    INTO
  IMPORT TUPLE    INTO
  IMPORT RELATION INTO
  CLASS

    PRED uniform : Relation
    PAR  r:Relation
    DEF  EXISTS n:Nat
         ( FORALL tup:Tuple ( is_in(tup,r) => len(tup) = n ) )

    FUNC type : Relation -> Nat
    PAR  r:Relation
    DEF  SOME n:Nat
         ( FORALL tup:Tuple ( is_in(tup,r) => len(tup) = n ) )

    PRED check : Relation # Nat
    PAR  r:Relation,n: Nat
    DEF  uniform(r);
         r = empty OR type(r) = n

    FUNC type : RName -> Nat VAR

    AXIOM INIT => FORALL r:RName ( NOT type(r)! )

    PROC type_it : RName # Nat ->
    MOD  type : RName -> Nat

    AXIOM FORALL r:RName,n:Nat ( NOT type(r)! =>
          < type_it(r,n) > TRUE;

          [ type_it(r,n) ]
          ( type(r) = n;
            FORALL r':RName,n':Nat
            ( NOT r' = r =>
                  ( n' = type(r') <=> n' = PREV type(r') ) ) ) )
```

```
END;
```

Let us explain the details of TYPING. The first part of TYPING introduces the notion of type correctness for relations. A relation is called *uniform* if all its tuples have the same length. Roughly speaking, we say that the type of the relation r is n when all tuples in r have the length n. There is one caveat which is that we must pay special attention to the empty relation. The formal definition of `uniform` below is such that the empty relation *is* considered uniform. Yet it does not have a type; in particular, if `empty` denotes the empty relation, `type(empty)` is defined by means of a `SOME n:Nat` expression with the restricting clause `FORALL tup:Tuple (is_in(tup,empty) => len(tup) = n)`. Since *any* natural number `n` satisfies that clause and `type` is a function (requiring *uniqueness*), `type(empty)` is formally undefined. Type checking boils down to having a binary predicate called `check` such that `check`(r, n) means that the relation r is correct with respect to type n. When defining this binary predicate we cannot simply say that `check`(r, n) holds iff `type`$(r) = n$; we must explicitly single out the case that r = `empty`. One could say that `empty` is a 'polymorphic' object.

The second part of TYPING introduces the *system* aspect in the form of a variable mapping from relation names to relation types. Formally it is introduced as a function `type: RName -> Nat` which is labelled `VAR`. The invariant simply is `TRUE`, making the proof obligations trivial. As it turns out there exists an invariant property that `type`(r) is defined for finitely many relation names r only, yet this invariant hardly serves as an aid in setting up the specification and we pay no further attention to it here. The procedure `type_it` serves to add new relation names together with their types. In this database system one can only *add* relation names, never remove them.

7.2.3 The contents of a database

The above class description TYPING allows the incremental introduction of database schemas. Now we turn our attention to the database contents. We introduce a class description called CONTENTS. Again this is a state-based specification and we employ an invariant CI for Contents Invariant, as an aid in setting up the state-based specification. We give CONTENTS below and because we want the database contents to be well-typed in the sense of CI, we need sorts and operations from TYPING, which is therefore imported.

```
LET CONTENTS :=
EXPORT
  SORT Nat,
```

```
   SORT RName,
   SORT Relation,
   FUNC contents : RName -> Relation,
   PROC store    : RName # Relation  -> ,
   PROC create   : RName # Nat       ->
 FROM
 IMPORT RNAME    INTO
 IMPORT RELATION INTO
 IMPORT TYPING   INTO
 CLASS

   FUNC contents : RName -> Relation VAR

   PRED CI :
   DEF  FORALL n:RName
        ( contents(n)! => check(contents(n),type(n)) )

   AXIOM INIT => FORALL n:RName ( NOT contents(n)! )

   % AXIOM INIT => CI

   PROC store : RName # Relation ->
   MOD  contents

   AXIOM FORALL n:RName,r:Relation ( check(r,type(n)) =>
         < store(n,r) > TRUE;

         [ store(n,r) ]
         ( contents(n) = r;
           FORALL n':RName,r':Relation
           ( NOT n' = n =>
             ( r' = contents(n') <=> r' = PREV contents(n') ) ) ) )

   % AXIOM FORALL n:RName (
   % CI => [ store(n,SOME r:Relation (check(r,type(n)))) ] CI )

   PROC create : RName # Nat ->
   PAR  r:RName,n:Nat
   DEF  type_it(r,n);
        store(r,empty)

 END;
```

Let us explain the details of CONTENTS. We have explicitly indicated the invariance of CI with respect to the initial state and with respect to **store** as a proof obligation. It is a routine matter to check that CI is also an invariant with respect to **type_it**(r, n), provided the precondition NOT type(r)! of **type_it** is respected, which means that r must be a fresh relation name. There is also an algorithmically defined procedure **create** which combines **type_it** and **store** by means of the (sequential) composition operator ';' which will be introduced formally in Section 8.2. Again the effect of **create**(r, n) is only guaranteed if r is a fresh relation name. Since the newly 'created' relation becomes **empty**, which behaves as a polymorphic object, there is no dynamic typing problem when invoking **create**.

In practice, **create** is a command which is made available at the user level, e.g. with a concrete syntax as follows:

```
create <RName> ( <Nat> )
```

where <RName> and <Nat> refer to the syntactic categories of relation names and natural numbers respectively (cf. the sorts RName and Nat).

It is very natural to consider the database as a state-based system in this way because just as at the user level, the COLD-K operations do not require explicit arguments to denote states. For example, to create three relations in the COLD-K approach means writing

```
create(employee,2);
create(salary,2);
create(products,10)
```

whereas to do this with explicit state arguments would require something like the nested state-valued expression in

$$s_3 := \texttt{create}(\texttt{create}(\texttt{create}(s_0, \texttt{employee}, 2), \texttt{salary}, 2), \texttt{products}, 10)$$

7.2.4 Tuple variables

The above class description CONTENTS provides the storage of the database contents so now we turn our attention to the query language which serves for performing data retrieval actions. There are several approaches to formulating queries and we shall adopt a style known as *tuple relational calculus*. This is the approach adopted for the QUEL language [32], which used to be available for the early INGRES systems. It is called a *calculus* approach, as contrasted to an *algebraic* approach (such as SQL), because of the phenomenon of *bound variables.* Bound variables must be explictly declared according to a regime of first introducing and then using them. These bound variables are not to be confused with the sorts and operations declared VAR in COLD-K or the logical variables introduced by a FORALL or an EXISTS quantifier. Bound variables are just names which we can define ourselves – using COLD-K as a meta-language. Therefore we introduce the sort VName for *V*ariable *N*ame. Just like RName objects, VName objects could be e.g. strings.

```
LET VNAME :=
CLASS
  SORT VName
END;
```

The fact that tuple variables must be declared before use gives rise to another state-based aspect in the specification. This is described in BINDING below. Again this is a state-based specification and we employ an invariant BI, for Binding Invariant, as an aid in setting up the state-based specification. The motivation for using a *state-based description* here instead of an algebraic one comes from the fact that the system presents itself as a dynamic and state-based system in a natural way. The user can interactively type commands that modify the state of the system.

```
LET BINDING :=
EXPORT
  SORT VName,
  SORT RName,
  FUNC binding  : VName          -> RName,
  PROC range_of : VName # RName ->
FROM
IMPORT VNAME  INTO
IMPORT TYPING INTO
CLASS

  FUNC binding : VName -> RName VAR

  PRED BI :
  DEF  FORALL v:VName
       ( binding(v)! => type(binding(v))! )

  AXIOM INIT => FORALL v:VName ( NOT binding(v)! )
```

```
% AXIOM INIT => BI

PROC range_of : VName # RName ->
MOD  binding

AXIOM  FORALL r:RName,v:VName ( type(r)! =>
    < range_of(v,r) > TRUE;

    [ range_of(v,r) ]
    ( binding(v) = r;
      FORALL v':VName,r':RName
      ( NOT v = v' =>
        ( r' = binding(v') <=> r' = PREV binding(v') ) ) ) )

% AXIOM  FORALL v:VName (
% BI => [ range_of(v,SOME r:RName (type(r)!)) ] BI )

END;
```

We shall add some explanation to the above specification. When a tuple variable v is declared, it becomes bound to a relation name r, say. The meaning of this binding is that in all subsequent queries, v takes the values of all tuples in the relation of r – one after the other. Of course this is a poor explanation of the effect of the binding and we hope to clarify this later by means of a more formal specification of the query language and its semantics. The binding is modelled by means of a variable function `binding`, mapping variable names to relation names. In practice the `range_of` procedure, which acts as a declaration command, is made available to the user by means of the following concrete syntax:

range of <VName> is <RName>

where <VName> and <RName> refer to the syntactic categories of variable names and relation names respectively (cf. the sorts `RName` and `VName`). So when `employee` is a relation name, the command **range of** t **is** `employee` binds t to `employee`.

The explicitly indicated proof obligation states the invariance of `BI` with respect to the initial state and with respect to `range_of`(v, r), at least for relation names r known to the database system. It can also be checked that `BI` is an invariant with respect to `type_it` and `create`.

7.2.5 Expressions and qualifications

Now we turn our attention to the syntax of the query language. The query language is very simple and yet it requires some work to define its syntax using COLD-K. We need to introduce four sorts, each sort modelling a syntactic category. These are the sorts `Attr`, `Expr`, `Qual` and `ExprList`, of *attributes*, *expressions*, *qualifications* and *expression lists* respectively. To give some intuition, we could consider the following command which is presented at the level of the concrete user syntax:

retrieve (t.0 , t.1) **where** t.0 = `'Eindhoven'`.

In this example t.0 and t.1 are attributes, but they are also expressions. The string `'Eindhoven'` is an expression whereas (t.0 , t.1) is an expression list and t.0 = `'Eindhoven'` is a qualification. In general, attributes play the role of field selectors and qualifications play the role of selection criteria. In the formal specification we focus on the abstract syntax, rather than on the concrete user syntax.

We have put everything dealing with the abstract syntax in a class description `SYNTAX`. It is a purely algebraic specification.

```
LET SYNTAX :=
EXPORT
  SORT VName,
  SORT String,
  SORT Nat,
  SORT Attr,
  FUNC attr : VName # Nat -> Attr,
  FUNC v : Attr           -> VName,
  FUNC n : Attr           -> Nat,
  SORT Expr,
  FUNC expr : String     -> Expr,
  FUNC expr : Attr       -> Expr,
  FUNC add : Expr # Expr -> Expr,
  SORT Qual,
  FUNC true :              -> Qual,
  FUNC not : Qual          -> Qual,
  FUNC and : Qual # Qual   -> Qual,
  FUNC equal : Expr # Expr -> Qual,
  SORT ExprList,
  FUNC exprlist : Expr              -> ExprList,
  FUNC exprlist : Expr # ExprList -> ExprList
FROM
IMPORT STRING INTO
```

```
IMPORT NAT    INTO
IMPORT CHAR   INTO
IMPORT VNAME  INTO
CLASS

  SORT Attr
  SORT Expr
  SORT Qual
  SORT ExprList

  % attributes:

  FUNC attr : VName # Nat -> Attr

  PRED is_gen : Attr
  IND  FORALL v:VName,n:Nat
       ( is_gen(attr(v,n)) )

  AXIOM FORALL a:Attr ( is_gen(a) )

  FUNC v : Attr -> VName
  FUNC n : Attr -> Nat

  AXIOM FORALL v:VName,n:Nat
        ( v(attr(v,n)) = v;
          n(attr(v,n)) = n )

  % expressions:

  FUNC expr : String -> Expr
  FUNC expr : Attr   -> Expr
  FUNC add  : Expr # Expr -> Expr

  PRED is_gen : Expr
  IND  FORALL s:String
       ( is_gen(expr(s)) );
       FORALL a:Attr
       ( is_gen(a) => is_gen(expr(a)) );
       FORALL e1:Expr,e2:Expr
       ( is_gen(e1) AND is_gen(e2) => is_gen(add(e1,e2)) )

  AXIOM FORALL e:Expr ( is_gen(e) )

  FUNC kind : Expr -> Nat
```

```
AXIOM FORALL s:String,a:Attr,e1:Expr,e2:Expr
      ( kind(expr(s)) = 0;
        kind(expr(a)) = 1;
        kind(add(e1,e2)) = 2 )

FUNC s  : Expr -> String
FUNC a  : Expr -> Attr
FUNC e1 : Expr -> Expr
FUNC e2 : Expr -> Expr

AXIOM FORALL s:String,a:Attr,e:Expr,e1:Expr,e2:Expr
      ( s(e) = s <=> e = expr(s);
        a(e) = a <=> e = expr(a);
        e1(e) = e1 AND e2(e) = e2 <=> e = add(e1,e2) )

% qualifications:

FUNC true : -> Qual
FUNC not : Qual -> Qual
FUNC and : Qual # Qual -> Qual
FUNC equal : Expr # Expr -> Qual

PRED is_gen : Qual
IND  is_gen(true);
     FORALL q: Qual
     ( is_gen(q) => is_gen(not(q)) );
     FORALL q1:Qual,q2:Qual
     ( is_gen(q1) AND is_gen(q2) => is_gen(and(q1,q2)) );
     FORALL e1:Expr,e2:Expr
     ( is_gen(e1) AND is_gen(e2) => is_gen(equal(e1,e2)) )

AXIOM FORALL q:Qual ( is_gen(q) )

FUNC kind : Qual -> Nat

AXIOM FORALL q:Qual,q1:Qual,q2:Qual,e1:Expr,e2:Expr
      ( kind(true) = 0;
        kind(not(q)) = 1;
        kind(and(q1,q2)) = 2;
        kind(equal(e1,e2)) = 3 )

FUNC q  : Qual -> Qual
FUNC q1 : Qual -> Qual
FUNC q2 : Qual -> Qual
FUNC e1 : Qual -> Expr
```

```
    FUNC e2 : Qual -> Expr

    AXIOM FORALL q:Qual,ql:Qual,q1:Qual,q2:Qual,e1:Expr,e2:Expr
          ( q(ql) = q <=> ql = not(q);
            q1(ql) = q1 AND q2(ql) = q2 <=> ql = and(q1,q2);
            e1(ql) = e1 AND e2(ql) = e2 <=> ql = equal(e1,e2) )

    % expression lists:

    FUNC exprlist : Expr -> ExprList
    FUNC exprlist : Expr # ExprList -> ExprList

    PRED is_gen : ExprList
    IND  FORALL t:Expr
         ( is_gen(t) => is_gen(exprlist(t)) );
         FORALL t:Expr,l:ExprList
         ( is_gen(t) AND is_gen(l) => is_gen(exprlist(t,l)) )

    AXIOM FORALL l:ExprList ( is_gen(l) )

    FUNC kind : ExprList -> Nat

    AXIOM FORALL e:Expr,e1:Expr,l:ExprList
          ( kind(exprlist(e)) = 0;
            kind(exprlist(e1,l)) = 1 )

    FUNC e  : ExprList -> Expr
    FUNC e1 : ExprList -> Expr
    FUNC l  : ExprList -> ExprList

    AXIOM FORALL e:Expr,el:ExprList,l:ExprList
          ( e(el) = e <=> el = exprlist(e);
            e1(el) = e AND l(el) = l <=> el = exprlist(e,l) )

  END;
```

By way of an example we shall explain the definitions dealing with the sort **Expr**. There are three ways of constructing an expression which gives rise to three constructor functions, two of them called **expr** – where we employ the COLD-K mechanism of *overloading* – and a third constructor function called **add**. These are the *only* ways to make **Expr** objects and this minimality condition is made explicit using an inductive definition (viz. of **is_gen**) and a 'no-junk' axiom. Furthermore we need 'no-confusion' axioms, to make sure that e.g. **expr**$(s) \neq$ **expr**(a) for arbitrary strings s and attributes a. Therefore we use an auxiliary function **kind**. In addition to the constructor functions, we also have functions for taking expressions apart: for example **e1** takes the first subexpression of an addition expression and **e2** takes its second subexpression. Note that there are *two* axioms necessary which together guarantee no confusion, because the first one does not, e.g. it does not guarantee that **expr**(s_1) $\neq$**expr**(s_2) if $s_1 \neq s_2$.

We do not need explicit 'definedness' axioms for the constructor functions because the definedness of the constructor functions follows already from the no junk axioms. All this is more conveniently written down when formulating the concrete syntax at the user level by a Backus-Naur form (BNF) grammar as follows:

```
<Attr> ::= <VName> . <Nat>

<Expr> ::= <String>
         | <Attr>
         | ( <Expr> + < Expr> )

<Qual> ::= true
         | ( not <Qual> )
         | ( <Qual> and <Qual> )
         | ( <Expr> = <Expr> )

<ExprList> ::= <Expr>
             | <Expr> , <ExprList>
```

It is certainly a good question to ask why the COLD-K specification is more cumbersome than that using BNF. It is a good idea to use Backus-Naur form (BNF) as syntactic sugar. BNF is more compact, because it is a special-purpose formalism with certain built-in principles, such as the minimality principle which we had to express using **is_gen** predicates. At first sight it would seem to be a weakness of COLD-K that we have to advise using BNF, but the advantage of viewing BNF as syntactic sugar for a fragment of COLD-K is that we still have the other concepts of COLD-K available, such as the modularisation constructs and the state-based description mechanisms – in a single linguistic framework. This concludes the abstract syntax for the syntactic categories of attributes, expressions, qualifications and expression lists.

7.2.6 Well-formedness

The class description SYNTAX can be viewed as a context-free grammar, but it is *not* the case that every Attr, Expr, Qual or ExprList object is well-formed in the sense that it can be part of a meaningful query. The notion of well-formedness arises from the conditions that all tuple variables must have been declared and that the field selections must make sense. Using overloading we introduce various *w*ell-*f*ormedness predicates wf. For later use we need various functions called vars, with the intuition of 'set of occurring tuple variables'.

```
LET SET_VNAME :=
EXPORT
  SORT VName,
  SORT Nat,
  SORT Set_VName,
  PRED is_in : VName # Set_VName,
  FUNC empty :                          -> Set_VName,
  FUNC ins   : VName # Set_VName        -> Set_VName,
  FUNC rem   : VName # Set_VName        -> Set_VName,
  FUNC union : Set_VName  # Set_VName -> Set_VName,
  FUNC isect : Set_VName  # Set_VName -> Set_VName,
  FUNC diff  : Set_VName  # Set_VName -> Set_VName,
  PRED subset: Set_VName  # Set_VName,
  FUNC card  : Set_VName                -> Nat
FROM
IMPORT NAT INTO
IMPORT VNAME INTO
CLASS

  % ... as SET (see appendix)
  % (with Set replaced by Set_VName and Item by VName)
END;


LET WF :=
EXPORT
  SORT Attr,
  PRED wf : Attr,
  SORT Expr,
  PRED wf : Expr,
  SORT Qual    ,
  PRED wf : Qual,
  SORT ExprList    ,
  PRED wf : ExprList,
  SORT Set_VName,
  FUNC vars : Attr      -> Set_VName,
```

```
    FUNC vars : Expr     -> Set_VName,
    FUNC vars : Qual     -> Set_VName,
    FUNC vars : ExprList -> Set_VName
  FROM
  IMPORT NAT       INTO
  IMPORT TYPING    INTO
  IMPORT BINDING   INTO
  IMPORT SYNTAX    INTO
  IMPORT SET_VNAME INTO
  CLASS

    % well-formedness:

    PRED wf : Attr
    IND  FORALL v:VName,n:Nat
         ( lss(n,type(binding(v))) => wf(attr(v,n)) )

    PRED wf : Expr
    IND  FORALL s:String,a:Attr,e1:Expr,e2:Expr
         ( wf(expr(s));
           wf(a) => wf(expr(a));
           wf(e1) AND wf(e2) => wf(add(e1,e2)) )

    PRED wf : Qual
    IND  FORALL q:Qual,q1:Qual,q2:Qual,e1:Expr,e2:Expr
         ( wf(true);
           wf(q) => wf(not(q));
           wf(q1) AND wf(q2) => wf(and(q1,q2));
           wf(e1) AND wf(e2) => wf(equal(e1,e2)) )

    PRED wf : ExprList
    IND  FORALL e:Expr,l:ExprList
         ( wf(e) => wf(exprlist(e));
           wf(e) AND wf(l) => wf(exprlist(e,l)) )

    % set of occurring tuple variables:

    FUNC vars : Attr -> Set_VName
    IND  FORALL v:VName,n:Nat
         ( vars(attr(v,n)) = ins(v,empty) )

    FUNC vars : Expr -> Set_VName
    IND  FORALL s:String,a:Attr,e1:Expr,e2:Expr
         ( vars(expr(s)) = empty;
           vars(expr(a)) = vars(a);
```

```
          vars(add(e1,e2)) = union(vars(e1),vars(e2)) )

  FUNC vars : Qual -> Set_VName
  IND  FORALL q:Qual,q1:Qual,q2:Qual,e1:Expr,e2:Expr
       ( vars(true) = empty;
         vars(not(q)) = vars(q);
         vars(and(q1,q2)) = union(vars(q1),vars(q2));
         vars(equal(e1,e2)) = union(vars(e1),vars(e2)) )

  FUNC vars : ExprList -> Set_VName
  IND  FORALL e:Expr,l:ExprList
       ( vars(exprlist(e)) = vars(e);
         vars(exprlist(e,l)) = union(vars(e),vars(l)) )

END;
```

We add some explanation to `WF`. For the definition of `wf` we used inductive definitions following the structure of the inductive definitions of the `SYNTAX` specification. The reader should note that most clauses in the definition of `wf` are devoted to just saying "that a certain construct is `wf` iff its constituents are". The only non-standard clause occurs in the definition of `wf` on `Attr` from which we see how something could become non-`wf`: an atomic `Attr` object `attr(v,n)` is non-`wf` if `n` $\geq$ `type(binding(v))`.

Like `wf`, the identifier `vars` is overloaded. To explain e.g. the `vars` function on `ExprList`, consider the expression list

(t.0 , u.1)

at the level of concrete syntax, then it is clear that its set of occurring tuple variables is $\{\mathtt{t}, \mathtt{u}\}$. At the level of the abstract syntax this is formulated as follows:

```
vars(exprlist(expr(attr(t,0)),exprlist(expr(attr(u,1)))))
```

which is equal to the set with elements `t` and `u`.

7.2.7 Semantics of queries

In the previous section we completed the definition of the well-formedness of the syntactic categories of attributes, expressions, qualifications and expression lists. The class description `MAP_VNAME_TUPLE` below introduces the sort `Map_VName_Tuple` of maps from tuple variables to tuples. Sometimes we call the objects of `Map_VName_Tuple` simply *tables* and we use `tab` as a typical element of this sort.

```
LET MAP_VNAME_TUPLE :=
EXPORT
  SORT VName,
  SORT Tuple,
  SORT Set_VName,
  SORT Relation,
  SORT Map_VName_Tuple,
  FUNC empty :                                   -> Map_VName_Tuple,
  FUNC add : Map_VName_Tuple # VName # Tuple -> Map_VName_Tuple,
  FUNC rem : Map_VName_Tuple # VName          -> Map_VName_Tuple,
  FUNC app : Map_VName_Tuple # VName          -> Tuple,
  FUNC dom : Map_VName_Tuple                  -> Set_VName,
  FUNC ran : Map_VName_Tuple                  -> Relation
FROM
IMPORT VNAME INTO
IMPORT TUPLE INTO
% ...
CLASS

  % ... as MAP (see appendix)
  % (with Map replaced by Map_VName_Tuple, Item1 by VName,
  % Item2 by Tuple, Set1 by Set_VName, Set2 by Relation )
END;
```

We shall have a meaning function **sem**, for *sem*antics. It is defined in a compositional manner, following the structure of the abstract syntax; therefore we have in fact several overloaded functions called **sem** and also a predicate. The predicate **sem** gives meaning to qualifications; since these are kinds of 'assertions' their meaning is either TRUE or FALSE – which is the motivation for employing a predicate instead of a function. Each meaning function (or predicate) takes an additional table argument. In the class description below called RETRIEVAL the semantics of the queries is defined.

```
LET RETRIEVAL :=
EXPORT
  SORT Qual,
  SORT RName,
  SORT ExprList,
  SORT Relation,
  FUNC retrieve       : ExprList # Qual         -> Relation,
  PROC retrieve_into  : ExprList # Qual # RName -> ,
  PROC append         : ExprList # Qual # RName ->
```

```
FROM
IMPORT STRING          INTO
IMPORT TUPLE           INTO
IMPORT SYNTAX          INTO
IMPORT RELATION        INTO
IMPORT BINDING         INTO
IMPORT WF              INTO
IMPORT CONTENTS        INTO
IMPORT SET_VNAME       INTO
IMPORT MAP_VNAME_TUPLE INTO
CLASS

  FUNC sem : Map_VName_Tuple # Attr -> String
  PAR  tab:Map_VName_Tuple,a:Attr
  DEF  sel(app(tab,v(a)),n(a))

  FUNC sem : Map_VName_Tuple # Expr -> String

  AXIOM FORALL tab:Map_VName_Tuple,s:String,a:Attr,e1:Expr,e2:Expr
        ( wf(expr(s)) =>
            sem(tab,expr(s)) = s;
          wf(expr(a)) =>
            sem(tab,expr(a)) = sem(tab,a);
          wf(add(e1,e2)) =>
            sem(tab,add(e1,e2)) = cat(sem(tab,e1),sem(tab,e2)) )

  PRED sem : Map_VName_Tuple # Qual

  AXIOM FORALL tab:Map_VName_Tuple,q1:Qual,q2:Qual,e1:Expr,e2:Expr
        ( wf(not(q1)) =>
            sem(tab,not(q1)) <=> NOT sem(tab,q1);
          wf(and(q1,q2)) =>
            sem(tab,and(q1,q2)) <=> sem(tab,q1) AND sem(tab,q2);
          wf(equal(e1,e2)) =>
            sem(tab,equal(e1,e2)) <=> sem(tab,e1) = sem(tab,e2) )

  FUNC sem : Map_VName_Tuple # ExprList -> Tuple

  AXIOM FORALL tab:Map_VName_Tuple,e:Expr,el:ExprList
        ( wf(exprlist(e)) =>
            sem(tab,exprlist(e)) = cons(sem(tab,e),empty);
          wf(exprlist(e,el)) =>
            sem(tab,exprlist(e,el)) = cons(sem(tab,e),sem(tab,el)) )

  PRED valid : Map_VName_Tuple
```

```
PAR  tab:Map_VName_Tuple
DEF  FORALL v:VName
     ( is_in(v,dom(tab)) =>
        is_in(app(tab,v),contents(binding(v))) )

FUNC retrieve : ExprList # Qual -> Relation
PAR  el:ExprList,q:Qual
DEF  wf(el) ?,
     wf(q ) ?,
     subset(vars(q),vars(el)) ?,

     SOME rel:Relation
     ( FORALL tup:Tuple
       ( is_in(tup, rel) <=>
         EXISTS tab:Map_VName_Tuple
         ( valid(tab);
           sem(tab,q);
             sem(tab,el) = tup ) ) )

PROC retrieve_into : ExprList # Qual # RName ->
PAR  el:ExprList,q:Qual,r:RName
DEF  store(r,retrieve(el,q))

PROC append : ExprList # Qual # RName ->
PAR  el:ExprList,q:Qual,r:RName
DEF  store(r,union(contents(r),retrieve(el,q)))

END
```

In denotational semantics one would use the double-brackets convention, and an equation like sem(tab,add(e1,e2)) = cat(sem(tab,e1),sem(tab,e2)) could be denoted as

$$[\![\texttt{add(e1,e2)}]\!]_{\texttt{tab}} = \texttt{cat}([\![\texttt{e1}]\!]_{\texttt{tab}}, [\![\texttt{e2}]\!]_{\texttt{tab}}).$$

The definition of the predicate valid refers to the variable contents of the database and also to the variable binding. More precisely, a 'table' is valid if it 'contains' only tuples which are actually present in the 'contents' of the database. The meaning functions sem are not inductively defined, which means that they may yield any result for constructs that are not well-formed. This is o.k. here because retrieve(*el*, *q*) has been guarded by wf(*el*) and wf(*q*). We employ a SOME rel:Relation expression in the definition of retrieve which can be viewed as a finite-set comprehension, quantifying over tab. In set-theoretical notation one would write { `sem(tab,el)` | `valid(tab) AND sem(tab,q)` }. The `retrieve`, `retrieve_into` and `append` operations are to be made available to the database user and have the following concrete syntax:

```
retrieve ( <ExprList> ) where <Qual>
retrieve ( <ExprList> ) where <Qual> into <RName>
append ( <ExprList> ) where <Qual> to <RName>
```

This completes our example specification of the INGRES-like database system.

7.2.8 Example of an interactive session

An example of an interactive session using the INGRES-like database system is given below. We show the results as relation pictures. This session shows that the database system described is quite realistic and interesting, even though we introduced several simplifications.

```
create employee ( 2 )

append ( 'Loe'     , 'Geldrop'   ) where true to employee
append ( 'Hans'    , 'Stiphout'  ) where true to employee
append ( 'Reinder' , 'Eindhoven' ) where true to employee

range of t is employee
retrieve ( t.0 , t.1 ) where true
```

The above command sequence first creates an (empty) relation called `employee`. Its type is 2, i.e. it is a relation whose (still-to-be-added) tuples are meant to have length 2. Then three **append** commands are given, each of which adds one tuple. After that a **range of** command binds t to `employee`. Finally the **retrieve** command has the effect that the full contents of the relation is shown. Its outcome is as follows:

field 0	*field 1*
'Hans'	'Stiphout'
'Loe'	'Geldrop'
'Reinder'	'Eindhoven'

Fig 7.3. Outcome of first **retrieve** command.

After this, the session proceeds with a query command where both a projection and a selection take place. The projection is to show the first field only; the selection is to take only those tuples where the second field does not have the value `'Geldrop'`.

retrieve (t.0) **where** (**not** (t.1 = `'Geldrop'`))

This **retrieve** command yields the following result:

field 0
'Hans'
'Reinder'

Fig 7.4. Outcome of second **retrieve** command.

Then the session proceeds with the introduction of another tuple variable u and a query as follows:

range of u **is** `employee`
retrieve (t.1, u.1) **where true**

Its effect is to calculate the binary Cartesian product of the set of values for the second field occurring in `employee`. It yields the following result:

field 0	*field 1*
'Stiphout'	'Stiphout'
'Stiphout'	'Eindhoven'
'Stiphout'	'Geldrop'
'Eindhoven'	'Eindhoven'
'Eindhoven'	'Geldrop'
'Eindhoven'	'Stiphout'
'Geldrop'	'Geldrop'
'Geldrop'	'Stiphout'
'Geldrop'	'Eindhoven'

Fig 7.5. Outcome of third **retrieve** command.

7.3 Discussion

Let us come back to our remark that *the example serves to illustrate a number of techniques.*

1. The use of the library to get started turned out to be useful since we had to employ relatively complex data types such as sets of tuples of strings etc. In this way we obtained the sorts `String`, `Tuple`, `Relation`, `RName` and `VName` with all standard operations.

2. We employed constructor functions and inductive definitions for modelling the syntax of a language. In this case it is a simple query language, but the technique also works for other kinds of languages.

3. We employed inductive definitions to define the well-formedness `wf` of the various language constructs. This `wf` depends on the state through the variable function `type: RName -> Nat`, although `wf` is actually described using purely algebraic techniques.

4. We used a standard technique known from the field of denotational semantics by interpreting elements of a language where bound variables play a role. The meaning functions take an additional argument which is a mapping from tuple variables to tuples.

5. We associated abstract semantics with queries using set-comprehension. In this way the top-level function `retrieve` is as abstract as possible – without any implementation bias.

Another technique that has been used is that of *sharing* of a (state-based) description, as indicated by Figure 7.6.

This picture shows that `TYPING` is imported by both `CONTENTS` and by `BINDING`. At the top level we see `RETRIEVAL` which imports the latter two descriptions. We say that `TYPING` is *shared* by `CONTENTS` and `BINDING`. The origin mechanism that will be explained in Section 9.5 guarantees that at the top-level, there is exactly one instance of TYPING, instead of two 'copies'.

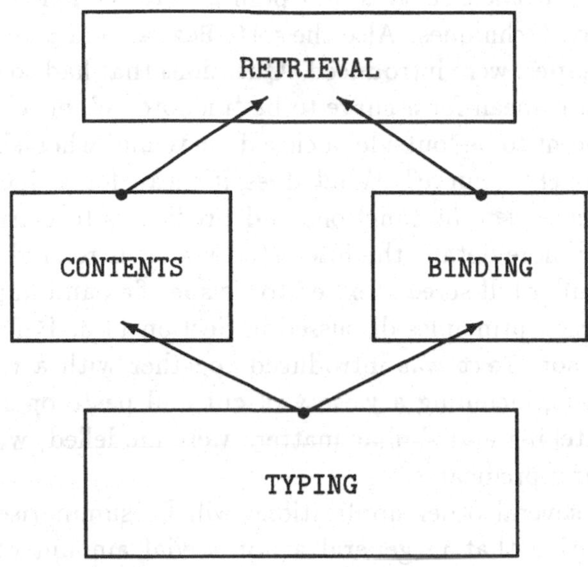

Fig 7.6. Sharing of the state-based description TYPING.

We end the present chapter with a discussion of the concept of *application domain modelling* mentioned in the introduction to this chapter. As it happens, in most of the examples in this text, only a very limited amount of application domain modelling is needed. In the traffic light example, all we needed was a three-valued enumeration type of `Colour`. In the VDU-like display example, all we needed were the data types of characters and strings (= sequences of characters). In the INGRES-like database example we encountered the syntax and well-formedness of a query language, which required a kind of application domain modelling.

This situation is a consequence of the size of the examples, which have to fit in with the size and the scope of this text. In larger applications, there will almost certainly be a non-trivial amount of application domain modelling and we shall illustrate this by briefly reporting on some case studies where this was indeed done.

Corthout and Jonkers describe in [33] the development of a new algorithm, that implements a point containment test for shapes on a discrete grid that are bounded by Bezier curves. This is a basic problem in raster graphics. Before the actual specification and implementation could be undertaken, the sort `Point` was introduced with operations to take the x and y coordinates of a point, a notion of 'distance' of two points, the 'width' of a non-empty sequence of points, containment in a bounding box etc. Furthermore a sort `Curve` and various relations between curves and points were modelled by means of algebraic specification techniques. Also the sorts `Bezier` and `Shape`, modelling Bezier curves and shapes, were introduced. Questions that had to be addressed included: what does it mean for a curve to be 'monotonic', or 'closed'? What does it mean for a point to be 'outside' a closed curve and when should a point be considered to 'touch' a curve? What does it mean for a line to intersect a curve? In total there were 58 functions and predicates to clarify these and similar matters. For more details the interested reader is refered to [33, 34].

In [35] a multi-buffer full-screen text editor is specified and implemented to illustrate certain design principles discussed in Section 11.3. Before this could be undertaken, the sort `Text` was introduced together with a rich collection of operations on texts, including a variety of cut and paste operations. Also blanking, string-matching and similar matters were modelled, with a total of some 50 functions and predicates.

In Section 11.4 several other applications will be summarised and these confirm the proposition that in general a non-trivial amount of application domain modelling is necessary.

Chapter 8

Implementing state-based specifications

8.1 Introduction

In this chapter we shall present language constructs for describing state-based algorithms and methodological guidelines for using them. In Part I, the only kind of algorithmic descriptions were (algebraic) expressions. Here, in Part II, we are dealing with state-based specifications and we shall consider a special kind of expression embodying the concept of *side-effect*. In this text we focus on those expressions with side-effect which have the empty type and we call these expressions *statement expressions* or just *statements* . In the concrete syntax as given in the appendix, expressions and statements are put together into one category called expressions. This is in accordance with the fact that expressions and statements are fully integrated in COLD-K but in order to keep things simple, we keep them separated here, avoiding constructs like procedures with result parameters. The meaning of a statement X is a transition relation $\mathcal{T}_X$ which is a binary relation on

$$\mathsf{State} \times \mathsf{State}$$

Statements are meant to establish a certain side-effect. Note that the concept of non-determinism applies to the side-effect of a statement. In Section 8.2 we shall present the various kinds of statements. Some of these are very similar to certain kinds of expressions as defined in Part I. Section 8.3 is concerned with algorithmic procedure definitions and Section 8.4 gives an example of a simple division algorithm. Statements are the main description mechanism offered by COLD-K for dealing with sequential algorithms. In this way classical imperative programs can be described and, even more importantly, they can be compared with other state-based specifications – either axiomatic ones or those which are algorithmic themselves. In Sections 8.5, 8.6 and further we shall present a systematic approach for implementing certain axiomatic state-based specifications by means of algorithmic implementations. The systematic approach presented is not meant to be exclusive; although it embodies a general and powerful technique based on abstraction functions and representation invariants, there is a wealth of other options. In particular it is a valid option to use COLD-K as a specification language only and to make implementations directly in some available implementation technology: Pascal, C, Prolog, LISP, TTL-hardware, microcode, etc. The approach of Sections 8.5, 8.6 onwards is to employ two comparable COLD-K descriptions, viz. an axiomatic description and an algorithmic description and to have a manual translation from the latter COLD-K description to C. An alternative approach is to use a COLD-K compiler; an experimental version for a small subset of COLD-K exists. It is not the aim of this text to give standard advice on choosing between these options. In the long term it might be advisable not to use COLD-K at all, but to use a sugared version of it. The main purpose of this chapter is to offer the basic description mechanisms and to explain one important implementation technique based on abstraction functions and representation invariants.

8.2 Statements

First, let us have another look at some of the expressions defined earlier in an algebraic setting to see what their interpretation could be, when viewed as a statement in a state-based setting.

The *guard statement* serves for guarding a state transition and it is among other things meant as a basic building block of **if then else**-like constructs. If A is an assertion, then the following is a guard statement:

$A\,?$

Its interpretation is a transition relation $\mathcal{T}_{A\,?}$ containing precisely the transitions $(s \to t)$ for which A holds in s and for which $s = t$.

If X and Y are statements, then the following is a *choice statement*:

$X \mid Y$

It denotes a binary transition relation $\mathcal{T}_{X \mid Y}$ on $\mathsf{State} \times \mathsf{State}$ which is given by $\mathcal{T}_{X \mid Y} = \mathcal{T}_X \cup \mathcal{T}_Y$. So $X \mid Y$ can 'do' all transitions of X but also all transitions of Y. Using this (and the ';' operator to be explained below) the **if** A **then** X **else** Y statement as usually present in other programming languages, can be viewed as syntactic sugar for the statement (A?; X | NOT A?; Y).

The interpretation of the *declaration statement* `LET` x : T as well as the *binding statement* x := Y (where Y must be an expression) and the *block statement* `BEGIN` X `END` (where X is a statement) are the same as for expressions: `LET` x : T introduces an object name x, and x := Y binds the result of the expression Y to x. `BEGIN` X `END` delimits the scope of the object names.

There is an obvious *parenthesized statement*:

(X)

Its meaning is equal to that of X.

In addition to these statements, which are derived from expressions already presented in Part I, we shall introduce several new kinds of statements. In particular these are the composition statement X ; Y, the procedure statement p X, the repetition statement X *, the skip statement `SKIP`, the modification statement `MOD` V `END`, the use statement `USE` P `END`, and the combined modification and use statement `MOD` V `USE` P `END`. We shall introduce each of these below.

The meaning of the *composition statement*

X ; Y

is the sequential composition of X and Y. Formally, if X and Y are statements, then X ; Y denotes a binary transition relation $\mathcal{T}_{X,Y}$ on State × State which contains precisely the transitions $(s \rightarrow t)$ for which there exists an intermediate state s' such that the interpretation $\mathcal{T}_X$ of X contains a transition $(s \rightarrow s')$ and the interpretation $\mathcal{T}_Y$ of Y contains a transition $(s' \rightarrow t)$.

Note that we use a composition expression with ',' when building a list of arguments for a function expression or a procedure statement such as `create(employee,2)` whereas we use a composition statement with ';' for sequential composition of statements as in the following example.

```
create(salary,2);
create(employee,2)
```

A *procedure statement* serves to apply a procedure to an actual parameter. If p : S_1 # ... # S_m -> is a procedure name and X is an expression of type S_1 # ... # S_m, then

p X

is a statement. Its evaluation amounts to evaluating the actual parameter(s) X and after that taking the results as arguments for invoking p. Formally, the interpretation of p X is a binary transition relation $\mathcal{T}_{pX}$ on State × State. The relation $\mathcal{T}_{pX}$ contains precisely the transitions $(s \rightarrow t)$ for which there exist intermediate results x such that the interpretation $\mathcal{T}_X$ of X in s yields x and $(s, x \rightarrow t)$ is a transition of $\mathcal{T}_p$.

In the example of the INGRES-like database system we employed procedure statements on several occasions. In particular the `DEF` clause of `retrieve_into` contains a procedure statement `store(r,retrieve(el,q))` where `store` is a procedure and where `(r,retrieve(el,q))` is the expression serving as its argument.

Now we turn our attention to the *repetition statement.* In COLD-K there are no **while** ... **do**, **repeat** ... **until**, **do** ... **od** or **for** loops: instead of these there is just one elementary but powerful repetition statement. If X is a statement, then

X *

is a statement again. Its evaluation amounts to executing X zero or more times. Formally, the interpretation of $X *$ is a binary transition relation $\mathcal{T}_{X*}$ on State × State containing the transitions $(s \rightarrow t)$ for which there exist states $t_0, \ldots, t_n$ such that $t_0 = s$, $t_n = t$ and such that for the intermediate states we have that $(t_i \rightarrow t_{i+1}) \in \mathcal{T}_X$ for $i = 0, \ldots, n-1$. Here $\mathcal{T}_X$ denotes the interpretation of X. The notation is similar to the notation often used for regular expressions where $a*$ is a regular expression generating all strings of zero or more as. The repetition statement is powerful enough to simulate many other repetition constructs. This means that constructs like **while** ... **do**, **repeat** ... **until**, **do** ... **od** and **for** loops can be employed as syntactic sugar for certain composite COLD-K expressions. For example the well-known **while** A **do** X construct from classical programming languages can be viewed as syntactic sugar for the statement `(`A`?;` X`)* ; (NOT` A`)?`.

A *skip statement* has no side-effect. It is simply denoted by the keyword

```
SKIP
```

and its interpretation is a transition relation containing the transitions $(s \rightarrow s)$ for all states s. It is semantically equivalent to the guard `TRUE?`.

A *modification statement* is closely related to the `MOD` clause which we discussed in the context of procedure definitions in Section 5.7. The notation for it is as follows

`MOD` V `END`

where V is a list of variables, i.e. names labelled `VAR`. It describes an arbitrary modification of the variables in V. So, its interpretation is a transition relation containing only transitions $(s \rightarrow t)$ such that the values of all variables in t are the same as in s except for the variables mentioned in V. It is not allowable to modify variables directly if these variables are introduced in another (imported) class description: in this case, a use statement may be employed (see below).

A *use statement* is closely related to the `USE` clause discussed in the context of procedure definitions. The notation is as follows

`USE` P `END`

where P is a list of procedure names. It describes the effect of an arbitrary sequence of invocations of the procedures in P. So, its interpretation is a transition relation containing precisely all transitions $(s \rightarrow t)$ such that t can be obtained from s by using the procedures mentioned.

A *combined modification and use statement* has the following notation:

`MOD` V `USE` P `END`

where V is a list of variables and P is a list of procedure names. It describes the effect of an arbitrary sequence of modifications of the variables in V and invocations of the procedures in P. So, its interpretation is a transition relation containing the transitions $(s \rightarrow t)$ for which there exist states $t_0, \ldots, t_n$ such that $t_0 = s$, $t_n = t$ and such that for each step $(t_i \rightarrow t_{i+1})$ with $i = 0, \ldots, n-1$ we have:

- all variables in t_{i+1} have the same values as in t_i except for the variables mentioned in V, or
- t_{i+1} can be obtained from t_i by using one of the procedures mentioned in P.

We end this section with a survey of all statements.

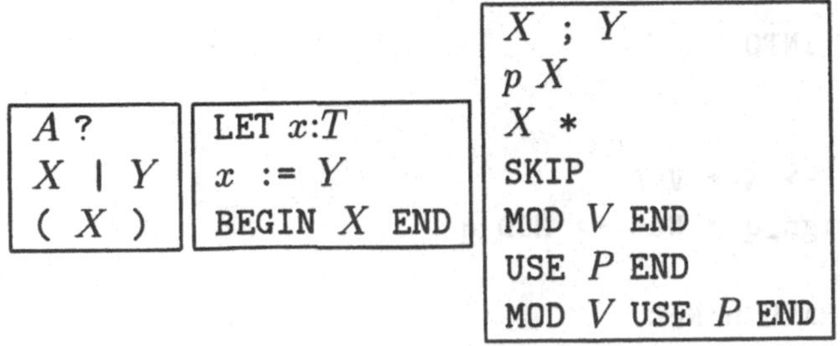

Table 8.1. Survey of all statements.

8.3 Algorithmic procedure definitions

In this section we shall discuss the mechanisms for introducing algorithmic procedures. An *algorithmic procedure definition* introduces a transition relation given by a statement. The notation for an algorithmic procedure definition is as follows.

PROC p : S_1 # ... # S_m ->
PAR $x_1 : S_1, \ldots, x_m : S_m$
DEF X

p denotes the $m+2$-ary transition relation $\mathcal{T}_p$ on $\mathsf{State} \times S_1 \times \ldots \times S_m \times \mathsf{State}$ containing the transitions $(s, x_1, \ldots, x_m \rightarrow t)$ for which $(s \rightarrow t)$ is contained in $\mathcal{T}_{X(x_1,\ldots,x_m)}$, i.e. in the transition relation that is the interpretation of X.

8.4 Example: implementation of division

We give an example of a classical algorithm concerning the division of two natural numbers by means of repeated subtraction. The algorithm operates on two simple programming variables of sort Nat, modelled by means of two variable functions named q and r, for *q*uotient and *r*emainder respectively. The main procedure of this example is called divide. Its purpose is to calculate the truncated quotient of two numbers such that for example divide(77,3) yields q = 25.

```
LET DIVIDE :=
EXPORT
  SORT Nat,
  FUNC q      : -> Nat,
  FUNC r      : -> Nat,
  PROC divide : Nat # Nat ->
FROM
IMPORT NAT INTO
CLASS

  FUNC q : -> Nat VAR
  PROC assign_q : Nat -> MOD q

  AXIOM FORALL n:Nat
      ( < assign_q(n) > TRUE;
        [ assign_q(n) ] q = n )
```

```
FUNC r : -> Nat VAR
PROC assign_r : Nat -> MOD r

AXIOM FORALL n:Nat
      ( < assign_r(n) > TRUE;
        [ assign_r(n) ] r = n )

PROC divide : Nat # Nat ->
PAR  x:Nat,y:Nat
DEF  assign_r(x);
     assign_q(0);
     ( leq(y,r) ?;
       assign_r(sub(r,y));
       assign_q(add(q,1))
     ) *;
     NOT leq(y,r) ?

END
```

Let us discuss the above COLD-K text in detail. Each variable has its own assignment procedure (**assign_r** and **assign_q**). The algorithm of repeated subtraction is modelled by the expression in the DEF clause of **divide**. Clearly this expression has side effects, for it invokes **assign_q** and **assign_r**. The initialisation serves to make r equal to the first input parameter x and to set q to 0. The repetition construct has a loop body which assigns $r - y$ to r followed by an increment of q. In operational terms, the algorithm proceeds by executing its loop body until the test $y \leq r$ fails. Finally the value of the variable q contains the result of **divide**.

To see the correctness of this algorithm, the well-known technique of repetition invariants can (and should) be used. Using obvious syntactic sugar, the repetition invariant is

$$x = r + y \times q$$

and it is easily verified that the initialisation **assign_r(x); assign_q(0)** makes the repetition invariant hold. It can be verified easily that the loop body preserves this invariant. Therefore, if the algorithm terminates, it does so in a state where $x = r + y \times q$ and $y \not\leq r$ which implies that the final value of q is the truncated quotient.

The language COLD-K can also be used for expressing one or more desired properties of this algorithm. In particular we can specify pre- and postconditions and the following properties PROP1 and PROP2:

```
PRED PROP1 :
DEF  FORALL x:Nat,y:Nat
     ( [ divide(x,y) ]
       ( x = add(r,mul(y,q)) AND NOT leq(y,r) ) )

PRED PROP2 :
DEF  FORALL x:Nat,y:Nat
     ( NOT y = 0 => < divide(x,y) > TRUE )
```

The language as such does not prescribe an operational interpretation of the algorithm since in its semantics, subjects like state transitions and side effects are explained in terms of relations. Yet a classical and straightforward operational view of the algorithm is not in contradiction with this relational semantics and the definition of **divide** can be directly executed. In order to demonstrate how close these algorithmic descriptions are to classical imperative programs, we have made a manual translation, mapping the above algorithmic definition of **divide** to the widely used programming language C. In this way we get a real program which runs on a computer. We employ macros to model the sort **Nat** and a few of its operations (this mapping is not perfect because in fact C integers have an upperbound **maxint**). We added a C main function to get a complete program.

```
#define Nat int
#define add(N,M) ((N)+(M))
#define sub(N,M) ((N)-(M))
#define leq(N,M) ((N)<= (M))

Nat r;
Nat q;

#define assign_r(N) r = (N)
#define assign_q(N) q = (N)

Nat divide(x,y)
Nat x;
Nat y;
{ assign_r(x);
  assign_q(0);
  while (leq(y,r))
  {  assign_r(sub(r,y));
     assign_q(add(q,1));
  }
```

```
  return(q);}

main() {printf("%d",divide(77,3));}
```

8.5 Towards an implementation strategy

State-based specifications can be implemented by using abstraction functions in a way similar to algebraic specifications. We show one simple example both in an algebraic and in a state-based setting. Here it is convenient to use some elementary set-theoretic notation as a form of syntactic sugar. Consider the algebraic specification

$\mathtt{T} = \{0, 1, 2, 3\}$

next : T -> T
  $\mathtt{next}(a) = (a + 1) \,\mathbf{mod}\, 4$

where $m \,\mathbf{mod}\, n$ denotes the rest of m when divided by n. According to the implementation strategy presented in Part I we can implement the above algebraic specification by another, more detailed algebraic specification. Let us consider the following 'algebraic implementation'.

$\mathtt{S} = \{0, 1\} \times \{0, 1\}$

next : S -> S
  $\mathtt{next}(0,0) = (0,1)$
  $\mathtt{next}(0,1) = (1,0)$
  $\mathtt{next}(1,0) = (1,1)$
  $\mathtt{next}(1,1) = (0,0)$

f : S -> T
  $\mathtt{f}(x, x') = 2 \times x + x'$

The function `f` is an *abstraction function* or *retrieve function*. This function `f` serves for *interpreting* a pair of bits x, x' as a natural number less than 4; its definition shows that a standard binary representation is chosen, where the second bit is the least significant one. `f` is an adequate abstraction function because of the property that for all $\vec{x}$ of type S we have $\mathtt{f}(\mathtt{next}(\vec{x})) = \mathtt{next}(\mathtt{f}(\vec{x}))$. Roughly speaking, this property states that it does not matter whether `next` is performed at the bit level or at the level of numbers: the results are the same. This is a well-known property, often explained in terms of commuting diagrams; it amounts to the fact that `f` is a homomorphism.

State-based specifications can be implemented by means of a slightly different but related approach. We shall show this approach first by means of a simple example concerning two state-based descriptions called MOD4_SPEC and MOD4_IMPL given below. The example essentially boils down to re-doing the above algebraic example in a state-based setting. Consider the following axiomatic state-based specification.

```
LET MOD4_SPEC :=
IMPORT NAT INTO
CLASS

  FUNC a : -> Nat VAR

  AXIOM {M1} lss(a,4)

  PROC next : -> MOD a

  AXIOM {M2} a = 3 => [ next ] a = 0

  AXIOM {M3} lss(a,3) => [ next ] a = succ(PREV a)

  AXIOM {M4} < next > TRUE

END;
```

We propose the state-based description MOD4_IMPL below as an implementation. It employs two variables x and x', each of which can store either a 0 or a 1. To update x and x' there are assignment procedures named upd_x and upd_x'. The function a is defined in terms of x and x'. The procedure next is defined algorithmically using the assignment procedures operating on x and x'.

```
LET MOD4_IMPL :=
IMPORT NAT INTO
CLASS

  FUNC x : -> Nat VAR

  AXIOM lss(x,2)

  PROC upd_x : Nat ->
  MOD  x
```

```
    AXIOM [ upd_x(0) ] x = 0;
          [ upd_x(1) ] x = 1;
          < upd_x(0) > TRUE;
          < upd_x(1) > TRUE

    FUNC x' : -> Nat VAR

    AXIOM lss(x',2)

    PROC upd_x' : Nat ->
    MOD  x'

    AXIOM [ upd_x'(0) ] x' = 0;
          [ upd_x'(1) ] x' = 1;
          < upd_x'(0) > TRUE;
          < upd_x'(1) > TRUE

    FUNC a : -> Nat
    DEF  add(mul(2,x),x')

    PROC next : ->
    DEF  ( x' = 0             ?; upd_x'(1)
         | x' = 1 AND x = 0 ?; upd_x'(0); upd_x(1)
         | x' = 1 AND x = 1 ?; upd_x'(0); upd_x(0)
         )

END
```

It can be verified that MOD4_IMPL provides the sort Nat and its associated operations, a function a : -> Nat and a procedure next : -> such that the specified constraints M1, M2, M3 and M4 have become logical consequences of the constraints described in MOD4_IMPL. We shall come back to this verification below. It should be noted that the implementation provides certain operations that were not required by the specification, i.e. x, x', upd_x and upd_x'. This is typical and does no harm. The variables x and x' act as storage functions instead of the variable a, which is defined algorithmically in terms of the variables x and x'. At the same time, the abstraction function has been 'coded' in the definition of a.

The statement that MOD4_IMPL implements MOD4_SPEC can be made more precise if we apply the following two criteria:

- signature inclusion: the signature of the implementation must include the signature of the specification;
- theory inclusion: the constraints specified in the specification must be

logical consequences of the constraints described (by axioms, MOD clauses, definitions, etc.) in the implementation.

The criterion of signature inclusion means that the implementation (that is MOD4_IMPL), provides *at least* the sorts, functions predicates and procedures of the specification MOD4_SPEC – which is the case. The criterion of theory inclusion means that the constraints specified must be derivable from the implementation. For example, let us verify this for the second constraint M2 which requires in states with a = 3 that next sets a to 0. From the DEF clause of a we see that a = 3 can only be the case if x = x' = 1. In that situation the last clause in the algorithmic definition of next applies which sets both x and x' to 0. But when x = x' = 0 the DEF clause of a tells us that a = 0. This shows that M2 is derivable.

The above example should give the basic idea and in the next section we shall elaborate this idea for a more general case. In particular the above example did not require an invariant, or in other words, its invariant was TRUE. In the general case, both at the specification level, and at the implementation level an invariant may be necessary.

8.6 The implementation strategy

We start with a general form of an axiomatic state-based specification which we give as a template below. We shall refer to this template as the 'general form of an axiomatic state-based specification', although it is not the *most* general format: many generalisations and variations are conceivable. Below we assume a number of variable functions $a_0, a_1, a_2, \ldots$ and an invariant *inv* that depends on these variables. We show only two variables (a_0 and a_1) but of course our strategy also works for any other number of variables. We assume an initialisation procedure *init* which, from a practical point of view, is more realistic than the INIT-based approach of the previous chapter. Furthermore we assume a collection of procedures $p_0, p_1, p_2, \ldots$, each with its own precondition *inv* AND pre_p_i and postcondition post_p_i. We show only two procedures (p_0 and p_1). We focus on partial correctness, that is on assertions with [...] only, leaving termination issues aside (in examples we can add them easily). We use the hook notation $\overleftarrow{a}$ as a shorthand for PREV a, as proposed in Section 5.9. THEOREM ... is meant as special notation for % AXIOM ... (i.e. a proof obligation).

```
LET GEN_SPEC :=
CLASS

  FUNC a0: A0 -> S0 VAR
  FUNC a1: A1 -> S1 VAR

  PRED inv: DEF inv(a0, a1)

  PROC init: -> MOD a0, a1

  AXIOM [ init ] post_init(a0, a1)

  PROC p0: -> MOD a0, a1
  PROC p1: -> MOD a0, a1

  AXIOM inv AND pre_p0(a0, a1) => [ p0 ] post_p0(a0, a1, ←a0 , ←a1 )
  AXIOM inv AND pre_p1(a0, a1) => [ p1 ] post_p1(a0, a1, ←a0 , ←a1 )

  THEOREM [ init ] inv;
          inv AND pre_p0(a0, a1) => [ p0 ] inv;
          inv AND pre_p1(a0, a1) => [ p1 ] inv

END
```

Fig 8.1. Template of an axiomatic state-based specification.

Here we have assumed that each precondition is of the form *inv* `AND` `pre_`p_i, which means that the procedures p_i are left unspecified for states where the invariant *inv* or `pre_`p_i does not hold. The invariant is assumed to serve as an aid in setting up the state-based specification and hence the invariance axiom must be derivable from the remaining axioms. Of course some of the procedures p_i need not have modification rights with respect to all variables $a_0, a_1, \ldots$. It is easy to add variable predicates, which are similar to functions.

Next we propose a general form of an algorithmic state-based implementation which we again give as a template. It corresponds with the above 'general form of an axiomatic state-based specification'. We employ a number of variable functions $x_0, x_1, x_2, \ldots$ and a defined invariant *inv'* that depends on these variables. The initialisation procedure *init* is defined algorithmically by a `DEF` clause rather than by its postcondition only. Furthermore each procedure p_i

is defined algorithmically.

```
LET GEN_IMPL :=
CLASS

  FUNC x0: X0 -> T0 VAR
  FUNC x1: X1 -> T1 VAR
  FUNC x2: X2 -> T2 VAR

  FUNC a0: A0 -> S0 DEF inv'?, a0'(x0, x1, x2)
  FUNC a1: A1 -> S1 DEF inv'?, a1'(x0, x1, x2)

  PRED inv: DEF inv(a0, a1) as before

  PROC init: ->
  DEF  modify x0, x1, x2 such that inv' and post_init(a0, a1) hold

  PROC p0: ->
  DEF  modify x0, x1, x2 such that, assuming that pre_p0 holds,
       inv' is preserved and post_p0(a0, a1, ←a0, ←a1) holds

  PROC p1: ->
  DEF  modify x0, x1, x2 such that, assuming that pre_p1 holds,
       inv' is preserved and post_p1(a0, a1, ←a0, ←a1) holds

  PRED inv': DEF inv'(x0, x1, x2) such that inv' implies inv

END
```

Fig 8.2. Template of an algorithmic state-based implementation.

In typical situations we have more variable functions (x_0, x_1, x_2) in the implementation than in the specification (a_0, a_1) and they tend to have more arguments. Again variations with respect to this general form exist.

The implementation provides certain operations that were not required by the specification: $x_0, x_1, x_2 \ldots$. As we saw before, the a variables are replaced by x variables, and the former can be defined in terms of the latter. At the same time, the abstraction function has been 'coded' in the definition of the a's. In general the invariant *inv'* may introduce constraints which were not stated already in *inv*. We call *inv'* the *representation invariant* and we say that the x variables are the *representation* of the a variables. The DEF clause of the a variables is guarded with the representation invariant; this makes it very explicit that when the constraints of *inv'* are not fulfilled, the x s do not make sense.

For particular instances of *GEN_IMPL* and *GEN_SPEC* it must be verified that the implementation provides the functions a_0 and a_1 of the right input and output types, the predicate *inv*, the procedure *init* and the procedures p_i such that all the constraints specified like

$$\texttt{[} init \texttt{] post\_}init(a_0, a_1)$$

and

$$inv \texttt{ AND pre\_}p_i(a_0, a_1) \texttt{ => [} p_i \texttt{] post\_}p_i(a_0, a_1, \overleftarrow{a_0}, \overleftarrow{a_1})$$

have become logical consequences of the constraints specified in the implementation. Note that there may be two kinds of such constraints, viz. the explicit axiomatic constraints and the constraints due to `MOD` and `USE` clauses. In order to make this verification step succeed it is a good idea to let all a_i occur positively in the `DEF` clause of *inv* – so not in the scope of a `NOT`.

In that case *GEN_IMPL* implements *GEN_SPEC* in the sense of the two criteria mentioned in Section 8.5:

- signature inclusion,
- theory inclusion.

A more theoretical discussion of the nature of the relation between *GEN_IMPL* and *GEN_SPEC* will be presented in Section 8.8.

8.7 Example: implementation of a line editor

8.7.1 Specifying the system

Most of the remainder of this chapter is devoted to a fairly large example of the strategy of Section 8.6. The example deals with a very simple 'editor' which provides capabilities for entering and modifying a one-line text. It has been shown that the approach of Section 8.6 applies to large and realistic systems as well, since in [35] a multi-buffer screen-oriented text editor was specified and implemented. The example here is chosen to fit within the size and the scope of this text and it is just enough to show our implementation strategy in a more or less realistic setting. We employ the standard data types `NAT` and `CHAR` from the standard library to get the data type of strings in a scheme `STRING` which is an instance of `SEQ`. We refer to Section 7.2.1.

The actual specification of the editor begins with importing NAT, CHAR and STRING and adding two application-domain specific algebraic definitions.

```
LET STRING_OPS :=
EXPORT
  SORT Nat,
  SORT Char,
  SORT String,
  FUNC insert : String # Char # Nat -> String,
  FUNC delete : String # Nat        -> String
FROM
IMPORT NAT INTO
IMPORT CHAR INTO
IMPORT STRING INTO
CLASS

  FUNC insert : String # Char # Nat -> String
  PAR  s:String,c:Char,n:Nat
  DEF  SOME  t:String
       ( sel(t,n) = c;
         FORALL i:Nat
         ( lss(i,n) => sel(t,i) = sel(s,i);
           leq(n,i) =>
             FORALL d:Char
             ( sel(t,succ(i)) = d <=> sel(s,i) = d ) ) )

  FUNC delete : String # Nat -> String
  PAR  s:String,n:Nat
  DEF  SOME t:String
       ( FORALL i:Nat
         ( lss(i,n) => sel(t,i) = sel(s,i);
           leq(n,i) =>
             FORALL d:Char
             ( sel(t,i) = d <=> sel(s,succ(i)) = d ) ) )

END {STRING_OPS};
```

The first definition introduces a function insert where insert(s, c, n) describes what is meant by insertion of a character c in a string s at the position n. The second definition introduces a function delete where delete(s, n) describes what is meant by deletion of the character at position n in a string s.

STRING_OPS provides the expressive power to express the effect of the actual editor operations `erase_buffer`, `insert_char`, `delete_char`, `forward_char` and `backward_char`, described below.

```
LET EDITOR_SPEC :=
EXPORT

  SORT Nat,
  SORT Char,
  SORT String,
  FUNC buffer : -> String,
  FUNC dot    : -> Nat,
  PROC erase_buffer  :       -> ,
  PROC forward_char  :       -> ,
  PROC backward_char :       -> ,
  PROC insert_char   : Char -> ,
  PROC delete_char   :       ->

FROM
IMPORT NAT INTO
IMPORT CHAR INTO
IMPORT STRING INTO
IMPORT STRING_OPS INTO
CLASS

  FUNC buffer : -> String VAR
  FUNC dot : -> Nat VAR

  PRED EI :
  DEF  leq(dot,len(buffer))

  PROC edit_op : ->
  DEF  ( forward_char
       | backward_char
       | insert_char(SOME c:Char ())
       | delete_char
       )

  PROC erase_buffer : -> MOD buffer,dot

  AXIOM < erase_buffer > TRUE;
        [ erase_buffer ] buffer = empty AND dot = 0

  % AXIOM [ erase_buffer ] EI
```

```
  PROC forward_char : -> MOD dot

  AXIOM EI AND dot = len(buffer) =>
        [ forward_char ] dot = PREV dot;

        EI AND lss(dot,len(buffer)) =>
        [ forward_char ] dot = succ(PREV dot)

  PROC backward_char : -> MOD dot

  AXIOM EI AND dot = 0 =>
        [ backward_char ] dot = PREV dot;

        EI AND gtr(dot,0) =>
        [ backward_char ] dot = pred(PREV dot)

  PROC insert_char : Char -> MOD buffer,dot

  AXIOM FORALL c:Char ( EI =>

        [ insert_char(c) ]
        ( dot = succ(PREV dot);
          buffer = PREV insert(buffer,c,dot) ) )

  PROC delete_char : -> MOD buffer

  AXIOM EI AND dot = len(buffer) =>
        [ delete_char ]
        ( buffer = PREV buffer );

        EI AND lss(dot,len(buffer)) =>
        [ delete_char ]
        ( buffer = delete(PREV buffer,dot) )

  AXIOM EI => ( < forward_char > TRUE;
                < backward_char > TRUE;
                < insert_char(SOME c:Char ()) > TRUE;
                < delete_char > TRUE )

  % AXIOM EI => [ edit_op ] EI

END; {EDITOR_SPEC}
```

First we have chosen the variables **buffer** and **dot** spanning the state-space of the editor. The first variable models the 'contents' of the buffer of the editor, which is a string. The second variable models the dot of the editor, which is a position in the buffer, acting as the 'point of interest' where the text modifications take place. The dot is simply a natural number. There is an invariant `EI` (for Editor Invariant) which arises in a very natural way and which expresses that the dot must be a valid position in the buffer. The following table indicates the relation between the template of Section 8.6 and the specific instantiation provided by `EDITOR_SPEC`. For example, the rôle of the initialisation procedure *init* as mentioned in Section 8.6 is played by the procedure `erase_buffer`.

GEN_SPEC	`EDITOR_SPEC`
a_0	`buffer`
a_1	`dot`
inv	`EI`
init	`erase_buffer`
p_0	`insert_char`
p_1	`delete_char`
p_2	`forward_char`
p_3	`backward_char`

Table 8.2. `EDITOR_SPEC` as an instance of the general template.

8.7.2 Documenting a building block

Let us assume that we want to provide an implementation of `EDITOR_SPEC` in terms of simple programming variables and a directly addressable character memory. The simple programming variables can be used for storing numbers, pointers, etc. whereas the memory can be used for storage of the buffer contents. We assume that the memory is given by the specification below.

```
LET MEMORY :=
EXPORT

   SORT Nat,
   SORT Char,
   FUNC mem  : Nat -> Char,
   FUNC size :     -> Nat,
   PROC grow : Nat -> ,
   PROC upd  : Nat # Char ->

FROM
```

```
IMPORT NAT INTO
IMPORT CHAR INTO
CLASS

  FUNC mem  : Nat -> Char VAR
  FUNC size :     -> Nat  VAR

  AXIOM FORALL n:Nat ( mem(n)! )

  AXIOM size!

  PROC grow : Nat ->  MOD size
  PROC upd : Nat # Char  ->  MOD mem

  AXIOM FORALL n:Nat (
        < grow(n) > TRUE;
        [ grow(n) ] size = add(n,PREV size) )

  AXIOM FORALL n:Nat,c:Char ( lss(n,size) =>
        < upd(n,c) > TRUE;
        [ upd(n,c) ]
        ( mem(n) = c;
          FORALL m:Nat
          ( NOT m = n => mem(m) = PREV mem(m) ) ) )

END; {MEMORY}
```

This memory is assumed to have a variable size which can be increased dynamically. We employ natural numbers as addresses. The contents of the memory cell with address n is denoted by mem(n). In order to store the character c in the memory cell with address n we have to write upd(n, c). To add n more cells to the memory we have to write grow(n). The invariant for MEMORY is TRUE – whence it is not made explicit. To keep things simple, we have made the assumption that mem(n) is always defined for all n, although in practice this might turn out to be somewhat unrealistic.

8.7.3 Choosing a representation

The buffer will be represented by characters in the memory locations mem(0) .. mem(size $-$ 1). Within this part of mem there is a *gap*. The contents of the gap is considered garbage (free space) and is kept contiguous. The gap is administrated by two programming variables gap1 and gap2. We define the *gap* as the positions gap1 up to (but not including) gap2. We shall keep the dot equal to **gap1**: therefore it is possible to make insertions easily and efficiently. The following picture sketches a buffer with its gap.

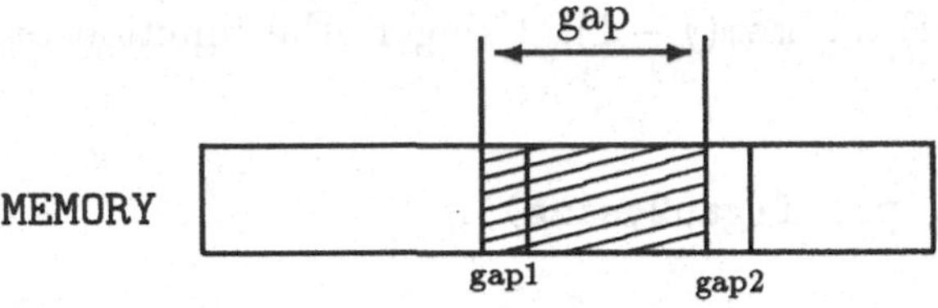

Fig 8.3. Buffer with gap.

Choosing the representation is the most essential step in the implementation phase. Below we give the formal implementation of the editor according to the strategy of Section 8.6 using the representation choice explained above and sketched in Figure 8.3. The rôle of the variable **buffer** is taken over by several other variables, i.e. **mem** and **size** from **MEMORY** and **gap1**, **gap2** which are introduced below. The function **dot** becomes an assignable programming variable.

```
LET EDITOR_IMPL :=
IMPORT NAT          INTO
IMPORT CHAR         INTO
IMPORT STRING       INTO
IMPORT STRING_OPS INTO
IMPORT MEMORY       INTO
CLASS

  FUNC gap1 : -> Nat VAR
  FUNC gap2 : -> Nat VAR
  FUNC dot  : -> Nat VAR

  PROC set_gap1 : Nat -> MOD gap1
  AXIOM FORALL n:Nat ( < set_gap1(n) > TRUE;
                       [ set_gap1(n) ] gap1 = n )

  PROC set_gap2 : Nat -> MOD gap2
  AXIOM FORALL n:Nat ( < set_gap2(n) > TRUE;
                       [ set_gap2(n) ] gap2 = n )

  PROC set_dot  : Nat -> MOD dot
  AXIOM FORALL n:Nat ( < set_dot(n) > TRUE;
                       [ set_dot(n) ] dot = n )
```

Next we must formally define the variable buffer in terms of mem, gap1 and gap2. We use an auxiliary function f such that f(i,j) denotes the string stored in the locations mem(i) .. mem($j-1$). Using f, the function buffer can be defined as

```
EI'?, cat(f(0,gap1),f(gap2,size)).
```

The definition of buffer is guarded by the invariant EI'? to make it very explicit that when the constraints of EI' are not fulfilled, the contents of the memory together with the size, dot and gap variables do not make sense.

Let us consider an example: assume that the memory contains the string "hello_ugly_world" in its cells starting from address 0 and that dot = gap1 = 6, gap2 = 11 and size = 16. In this state gap1 and dot point to the cell containing the character 'u' whereas gap2 points to the cell containing the character 'w'. EI' holds and the result of buffer equals the concatenation of the strings "hello_" and "world" so buffer equals "hello_world". This is shown in the figure below.

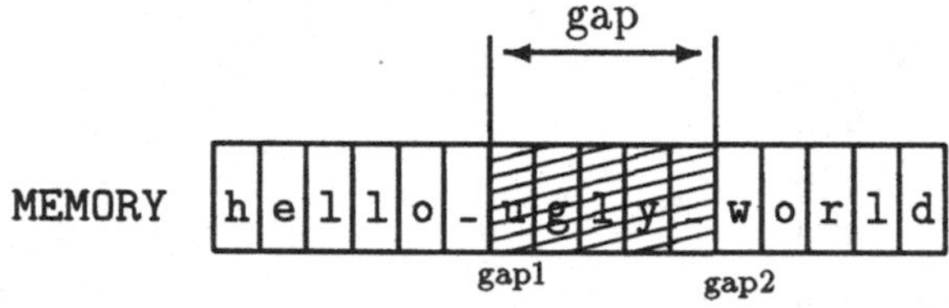

Fig 8.4. Buffer representing string "hello_world".

The algorithms for erase_buffer, insert_char, delete_char, forward_char and backward_char are fairly straightforward.

```
FUNC f : Nat # Nat -> String
PAR  i:Nat,j:Nat
DEF  ( i = j     ?, empty
     | lss(i,j) ?, cons(mem(i),f(succ(i),j))
     )

PRED EI' :
DEF  leq(gap1,gap2);
     leq(gap2,size);
     dot = gap1
```

```
FUNC buffer : -> String
DEF  EI'?, cat(f(0,gap1),f(gap2,size))

PRED EI : % as before

PROC edit_op    : -> % as in Section 8.7.1
PROC display_op : -> % as in Section 6.5

PROC erase_buffer : ->
DEF  set_gap1(0);
     set_gap2(size);
     set_dot(gap1)

PROC forward_char : ->
DEF  ( gap2 = size ?;
         SKIP
     | NOT gap2 = size ?;
         upd(gap1,mem(gap2));
         set_gap1(succ(gap1));
         set_gap2(succ(gap2));
         set_dot(succ(dot))
     )

PROC backward_char : ->
DEF  ( gap1 = 0 ?;
         SKIP
     | NOT gap1 = 0 ?;
         set_gap1(pred(gap1));
         set_gap2(pred(gap2));
         set_dot(pred(dot));
         upd(gap2,mem(gap1))
     )

PRED space :
DEF  NOT gap1 = gap2

PRED loop_invar :
DEF  leq(dot,gap1);
     leq(gap1,gap2);
     leq(gap2,size)

PROC gap_down : ->
DEF  set_gap1(pred(gap1));
     set_gap2(pred(gap2));
     upd(gap2,mem(gap1))
```

```
    PROC make_space : Nat ->
    PAR  n:Nat
    DEF  set_gap1(size);
         grow(n);
         set_gap2(size);
         (   lss(dot,gap1) ?;
             gap_down
         )*; NOT lss(dot,gap1) ?

    PROC insert_char : Char ->
    PAR  c:Char
    DEF  ( space ?;
             SKIP
         | NOT space ?;
             make_space(succ(size))
         );
         upd(gap1,c);
         set_gap1(succ(gap1));
         set_dot(succ(dot))

    PROC delete_char : ->
    DEF  ( gap2 = size ?;
             SKIP
         | NOT gap2 = size ?;
             set_gap2(succ(gap2))
         )

  END; {EDITOR_IMPL}
```

We added a predicate `loop_invar` which is the loop invariant of `make_space`. Clearly this `loop_invar` is a weakened version of `EI'`. Furthermore it should be noted explicitly that the loop body of `make_space` does not affect the value of `cat(f(0,gap1),f(gap2,size))`, provided `make_space` is invoked in a state where gap1 = gap2.

The implementation of `insert_char` increases the memory size to $2n + 1$ if the current memory size is n and there is no space for another character. Clearly there is some implementation freedom here. The choice for $2n + 1$ guarantees that there is always a non-zero increment. For large n, this means that the memory is roughly doubled. This could be a reasonable compromise between wasting memory (which certainly is the case if we increase to $100n+1$, say) and wasting processor time by moving the gap too often (which e.g. is the case if we increase to $n + 1$).

The following table indicates the relation between the template of Section 8.6 and the specific instantiation given by EDITOR_IMPL.

GEN_IMPL	EDITOR_IMPL
x_0	mem
x_1	size
x_2	gap1
x_3	gap2
x_4	dot
a_0	buffer
a_1	dot
inv	EI
init	erase_buffer
p_0	insert_char
p_1	delete_char
p_2	forward_char
p_3	backward_char
inv'	EI'

Table 8.3. EDITOR_IMPL as an instance of the general template.

It is interesting to see how the guard in the definition of buffer plays an essential rôle when verifying the criterion of theory inclusion where the constraints of the specification must logically follow from the implementation. For example consider the constraint

```
EI AND dot = len(buffer) => [ forward_char ] dot = PREV dot
```

which is a part of the specification of Section 8.7.1. To show this, we consider a state where EI and dot = len(buffer) hold. By strictness, len(buffer) and buffer are defined, which means that EI' must hold. To see this, recall that buffer is defined by

```
EI'?, cat(f(0,gap1),f(gap2,size)).
```

Now assume that in this state, forward_char as defined algorithmically, is invoked, then the test gap2 = size ? will succeed. To see this, note that

```
dot = len(buffer)  iff  gap1 = len(buffer)
```

due to the clause dot = gap1 in EI'. Therefore gap1 = len(cat(f(0,gap1), f(gap2,size))) which can only be the case if f(gap2,size)) is empty, i.e.

```
gap2 = size.
```

Because this test is used as the guard of SKIP in the algorithm of forward_char, the postcondition dot = PREV dot is obvious.

This concludes the implementation of the editor example according to the strategy of Section 8.6. For reasons of completeness and in order to fulfil a promise made in Section 6.6, we do not end here but we extend the example somewhat further below. On a first reading of the text, the reader may skip these further details and proceed with Section 8.8.

8.7.4 Adding display-oriented features

In this section we shall extend the editor example of the previous two sections. In particular, we shall extend the specification EDITOR_SPEC, adding axioms which explain which part of the buffer is visible on the screen of a display device. The extensions of the editor as presented in this and subsequent sections go strictly speaking, beyond the 'general' template of Section 8.6. Moreover, we shall demonstrate the use of invariants as a *specification technique* here – as was mentioned in Section 6.6. We assume a display device as specified in Section 6.5. We also need another set of string operations, collected in STRING_OPS' below.

```
LET STRING_OPS' :=
EXPORT
  SORT Nat,
  SORT Char,
  SORT String,
  FUNC prefix        : String # Nat -> String,
  FUNC mk_printable : Char          -> Char,
  FUNC mk_printable : String        -> String,
  FUNC fill          : String # Nat -> String
FROM
IMPORT NAT INTO
IMPORT CHAR INTO
IMPORT STRING INTO
CLASS

  FUNC prefix : String # Nat -> String
  PAR  s:String,n:Nat
  DEF  ( n = 0     ?, empty
       | NOT n = 0 ?, cons(hd(s),prefix(tl(s),pred(n)))
```

```
    )

PRED printable : Char
PAR  c:Char
DEF  leq(ord(blank),ord(c)) AND leq(ord(c),ord(tilde))

FUNC mk_printable : Char -> Char
PAR  c:Char
DEF  ( printable(c)     ?, c
     | NOT printable(c) ?, tilde
     )

FUNC mk_printable : String -> String
PAR  s:String
DEF  ( s = empty     ?, empty
     | NOT s = empty ?,
          cons(mk_printable(hd(s)),mk_printable(tl(s)))
     )

FUNC blanks : Nat -> String
PAR  j:Nat
DEF  ( j = 0 ?,       empty
     | NOT j = 0 ?, cons(blank,blanks(pred(j)))
     )

FUNC fill : String # Nat -> String
PAR  l:String,n:Nat
DEF  cat(l,blanks( lss(n,len(l))?, 0
                 | geq(n,len(l))?, sub(n,len(l))
                 ) )

END {STRING_OPS'};
```

The function `prefix` takes a prefix of a specified length from a given string. For example `prefix("hello world",5)` is `"hello"`. The predicate `printable` is specific for the ASCII character set and it serves to characterise those characters which can be made visible on a display – i.e. the non-control characters. The `mk_printable` functions have the intuition of 'making printable'; they replace unprintable characters by `'~'`. There are two overloaded functions called `mk_printable`: one for characters and one for strings. The function `blanks` yields white space strings of a given length. The function `fill` serves to extend a given string by adding blanks such that the result has a given minimal length. For example `fill("hello",7)` is `"hello  "`. This provides us with a sufficient vocabulary for expressing the relation between the contents of the buffer and its visualisation on the screen of the display, which is the topic of the next class description called EDITOR_SPEC'.

EDITOR_SPEC' is essentially the same as EDITOR_SPEC except that the procedure names are **erase_buffer_** and **forward_char_** etc. rather than **erase_buffer** and **forward_char** etc. Furthermore there are two additional invariance axioms dealing with a screen-invariant SI.

DISPLAY from Section 6.5 is imported and the procedures have use rights with respect to display_op. This is necessary because we must allow the editor to show parts of its buffer on a screen and hence to modify the screen and the cursor.

```
LET EDITOR_SPEC' :=
EXPORT
  SORT Nat,
  SORT Char,
  SORT String,
  FUNC screen : -> String,
  FUNC cursor : -> Nat,
  PROC erase_buffer_  :      -> ,
  PROC forward_char_  :      -> ,
  PROC backward_char_ :      -> ,
  PROC insert_char_   : Char -> ,
  PROC delete_char_   :      ->
FROM
IMPORT NAT          INTO
IMPORT CHAR         INTO
IMPORT STRING       INTO
IMPORT STRING_OPS   INTO
IMPORT STRING_OPS'  INTO
IMPORT DISPLAY      INTO
CLASS

  FUNC buffer : -> String VAR
  FUNC dot : -> Nat VAR

  PRED EI :
  DEF  leq(dot,len(buffer))

  PROC edit_op_ : ->
  DEF  ( forward_char_
       | backward_char_
       | insert_char_(SOME c:Char ())
       | delete_char_
       )
```

```
  PROC display_op : -> % as in Section 6.5

  PRED SI1 :
  DEF  lss(dot,po) => cursor = dot

  PRED SI2 :
  DEF  screen = mk_printable(prefix(fill(buffer,po),po))

  PRED SI :
  DEF  SI1 AND SI2

  AXIOM [ erase_buffer_ ] SI

  AXIOM EI AND SI => [ edit_op_ ] SI

  PROC erase_buffer_ : -> MOD buffer,dot USE display_op

  AXIOM < erase_buffer_ > TRUE;
        [ erase_buffer_ ] buffer = empty AND dot = 0

  % AXIOM [ erase_buffer_ ] EI

  PROC forward_char_ : ->       MOD dot        USE display_op
  PROC backward_char_ : ->      MOD dot        USE display_op
  PROC insert_char_ : Char -> MOD buffer,dot USE display_op
  PROC delete_char_ : ->        MOD buffer     USE display_op

  % axioms for forward_char_  as for forward_char
  % axioms for backward_char_ as for backward_char
  % axioms for insert_char_   as for insert_char
  % axioms for delete_char_   as for delete_char

  AXIOM EI => ( < forward_char_ > TRUE;
                < backward_char_ > TRUE;
                < insert_char_(SOME c:Char ()) > TRUE;
                < delete_char_ > TRUE )

  % AXIOM EI => [ edit_op ] EI

END; {EDITOR_SPEC'}
```

Recall that in Section 6.6 two rôles for invariants were mentioned. Here we demonstrate the second rôle for the invariant SI, which is to express additional constraints on the state space. The invariant SI has been split into two parts named SI1 and SI2. SI1 describes the relation between the dot of the editor and the cursor of the display device. SI2 describes the relation between the buffer of the editor and the screen of the display device. In the definition of SI2 we use prefix, fill and mk_printable. The use of prefix is necessary in order to cope with the possibility that the buffer is longer than the screen – in which case only a prefix of the buffer is displayed. The use of fill is needed in order to cope with the possibility that the buffer is shorter than the screen – in which case the remaining positions are blank.

8.7.5 Implementing the display-oriented features

This section is concerned with the implementation of the display-oriented features added in the previous section. The class description SI_PACKAGE_SPEC below specifies two procedures named cursor_restore and screen_restore which serve to re-establish the screen invariant SI. This screen invariant package is supposed to take the buffer contents from the dot and buffer variables as described in EDITOR_SPEC.

```
LET SI_PACKAGE_SPEC :=
EXPORT
  PROC cursor_restore : -> ,
  PROC screen_restore : ->
FROM
IMPORT STRING_OPS' INTO
IMPORT EDITOR_SPEC INTO
IMPORT DISPLAY     INTO
CLASS

  PRED SI : % as before
  PRED EI : % as before
  PRED SI1 : % as before
  PRED SI2 : % as before
  PROC display_op : -> % as before

  PROC cursor_restore : -> USE display_op

  AXIOM EI => [ cursor_restore ] SI1 AND screen = PREV screen

  PROC screen_restore : -> USE display_op

  AXIOM EI => [ screen_restore ] SI2
```

```
    AXIOM EI => ( < cursor_restore > TRUE;
                  < screen_restore > TRUE )

  END {SI_PACKAGE_SPEC};
```

The procedure cursor_restore serves to make the first part of the screen invariant hold: this means that it makes the dot position equal to the cursor, provided dot < po. Use of cursor_restore cannot modify the screen contents. The procedure screen_restore serves to make the second part of the screen invariant hold. Roughly speaking, this means that screen_restore makes the buffer visible on the screen. After execution of screen_restore, nothing is guaranteed about the cursor position. The implementation of the screen invariant package is given below:

```
LET SI_PACKAGE_IMPL :=
EXPORT
  PROC cursor_restore : -> ,
  PROC screen_restore : ->
FROM
IMPORT STRING_OPS' INTO
IMPORT EDITOR_IMPL INTO
IMPORT DISPLAY     INTO
CLASS

  PROC cursor_restore : ->
  DEF  ( lss(dot,po)     ?; cm(dot)
       | NOT lss(dot,po) ?; SKIP
       )

  FUNC i : -> Nat VAR

  PROC set_i : Nat -> MOD i

  AXIOM FORALL n:Nat ( < set_i(n) > TRUE;
                       [ set_i(n) ] i = n )

  FUNC j : -> Nat VAR

  PROC set_j : Nat -> MOD j

  AXIOM FORALL n:Nat ( < set_j(n) > TRUE;
                       [ set_j(n) ] j = n )
```

```
FUNC f : Nat -> Nat
PAR  k:Nat
DEF  ( lss(k,gap1) ?, k
     | geq(k,gap2) ?, sub(k,sub(gap2,gap1))
     )

PRED loop_invar' :
DEF  leq(i,po);
     i = f(j);
     lss(i,po) => cursor = i;
     prefix(screen,i) = mk_printable(prefix(fill(buffer,po),i))

PROC screen_restore : ->
DEF  set_i(0);
     ( gap1 = 0 ?    ; set_j(gap2)
     | NOT gap1 = 0 ?; set_j(0)
     );
     cm(0);
     ( NOT i = po ?;
       ( lss(j,size)     ?; pr(mk_printable(mem(j)))
       | NOT lss(j,size) ?; pr(blank)
       );
       set_j(succ(j));
       ( j = gap1     ?; set_j(gap2)
       | NOT j = gap1 ?; SKIP
       );
       set_i(succ(i))
     ) *;
     i = po ?

END {SI_PACKAGE_IMPL};
```

Let us add a few lines of explanation to the above implementation. The variable functions `i` and `j` serve as loop counters. `i` counts the number of screen positions which have already been dealt with. The `j` variable is a pointer in the buffer representation. The repetition construct of `screen_restore` has been designed according to the classical technique of finding a loop (repetition) invariant first and we refer to for example [36]. We have documented the loop invariant as a predicate `loop_invar'` which can be viewed as a generalisation of the postcondition `SI2` of `screen_restore`. The function `f` is just an auxiliary used in `loop_invar'`; it is used for relating the two counters `i` and `j`. The point is that the `j` variable must 'skip' the gap. The implementation chosen is fairly straightforward and we leave it to the reader to design more sophisticated and more efficient implementations (e.g. exploiting the display operations cl, ce and cm).

Using the above SI_PACKAGE_IMPL it is easy to make a new version of the editor which satisfies the strengthened specification EDITOR_SPEC'. We use the operations erase_buffer, forward_char etc. as already implemented in EDITOR_IMPL. Each new operation (the version whose name ends with _) is obtained as the sequential composition of an operation from EDITOR_IMPL and an operation from the screen invariant package.

```
LET EDITOR_IMPL' :=
EXPORT
  SORT Nat,
  SORT Char,
  SORT String,
  FUNC screen : -> String,
  FUNC cursor : -> Nat,
  PROC erase_buffer_  :      -> ,
  PROC forward_char_  :      -> ,
  PROC backward_char_ :      -> ,
  PROC insert_char_   : Char -> ,
  PROC delete_char_   :      ->
FROM
IMPORT STRING_OPS'      INTO
IMPORT EDITOR_IMPL      INTO
IMPORT SI_PACKAGE_IMPL INTO
CLASS

  PRED SI : % as before
  PRED SI1 : % as before
  PRED SI2 : % as before
  PROC display_op_ : -> % as before

  PROC erase_buffer_ : ->
  DEF  erase_buffer;
       screen_restore;
       cursor_restore

  PROC forward_char_ : ->
  DEF  forward_char;
       cursor_restore

  PROC backward_char_ : ->
  DEF  backward_char;
       cursor_restore
```

```
    PROC insert_char_ : Char ->
    PAR  c:Char
    DEF  insert_char(c);
         screen_restore;
         cursor_restore

    PROC delete_char_ : ->
    DEF  delete_char;
         screen_restore;
         cursor_restore

  END {EDITOR_IMPL'}
```

We should say something about the correctness of the implementation for the extended editor because of the deviation from the implementation strategy of Section 8.6.

First of all, considering `EDITOR_SPEC'` as an instance of the general template, we find that there are four variables a_i, viz. a_0 = `buffer`, a_1 = `dot` (but now these are hidden), a_2 = `screen` and a_3 = `cursor`. The fact that `buffer` and `dot` are hidden, does not cause problems because in the specification and the implementation they are hidden in precisely the same way. So formally speaking, we apply the strategy of Section 8.6 to the (normal forms of the) `CLASS` ... `END` parts of `EDITOR_SPEC'` and `EDITOR_IMPL'`; after that, we can apply the same `EXPORT` Σ `FROM` operation. This operation preserves the correctness of the specification-implementation pair.

Another detail in which we deviate from the implementation strategy of Section 8.6 is the axiom `EI AND SI => [ edit_op_ ] SI`. In principle this can be unfolded to become a number of additional axioms of the form `AXIOM` *inv* `AND pre_`p_j`(`a_0, a_1`) => [` p_j `] post_`p_j`(`$a_0, a_1, \overleftarrow{a_0}, \overleftarrow{a_1}$`)`, where both `pre_`$p_j$ and `post_`p_j happen to be `SI`. These axioms can be dealt with in the standard way.

Finally it should be noted that `buffer` and `dot` are their own representation. In other words, when viewed in the context of *GEN_IMPL* we find that a_2 coincides with one of the x_i and that a_3 coincides with another x_j. The abstraction functions are nothing but identity functions.

This concludes the implementation of the extended editor example.

8.7.6 Translation to C

We now perform a manual translation of the above implementation to the programming language C. It should be noted that old style C declarations have been used; it fits in better with the syntax of COLD-K but it is not a part of the latest ANSI specification. First of all we define several macros to achieve a certain syntactic similarity between the COLD-K texts and the C texts. After that we define macros to model the sorts **Nat** and **Char** and some of their operations. The names of the various class descriptions involved are inserted as comments.

```
#define PROC void
#define PRED Bool
#define DEF {
#define SKIP
#define AND &&
#define OR ||
#define NOT !
#define Bool int
#define true 1
#define false 0

/* NAT */

#define Nat int
#define pred(N) ((N)-1)
#define succ(N) ((N)+1)
#define lss(N,M) ((N)< (M))
#define leq(N,M) ((N)<= (M))

/* CHAR */

#define Char char
#define ord(N) N
#define blank ' '
#define tilde '~'
#define printable(C) leq(ord(blank),ord(C)) AND leq(ord(C),ord(tilde))

/* MEMORY */

Char memory[1000];
Nat size=3;
#define mem(N) memory[N]
#define upd(N,C) mem(N) = C
#define grow(N) size = size + (N)

/* EDITOR_IMPL */

Nat gap1;
```

```
Nat gap2;
Nat dot;

#define set_gap1(N) gap1 = (N)
#define set_gap2(N) gap2 = (N)
#define set_dot(N) dot = (N)

PROC erase_buffer()
DEF  set_gap1(0);
     set_gap2(size);
     set_dot(gap1);}

PROC forward_char()
DEF  if (gap2 == size) {
       SKIP
     } else {
       upd(gap1,mem(gap2));
       set_gap1(succ(gap1));
       set_gap2(succ(gap2));
       set_dot(succ(dot));
     }}

PROC backward_char()
DEF  if (gap1 == 0) {
       SKIP
     } else {
       set_gap1(pred(gap1));
       set_gap2(pred(gap2));
       set_dot(pred(dot));
       upd(gap2,mem(gap1));
     }}

PRED space()
DEF  return(NOT (gap1 == gap2));}

PROC gap_down()
DEF  set_gap1(pred(gap1));
     set_gap2(pred(gap2));
     upd(gap2,mem(gap1));}

PROC make_space(n)
Nat  n;
DEF  set_gap1(size);
     grow(n);
     set_gap2(size);
```

```
     while (lss(dot,gap1)) {
          gap_down();
     }}

PROC insert_char(c)
Char c;
DEF  if (space()) {
        SKIP
     } else {
        make_space(succ(size));
     };
     upd(gap1,c);
     set_gap1(succ(gap1));
     set_dot(succ(dot));}

PROC delete_char(c)
Char c;
DEF  if (gap2 == size) {
        SKIP
     } else {
        set_gap2(succ(gap2));
     }}

/* STRING_OPS' */

#define printable(C) leq(ord(blank),ord(C)) AND leq(ord(C),ord(tilde))

Char mk_printable(c)
Char c;
DEF  if (printable(c)) {
       return(c);
     } else {
       return(tilde);
     }}

/* SI_PACKAGE_IMPL */

PROC cursor_restore()
DEF  if (lss(dot,po)) {
       cm(dot);
     } else {
       SKIP
     }}
```

```
Nat i;
Nat j;

#define set_i(N) i = (N)
#define set_j(N) j = (N)

PROC screen_restore()
DEF  set_i(0);
     if (gap1 == 0) {
       set_j(gap2);
     } else {
       set_j(0);
     };
     cm(0);
     while (i != po)) {
         if (lss(j,size)) {
           pr(mk_printable(mem(j)));
         } else {
           pr(blank);
         };
         set_j(succ(j));
         if (j == gap1) {
           set_j(gap2);
         } else {
           SKIP
         };
         set_i(succ(i));
     }}

/* EDITOR_IMPL' */

PROC erase_buffer_()
DEF  erase_buffer();
     screen_restore();
     cursor_restore();}

PROC forward_char_()
DEF  forward_char();
     cursor_restore();}

PROC backward_char_()
DEF  backward_char();
     cursor_restore();}
```

```
PROC insert_char_(c)
Char c;
DEF  insert_char(c);
     screen_restore();
     cursor_restore();}

PROC delete_char_()
DEF  delete_char();
     screen_restore();
     cursor_restore();}
```

8.7.7 Executing the program

The pieces of C program given below constitute an execution environment which interfaces the editor with a true keyboard and display. Part of this execution environment has simply been programmed without having a formal specification. To simulate a single-line display device we have a constant po for 'number of *po*sitions' and commands pr and cm, for '*pr*int character' and '*c*ursor *m*otion'. Their implementation is meant for a VT100 type of terminal.

```
#define po 80
#define pr(c) putchar(c)
#define cm(n) {pr('\033');pr('[');\
               printf("%1u",1); pr(';');\
               if (n<9) printf("%1u",n+1);\
                  else printf("%2u",n+1);pr('H');}
```

The procedure key associates editor procedures with key strokes of the user. Typing a control-B invokes backward_char, control-D invokes delete_char whereas control-F invokes forward_char. The procedure main ties everything together. The user can exit the editor by typing control-C.

```
PROC key(c)
Char c;
DEF  if ( printable(c) )
          insert_char_(c);
     else switch (ord(c)) {
          case 2 : backward_char_();  break;
          case 4 : delete_char_();    break;
          case 6 : forward_char_();   break;
     }}
```

```
main()
DEF Char c;
    erase_buffer_();
    c = getchar();
    while (ord(c) != 3) {
            key(c);
            c = getchar();
    }}
```

8.8 Discussion

Let us have a closer look at the precise nature of the relation between an axiomatic state-based specification and its algorithmic implementation. First of all we want to stress that *implementation* and *specification* are relative notions in the sense that they are just roles played by descriptions. If we have given a certain class description, then there is no way to tell a priori whether this is a specification or an implementation. This depends on the way the description is used in a specific software development trajectory. As a rule of thumb, axiomatic specifications are mostly used as specifications and algorithmic specifications are used as implementations, but it can be the other way around. The notion of 'role' can become clearer by introducing a binary relation $\sqsubseteq$ on class descriptions. Referring to the templates of section 8.6 we have

$$GEN\_IMPL \ \sqsubseteq \ GEN\_SPEC.$$

The direction of the $\sqsubseteq$ sign is motivated by the fact that the class of models of *GEN_IMPL* is a subset of the model class of *GEN_SPEC*.

Recall that a normal-form state-based specification is a pair $(\Gamma, \mathcal{D})$ where Γ is a class signature and $\mathcal{D}$ may contain definitions of variables or dependent sorts, functions, predicates and also procedures; Γ may contain only names introduced in $\mathcal{D}$. For the general case of two given normal-form class descriptions $(\Gamma_i, \mathcal{D}_i)$ and $(\Gamma_s, \mathcal{D}_s)$ we must define the meaning of

$$(\Gamma_i, \mathcal{D}_i) \ \sqsubseteq \ (\Gamma_s, \mathcal{D}_s).$$

As a first approximation of the definition of $\sqsubseteq$ one could say that $(\Gamma_i, \mathcal{D}_i) \sqsubseteq (\Gamma_s, \mathcal{D}_s)$ if every class $\mathcal{C}$ which is a model of $(\Gamma_i, \mathcal{D}_i)$ is also a model of $(\Gamma_s, \mathcal{D}_s)$. However, this is a little too strict as we would like to allow the implementation to offer a richer signature than required by the specification. The intuition behind this is that it does no harm if one gets too much – except maybe for some name clashes which in practice can always be easily resolved. Therefore the correct definition of the implementation relation $\sqsubseteq$ is not to define it as model inclusion but as *model inclusion under a forgetful mapping.*

Definition. For the general case of two given normal-form class descriptions $(\Gamma_i, \mathcal{D}_i)$ and $(\Gamma_s, \mathcal{D}_s)$ we define that $(\Gamma_i, \mathcal{D}_i) \sqsubseteq (\Gamma_s, \mathcal{D}_s)$ iff for every class $\mathcal{C}$ of $(\Gamma_i, \mathcal{D}_i)$ we find that $\mathcal{F}(\mathcal{C})$ is a model of $(\Gamma_s, \mathcal{D}_s)$ where $\mathcal{F}$ is the forgetful mapping at the level of classes which forgets the sorts, functions, predicates and procedures which are in Γ_i but which are not in Γ_s.

For non-normal-form class descripions we say that one class description implements another if this is the case for their normal forms, where we refer to the process of normal form reduction by means of elimination of imports, renamings, etc.

□

In practice we do not always reason at the level of classes, but we verify that the implementation provides the sorts, functions, predicates and procedure required by the specification and that all the constraints specified have become logical consequences of the implementation.

Part III

Advanced techniques

Chapter 9

Theoretical topics

9.1 Introduction

In this chapter a number of existence proofs and theoretical discussions are presented. These are related to the earlier chapters, but were not presented there in order not to distract too much from the main line of those chapters. Sections 9.2 and 9.3 are related to Chapter 1. Sections 9.4 and 9.5 are related to Chapters 2 and 3, respectively. Finally Sections 9.6 and 9.7 are related to Chapter 5.

9.2 Undefinedness revisited

In this section we explain precisely how the truth and falsity of COLD-K assertions with respect to the partial many-sorted algebras is established. In particular the issue of undefinedness deserves a careful treatment. In this section we focus on the terms and assertions as presented in in Chapter 1 (see Tables 1.1 and 1.2).

Recall that a partial many-sorted Σ-algebra M is a system of carrier sets S^M (one for each sort name S in Σ), partial functions f^M (one for each function name f in Σ), and relations r^M (one for each relation name r in Σ). The functions f^M must be *compatible with their typing* in the following sense: if f : S_1 # ... # S_m -> V_1 # ... # V_n is in Σ we have that f^M is a partial function from $S_1^M \times \ldots \times S_m^M$ to $V_1^M \times \ldots \times V_n^M$. Similarly the predicates must be compatible with their typing, i.e. if r : S_1 # ... # S_m is in Σ we have that r^M is a relation on $S_1^M \times \ldots \times S_m^M$.

The main differences between these algebraic systems and the algebraic systems usually encountered in mathematical logic are the following:

- the sets S^M can be empty,
- the functions f^M are partial functions .

This should be compared with for example [37] where the carrier set is required to be non-empty and where all functions are total.

We aim at giving a precise definition of the *semantics* of terms $[\![\ ]\!]$ and *satisfaction* of assertions $\models$. First we introduce some technical machinery. We shall employ valuations, which are finite partial functions from typed logical variables, or object names as they are called in COLD-K, to values. We use the notation $\rightharpoondown$ in function types, instead of $\rightarrow$, to indicate partiality. For a partial function f we write $\operatorname{dom} f$ to denote the domains of f and similarly we use $\operatorname{rng} f$ as a notation for the range of f. For a set $\mathcal{S}$ we write "tuples over $\mathcal{S}$" to denote the set of tuples $(v_1, \ldots, v_m)$, where $(v_1, \ldots, v_m) \in \mathcal{S} \times \ldots \times \mathcal{S}$ (m times) for $m = 0, 1, \ldots$. Note that for $m = 0$ the set of tuples over $\mathcal{S}$ contains a single element: the empty tuple $()$.

Definition. For a given Σ-algebra M, a *valuation* Γ is a partial function

$$\Gamma : \text{variables} \rightharpoondown \text{tuples over} \bigcup_{\texttt{SORT}\, S \in \Sigma} S^M$$

which is compatible with the typing, i.e. for every $x \in \operatorname{dom}\Gamma$ of type S_1 # ... # S_m we find that $\Gamma(x)$ is a tuple $(v_1, \ldots, v_m)$ such that $v_1 \in S_1^M \wedge \ldots \wedge v_m \in S_m^M$. □

For a given signature Σ, the meaning function $[\![\ ]\!]$ is a mapping from Σ-algebras, valuations and expressions to values. For a given Σ-algebra M, valuation Γ and term X, we write $[\![X]\!]_\Gamma^M$ to denote the meaning of X. In this approach $[\![\ ]\!]_\Gamma^M$ is a partial function, reflecting the fact that certain COLD-K terms like `div(1,0)` and `pop(empty)` do *not* denote values. Instead, such terms are said to be undefined. Note that we do not need to introduce an artificial 'undefined value' (which is done in a related but technically different approach, to be discussed later).

In the definition below, we find a number of clauses which are of the form "$X \in \operatorname{dom}[\![\ ]\!]_\Gamma^M$ iff Q and when defined, $[\![X]\!]_\Gamma^M = R$". Each such clause is to be understood as consisting of two statements:

1. $X \in \operatorname{dom}[\![\ ]\!]_\Gamma^M \Leftrightarrow Q$;
2. $X \in \operatorname{dom}[\![\ ]\!]_\Gamma^M \Rightarrow [\![X]\!]_\Gamma^M = R$.

where the first statement is clearly about the definedness of the term X and the second clause is concerned with the result of $[\![\ ]\!]$ for defined terms.

Definition. Let M be a Σ-algebra and Γ a valuation, then the *meaning function* for terms is a partial function

$$[\![\ ]\!]_\Gamma^M : \text{well-typed terms} \rightharpoondown \text{tuples over} \bigcup_{\texttt{SORT}\, S \in \Sigma} S^M$$

which is compatible with the typing and is defined as follows:

1. $x \in \mathrm{dom}[\![\ ]\!]^M_\Gamma$ iff $x \in \mathrm{dom}\,\Gamma$ and when defined, $[\![x]\!]^M_\Gamma = \Gamma(x)$;
2. X,$Y \in \mathrm{dom}[\![\ ]\!]^M_\Gamma$ iff $X \in \mathrm{dom}[\![\ ]\!]^M_\Gamma \wedge Y \in \mathrm{dom}[\![\ ]\!]^M_\Gamma$ and when defined, $[\![X,Y]\!]^M_\Gamma = (x_1,\ldots,x_m,y_1,\ldots,y_n)$ where $[\![X]\!]^M_\Gamma = (x_1,\ldots,x_m)$ and where $[\![Y]\!]^M_\Gamma = (y_1,\ldots,y_n)$;
3. $f\ X \in \mathrm{dom}[\![\ ]\!]^M_\Gamma$ iff $X \in \mathrm{dom}[\![\ ]\!]^M_\Gamma \wedge [\![X]\!]^M_\Gamma \in \mathrm{dom}\, f^M$ and when defined, $[\![f\ X]\!]^M_\Gamma = f^M([\![X]\!]^M_\Gamma)$;
4. $(X) \in \mathrm{dom}[\![\ ]\!]^M_\Gamma$ iff $X \in \mathrm{dom}[\![\ ]\!]^M_\Gamma$ and when defined, $[\![(X)]\!]^M_\Gamma = [\![X]\!]^M_\Gamma$;
5. $() \in \mathrm{dom}[\![\ ]\!]^M_\Gamma$ and $[\![()]\!]^M_\Gamma = ()$, i.e. the only element of the Cartesian product of zero sets. □

The case of nullary functions requires a particular interpretation of the clause for $f\ X$ which for `FUNC` f `: ->` S should be read as: $f \in \mathrm{dom}[\![\ ]\!]^M_\Gamma$ iff $\mathrm{rng}\, f^M \neq \emptyset$ and when defined, $[\![f]\!]^M_\Gamma = f^M$.

Although some terms fail to have a meaning, this is remedied by the treatment of assertions, because for a given M and Γ all well-typed assertions are either true or false. Below we use the notation $\Gamma + (x \mapsto v)$ to denote the valuation which is like Γ except for the variable x which is mapped to the value v.

Definition. Let M be a Σ-algebra and Γ a valuation, then the truth (satisfaction) of assertions is a total function

$$M \models_\Gamma : \text{well-typed assertions} \rightarrow \{\text{ true, false }\}$$

defined as follows:

1. $M \models_\Gamma$ `NOT` $A \Leftrightarrow M \not\models_\Gamma A$;
2. $M \models_\Gamma A$ `AND` $B \Leftrightarrow M \models_\Gamma A \wedge M \models_\Gamma B$;
3. $M \models_\Gamma$ `FORALL` x:S $A \Leftrightarrow$ for all $v \in S^M$ $M \models_{\Gamma + (x \mapsto v)} A$;
4. $M \models_\Gamma$ `EXISTS` x:S $A \Leftrightarrow$ there is a $v \in S^M$ $M \models_{\Gamma + (x \mapsto v)} A$;
5. $M \models_\Gamma X! \Leftrightarrow X \in \mathrm{dom}[\![\ ]\!]^M_\Gamma$;
6. $M \models_\Gamma X = Y \Leftrightarrow X \in \mathrm{dom}[\![\ ]\!]^M_\Gamma \wedge Y \in \mathrm{dom}[\![\ ]\!]^M_\Gamma \wedge [\![X]\!]^M_\Gamma = [\![Y]\!]^M_\Gamma$;
7. $M \models_\Gamma r\ X \Leftrightarrow X \in \mathrm{dom}[\![\ ]\!]^M_\Gamma \wedge [\![X]\!]^M_\Gamma \in r^M$;
8. $M \models_\Gamma (A) \Leftrightarrow M \models_\Gamma A$;
9. $M \models_\Gamma () \Leftrightarrow$ true;
10. clauses for `TRUE`, `FALSE`, A `;` B, A `OR` B, A `=>` B and A `<=>` B. □

The case of the empty sort S^M requires a particular interpretation of the clause for `FORALL` x:S A which if $S^M = \emptyset$ should be read as: $M \models_\Gamma$ `FORALL` x:S A is true. The clauses for `TRUE`, `FALSE`, A `;` B, A `OR` B, A `=>` B and A `<=>` B are trivial and have not been included here. It is interesting to observe how the clauses for the quantifiers build up the valuations Γ by adding a maplet $(x \mapsto v)$. The following definition establishes the truth and falsity of COLD-K assertions with respect to partial many-sorted algebras.

Definition. Let M be a Σ-algebra, then the truth (satisfaction) of a closed assertion A in a model M is defined by

$$M \models A \Leftrightarrow M \models_{\emptyset} A$$

where $\emptyset$ denotes the valuation with the empty domain. □

The approach of Chapter 1, which is formalised in the present section, has been chosen because it is felt to be intuitive and avoids the use of artificial values. It should be noted that the above definitions do not contain a proof system for predicate logic based on partial many-sorted algebras (for a proof system some care is needed because the sorts can be empty). The logic MPL_ω has been devised for this purpose. It is described in [10] and [19]. The work described in [19] should be viewed as the mathematical basis of the predicate logic of COLD-K. In [19] a slightly different approach to the definition of $M \models A$ is taken: at the level of the algebras, 'undefined' is treated as as the 'bottom' value $\perp$ for which one can discuss equations such as e.g. the strictness principle that $f^M(\perp) = \perp$. In this way the partial functions can been avoided. The two approaches are essentially equivalent because it is always possible to add $\perp$ values, making all functions total, or to remove them, working with partial functions (because of the strictness properties).

9.3 Initial algebras

In this section we shall review several algebraic notions such as homomorphisms and initial algebras. The first notion to be defined is that of a homomorphism. To keep the presentation simple, we focus on Σ-algebras where Σ contains one sort name `S`, a constant function name `c: -> S` and a unary function name `f: S -> S`. The extension of our definitions to include n-ary functions and predicates is straightforward.

```
SORT S,
FUNC c : -> S,
FUNC f : S -> S
```

Fig 9.1. Signature Σ_{Scf} with sort, constant and unary function.

Definition. Consider the signature Σ_{Scf} and two Σ_{Scf}-algebras A and B. A *homomorphism* h from A to B is a mapping from $\mathtt{S}^A$ to $\mathtt{S}^B$ such that for all x in $\mathtt{S}^A$ we find that $h(\mathtt{c}^A)$ is defined iff $\mathtt{c}^B$ is defined, and if so,

$$h(\mathtt{c}^A) = \mathtt{c}^B$$

Moreover $h(\mathtt{f}^A(x))$ must be defined whenever $\mathtt{f}^B(h(x))$ is defined, and if so,

$$h(\mathtt{f}^A(x)) = \mathtt{f}^B(h(x))$$ □

Homomorphisms are structure-preserving mappings from one algebra to another. The generalisation from single-sorted algebras to many-sorted algebras can be made by adopting a mapping h_S for each sort S in the signature. The homomorphism property for a binary function `f` is that for all x and y in $\mathtt{S}^A$, $h(\mathtt{f}^A(x,y))$ is defined whenever $\mathtt{f}^B(h(x),h(y))$ is defined, and if so, $h(\mathtt{f}^A(x,y)) = \mathtt{f}^B(h(x),h(y))$; and similarly for n-ary functions. The extension to predicates is also straightforward.

Let us give an example. Consider the algebra of Figure 1.10 which has three objects and the algebra of Figure 1.9 which has one object. Now we define the homomorphism $h : Switch_{1.10} \rightarrow Switch_{1.9}$ as the mapping which maps all three objects in its domain to the unique object in its range. Let us verify the homomorphism property for the unary function `toggle` which is that $h(\mathtt{toggle}(x))$ is defined whenever $\mathtt{toggle}(h(x))$ is defined, and if so, $h(\mathtt{toggle}(x)) = \mathtt{toggle}(h(x))$, which is trivially the case. As another example, let us mention that there is also a homomorphism $Switch_{1.10} \rightarrow Switch_{1.11}$.

Definition. An algebra A is *initial* in a class V of Σ-algebras if A is in V and furthermore for each $B \in V$ there is a unique homomorphism from A to B. □

In fact there is also a dual notion: an algebra A is *final* in a class V of Σ-algebras if A is in V and for each $B \in V$ there is a unique homomorphism from B to A.

The lemma below shows that the meaning $\mathcal{M}(S)$ of a specification S can be defined as a unique special algebra: the initial algebra (provided that the syntactic algebraic specifications are suitably restricted). This has been used as a starting point for defining algebraic specification languages such as ASF [13], PLUSS [14], CLEAR [15], Act-one [16], and OBJ-2 [17].

In the lemma below we refer to *definedness axioms* by which we mean the following. The definedness axiom for a constant `c` is the axiom stating that `c!`. The definedness axiom for a unary function `f: S -> S` states that `FORALL x:S ( f(x)! )` etc. We also refer to *equations* by which we mean assertions of the form $X = Y$, where X and Y are 'terms', and which are universally quantified (i.e. by FORALL) over all free variables occurring in X and Y.

Lemma. (Initial algebra lemma). Consider a flat algebraic specification, such that

1. for each sort there is at least one closed term,
2. for each function there is a definedness axiom,
3. all other axioms are equations, with terms on either side,

then there is an initial algebra I in the class of all models of this flat algebraic specification.

Proof. We show this for a flat algebraic specification over the signature Σ_{Scf}. We shall give an explicit construction of I. Let CT denote the set of all closed terms built-up from elements of Σ_{Scf}. Let eq denote the binary relation on CT generated by the equational axioms, reflexivity, transitivity, symmetry and substitutivity. Thus eq(X,Y) means that $X = Y$ is derivable when reasoning with = in the usual way. Now eq is an equivalence relation and we can consider the set of closed terms *modulo* eq. Define $\mathtt{S}^I$ as follows:

$$\mathtt{S}^I = \mathrm{CT}/\mathrm{eq}$$

where CT/eq denotes the quotient set of CT as induced by eq. We write $[X]$ for the equivalence class containing the closed term X.

The next step is to construct interpretations for c and f. We define $\mathtt{c}^I = [\mathtt{c}]$. To define the interpretation of f we define $\mathtt{f}^I([X]) = [\mathtt{f}X]$. Of course we must check that this definition of $\mathtt{f}^I([X])$ is independent of the choice of the representative X. Therefore consider eq(X,Y), which means that $X = Y$ is derivable – reasoning with = in the usual way. We must check that $[\mathtt{f}X] = [\mathtt{f}Y]$. Clearly this is the case because of the substitutivity of eq.

We define I as the partial many-sorted algebra with $\mathtt{S}^I$, $\mathtt{c}^I$ and $\mathtt{f}^I$ and we claim that I is a model of the given COLD-K specification. Let us check that I is a model indeed. The definedness axioms hold in I because $\mathtt{c}^I$ is well-defined (it is an equivalence class) whereas $\mathtt{f}^I$ is defined for all arguments: (it is an equivalence class as well). Next, consider an axiom, FORALL x : S $(X(x) = Y(x))$ say. This holds in I if for arbitrary value $[V]$ we have that eq$(X(V),Y(V))$ which is the case because eq was derived from the axioms (including the axiom under consideration) using substitution, amongst other things.

Now we know that I is a model, we have to check that it is *initial* and therefore we consider an arbitrary algebra A satisfying our flat algebraic specification. Then we must indicate a unique homomorphism h from I to A. We define h as follows:

$$h([X]) = X^A$$

where X^A is the interpretation of the term X in A. Of course we must check that this definition of $h([X])$ is independent of the choice of the representative X: so suppose $\mathrm{eq}(X, Y)$ and suppose that $X^A \neq Y^A$, then A is not a model of the specification – contradicting our assumption on A.

Let us see if h is a homomorphism. The homomorphism property for $\mathtt{c}$ is obvious. For $\mathtt{f}$ we consider a value $[X]$ and we reason as follows:

$$\begin{aligned}
&h(\mathtt{f}^I([X])) \\
&= (1)\ \ h([\mathtt{f}X]) \\
&= (2)\ \ (\mathtt{f}X)^A \\
&= (3)\ \ \mathtt{f}^A(X^A) \\
&= (4)\ \ \mathtt{f}^A(h([X]))
\end{aligned}$$

where step (1) is motivated by the definition of $\mathtt{f}^I$, step (2) by the definition of h, step (3) by the compositionality of interpreting terms in A and finally step (4) is motivated again by the definition of h. This shows that h is a homomorphism.

Actually h is unique, for suppose there is another homomorphism h' say, then we claim that $h = h'$. To see this, note that for values $[X]$ we have $h'([X]) = X^A$, just as h does. The fact that $h'([X]) = X^A$ is a consequence of the homomorphism property of h'; we prove it by induction on the structure of the closed term X. The induction basis is $h(\mathtt{c}) = \mathtt{c}^A$. For the induction step we reason as follows:

$$\begin{aligned}
&h'([fX]) \\
&= (5)\ \ h'(\mathtt{f}^I([X])) \\
&= (6)\ \ \mathtt{f}^A(h'([X])) \\
&= (7)\ \ \mathtt{f}^A(X^A) \\
&= (8)\ \ (\mathtt{f}X)^A
\end{aligned}$$

where step (5) is motivated by the definition of $\mathtt{f}^I$, step (6) by the homomorphism property of h', step (7) by the induction hypothesis and finally step (8) is motivated again by the compositionality of the interpretation process in A. This shows that $h' = h$ and since h' was arbitrary this means that h is unique. Therefore the constructed algebra I is initial. □

There is a stronger version of this lemma, stating the existence of an initial algebra when using conditional equations instead of equations. A conditional equation is a (universally quantified) assertion of the form:

$$C \texttt{ => } term_1 \texttt{ = } term_2$$

where the condition C is a conjunction of equations.

In specification languages which do *not* have special provisions for treating definedness and undefinedness, the initial algebra lemma and its proof can be simplified accordingly. In that case we have normal many-sorted algebras instead of *partial* many-sorted algebras and no definedness axioms are needed.

Definition. A Σ-algebra A is said to be *total* if all functions of A are total. A sort S of a Σ-algebra A is said to be *minimal* if each object in S^A can be denoted by a closed Σ-term of type S. A Σ-algebra A is said to be *minimal* if all sorts of A are minimal. □

As it happens, the algebra I constructed in the initial algebra lemma has the following properties:

1. A is total;
2. A is minimal;
3. A satisfies the signature and axioms of the specification;
4. two objects in a sort of A are equal iff their equality can be proven from the axioms.

The notion of an algebra being minimal is closely related to the 'no junk' axioms, an example of which was already used as SWITCH6 in Section 1.8. In fact, a 'no junk' axiom serves precisely for expressing this minimality.

We give an example. If we were to adopt the initial-algebra semantics (unlike COLD-K), the following specification would have the model of Figure 1.11. as its meaning. There is no need for a 'no junk' axiom, because of property 2 above. There is also no need for a 'no confusion' axiom, because of property 4 above. Actually the axioms SWITCH1 and SWITCH2 are redundant because they follow by strictness from SWITCH3 and SWITCH4. We kept SWITCH1 and SWITCH2 in order to stick as closely as possible to the premises of the initial algebra lemma.

```
CLASS

  SORT Switch
  FUNC on     : -> Switch
  FUNC off    : -> Switch
  FUNC toggle : Switch -> Switch
```

```
    AXIOM
    {SWITCH1} on!;
    {SWITCH2} off!;
    {SWITCH2'} FORALL s:Switch ( toggle(s) ! )

    AXIOM
    {SWITCH3} toggle(on)  = off;
    {SWITCH4} toggle(off) = on

END
```

It is an interesting exercise to find the homomorphisms from this initial algebra to other algebras satisfying the assertions SWITCH1, SWITCH2, SWITCH2', SWITCH3 and SWITCH4. In particular, the algebra of Figure 1.9 can be viewed as a homomorphic image of the initial algebra of Figure 1.11. To see this, consider the mapping $h : Switch_{1.11} \rightarrow Switch_{1.9}$ with $h(on) = on$ and $h(off) = off$. This h is the unique homomorphism from the algebra of Figure 1.11 to the algebra of Figure 1.9. For more information on the initial algebra approach we refer to e.g. [38].

We end this section with a discussion about the advantages of the COLD-K approach, which seems to have the disadvantage that more axioms are required than with the initial algebra approach.

An example where we employ the greater flexibility of COLD-K is given in Section B.3 (see the standard library) where a loosely specified scheme CHAR is given. There are definitions of the form FUNC min : -> Nat and FUNC max : -> Nat, but there is no explicit DEF clause or axiom which could provide for normal forms of min and max. If we had adopted the initial algebra approach, this kind of looseness would have led to serious problems. Due to the built-in no-confusion and no-junk properties of the initial algebra approach, min and max would have to be considered as 'new' natural numbers, unequal to 0, 1, 2, ...! In the approach chosen in CHAR, only the property min < max is postulated; therefore we still have many possible models, including the well-known ASCII and EBCDIC character sets.

A second example where we employ the greater flexibility of COLD-K is given in Section 7.2.7. In RETRIEVAL there are several loosely specified auxiliary meaning functions called sem (on expressions, qualifications and expression lists). We do not care about their value for arguments which are not wf and so we do not specify anything about it. It should be noted that, although the INGRES example as a whole is state-based, the retrieve operation and all other meaning functions are modelled by purely algebraic techniques.

Finally, let us give one more demonstration of the looseness of COLD-K. The following example adds a selection function to the specification of finite sets of items.

```
LET SET' :=
EXPORT
  SORT Item,
  SORT Set,
  FUNC select : Set -> Item
FROM
IMPORT SET INTO
CLASS

  FUNC select : Set -> Item

  AXIOM NOT select(empty)!

  AXIOM FORALL s:Set
        ( NOT s = empty => is_in(select(s),s) )

END
```

The above specification SET' states that there is a function select such that for every non-empty set s the result select(s) is in s. Note that we did not specify *which* element of s must be selected: this may be decided by an implementor of SET and SET'. When using the initial algebra approach however this is a notorious specification problem: when select(s) cannot be proven equal to any other term, it must be a 'new' item, which was not the intention. When using loose semantics there is no problem.

9.4 Horn clauses

Inductive predicate definitions define predicates as the *least* predicate satisfying some assertion (provided that this predicate exists). Below we shall provide the proof of the proposition on which the practical approach to this existence problem of Section 2.3 was based.

Definition. An assertion A is an r-Horn clause iff it has the form of a conjunction, where each conjunct is a universally quantified assertion of the form:

t_1 AND ... AND t_m => $r(x_1, \ldots, x_n)$

Here $x_1, \ldots, x_n$ are object names (introduced by the universal quantifiers) and each t_i is either:

- an assertion not containing r,
- or an assertion of the form $r(y_1, \ldots, y_n)$ where $y_1, \ldots, y_n$ are object names. □

We provide a technical lemma and a proposition about Horn clauses: so if one adopts the syntactic pattern of Horn clauses, the least predicate is guaranteed to exist.

Lemma. Let A be an r-Horn clause. If R is a (possibly infinite) non-empty set of predicates satisfying A, then the intersection

$$\bigcap_{r \in R} r$$

of all predicates in R also satisfies A.

Proof. To keep things simple, we show this for the situation where A consists of *one* conjunct only. Let us moreover make the non-essential assumption that r is unary. Suppose that A is an r-Horn clause, then it can be written in the following form:

$$\forall x_0 x_1 \ldots x_n (\bigwedge_{i=1}^{m} r(x_i) \wedge \varphi(x_0, x_1, \ldots, x_n) \Rightarrow r(x_0)) \qquad (*)$$

with $m \leq n$ and $r \notin \varphi$. Let R be a non-empty set of predicates satisfying A, then we have that:

$$\forall r \in R\, \forall x_0 x_1 \ldots x_n (\bigwedge_{i=1}^{m} r(x_i) \wedge \varphi(x_0, x_1, \ldots, x_n) \Rightarrow r(x_0))$$

(were we use a higher-order quantification, so this fact is not expressed in COLD-K itself). This implies

$$\forall x_0 x_1 \ldots x_n\, \forall r \in R\, (\bigwedge_{i=1}^{m} r(x_i) \wedge \varphi(x_0, x_1, \ldots, x_n) \Rightarrow r(x_0))$$

from which we obtain using the logical rule that $\forall x(P(x) \Rightarrow Q(x))$ implies $\forall x(P(x)) \Rightarrow \forall x(Q(x))$:

$$\forall x_0 x_1 \ldots x_n\, (\forall r \in R\, (\bigwedge_{i=1}^{m} r(x_i) \wedge \varphi(x_0, x_1, \ldots, x_n)) \Rightarrow \forall r \in R(r(x_0)))$$

Now we can interchange the $\forall$ and the $\bigwedge$ constructs, noting that r does not occur in $\varphi(x_0, x_1, \ldots, x_n)$, whence

$$\forall x_0 x_1 \ldots x_n \; (\bigwedge_{i=1}^{m} \forall r \in R \; (r(x_i)) \wedge \varphi(x_0, x_1, \ldots, x_n) \Rightarrow \forall r \in R(r(x_0)))$$

We rewrite this, using the view that predicates are relations, into

$$\forall x_0 x_1 \ldots x_n \; (\bigwedge_{i=1}^{m} (\bigcap_{r \in R} r)(x_i) \wedge \varphi(x_0, x_1, \ldots, x_n) \Rightarrow (\bigcap_{r \in R} r)(x_0))$$

which just says that $A(\bigcap_{r \in R} r)$ holds. This concludes the proof. □

Proposition. Let A be an r-Horn clause, then there exists a least predicate satisfying A.

Proof. The existence of a least predicate satisfying A follows because we can apply the lemma to the set R of *all* predicates satisfying A. We only have to show that this set is non-empty. Therefore consider the predicate r defined by $r(x) :\Leftrightarrow \mathit{true}$ (for all x). It is easy to see that this predicate satisfies A. □

9.5 Origin consistency

In this section we shall have a closer look at one of the modularity principles behind the modular schemes and in particular we shall focus on the problem of tracing back the applied occurrence of a name to its definition. This should be viewed as a refinement of the explanation of modularisation already given in Chapter 3. Consider the following simple flat scheme:

```
CLASS
  SORT A
  FUNC a : -> A
  AXIOM a!
END
```

We see that the name `A` occurs twice. The first occurrence is said to be its *defining* occurrence, because this is the place where it is defined that `A` is a sort. The second occurrence is said to be an *applied* occurrence because here the name A is *used* to define the range type of a. Similarly the name a occurs twice. Its first occurrence is the defining occurrence, because it defines a as a function with a given domain type and range type. The second occurrence of a is an applied occurrence.

Some care is needed to avoid problems in connection with these kinds of occurrences. To see this, consider the following scheme:

```
LET X := EXPORT ΣX FROM
         CLASS ... FUNC f : A -> A ...... END;
LET Y := EXPORT ΣY FROM
         CLASS ...... FUNC f : A -> A ... END;
LET Z := IMPORT X INTO
         IMPORT Y INTO
         CLASS ... f ... END;
Z
```

Assume that f occurs in both Σ_X and Σ_Y. Now we ask the question: which f do we mean in the scheme Z, the one from X or the one from Y? The answer 'both' is only reasonable if the definitions of f (including all axioms characterizing f) are the same in X and Y. Otherwise, there is a fair chance that f from X and f from Y are different functions, leading to an inconsistency in Z.

The main tool in our discussion will be a notion called 'origin'. An origin is a unique label attached to a defining occurrence of a name. Alternatively, one might think of origins as pointers to the place in the text where the name is defined. Although we normally just write COLD-K texts, leaving the origins implicit, we shall sometimes visualise them as integer indices decorating names – just for the sake of the discussion in this chapter and in Chapter 10. For example, we could decorate the defining occurrence of A with its origin, 1 say and decorate a with another fresh origin (2).

```
CLASS
  SORT A₁
  FUNC a₂ : -> A
  AXIOM a!
END
```

To avoid problems like the problem of f in X and Y sketched above, we put forward the following requirement: it should be possible to trace back each applied occurrence of a name to a unique definition. In other words, each applied occurrence of a name should have a unique origin. In order to discuss whether a certain description satisfies this requirement we introduce the following terminology.

Definition. A scheme is *origin consistent* if it is possible to trace back each applied occurrence of a name to a unique definition (= origin). □

A scheme not satisfying the origin consistency requirement is called *origin inconsistent*. In this terminology, the above scheme Z with $f \in \Sigma_X$ and $f \in \Sigma_Y$ is origin inconsistent. When trying to resolve the origin inconsistency we must first analyse what was actually meant. There are two possibilities: either we defined two different functions with the same name `f` by accident, or we really mean the same function `f`. If by accident we defined two different functions with the same name `f`, we have to resolve the ambiguity by hiding or renaming the 'wrong' `f`. For example, if we mean the second `f` we can satisfy the origin consistency requirement by:

```
LET X := EXPORT Σ_X FROM
         CLASS ... FUNC f : A -> A ...... END;
LET Y := EXPORT Σ_Y FROM
         CLASS ...... FUNC f : A -> A ... END;
LET Z := IMPORT EXPORT Σ'_X FROM X INTO
         IMPORT Y INTO
         CLASS ... f ... END;
Z
```

where Σ'_X is Σ_X with `f` removed from it. If we really mean the same function `f` in both cases, we have to put the definition of `f` in a single flat scheme, e.g:

```
LET W := CLASS ... FUNC f : A -> A ... END;
LET X := EXPORT Σ_X FROM
         IMPORT W INTO CLASS ... END;
LET Y := EXPORT Σ_Y FROM
         IMPORT W INTO CLASS ... END;
LET Z := IMPORT X INTO
         IMPORT Y INTO
         CLASS ... f ... END;
Z
```

The above example shows that the `LET` construct is more than just an abbreviation mechanism: its use is essential in enforcing origin consistency.

The origin consistency requirement leads to a natural way of enforcing modularity of a scheme: it requires definitions of the same thing to be put in the same description instead of being spread over different descriptions. In fact, the requirement of origin consistency is a necessary precondition for finding the normal form of a scheme. Recall that in Section 3.4, considering an import scheme `IMPORT` K `INTO` L, we said that

> *in order to determine the denotation of L, we first have to add to L the definitions of the names exported by K and used in L.*

But by now it must be clear that this only makes sense if for each name exported by K and used in L, we know *which* definition to add. We can conclude that only origin consistent schemes can be brought into normal form.

The simple procedure for calculating the normal-form specification associated with a scheme should now be adjusted. The following steps describe the normalization of origin consistent modular schemes:

1. Assign values to the defining occurrences of names, uniquely identifying their definitions. The value associated with a name is called its *origin*.
2. Assign origins to all applied occurrences of names by tracing them back to their definitions. No origins are assigned to the names in a renaming: they are not considered applied occurrences of names since they are only used to define a mapping from names to names.
3. Normalize the scheme as before, treating identical names with different origins as different symbols.
4. Eliminate all name clashes of hidden names with other (hidden and non-hidden names) by suitable renamings of the hidden names.
5. Remove all origins from the names.

The first two steps serve to make explicit the origins, since origins are normally not a part of the COLD-K text. The third step serves to replace schemes by their denotations. This was described in Section 3.3 for export schemes – replacing `EXPORT` Σ `FROM` K by the normal-form specification $\langle \Sigma \cap \Sigma_K, \mathcal{D}_K \rangle$. In Section 3.4 this was described for import schemes – replacing `IMPORT` K `INTO` L by the normal-form specification $\langle \Sigma_K \cup \Sigma_L, \mathcal{D}_K \cup \mathcal{D}_L \rangle$. To justify the fourth step, we note that renamings of hidden names in the final normal-form specification can do no harm, since we cannot refer to these names anyway. Often it is convenient to employ a systematic renaming procedure here, e.g. replacing `f` by `f'`, using the fact that identifiers in COLD-K may contain quotes. Finally, step 5 serves to arrive at a normal-form specification without origins which can be interpreted as explained in Chapter 1 and Chapter 2.

We show this normalization procedure by means of an example. Consider the following origin consistent scheme:

```
LET X := EXPORT
           SORT A
         FROM
         CLASS
           SORT A
           SORT B
           FUNC f : B -> A
           AXIOM EXISTS b:B ()
           AXIOM FORALL b:B ( f(b)! )
```

```
          END;
IMPORT X INTO
RENAME FUNC g : B -> A TO f IN
CLASS
  SORT B
  FUNC g : B -> A
  AXIOM FORALL a:A EXISTS b:B ( g(b) = a )
END
```

After origin assignment (using integer indices as origins) this scheme becomes:

```
LET X := EXPORT
            SORT A_1
          FROM
          CLASS
            SORT A_1
            SORT B_2
            FUNC f_3 : B_2 -> A_1
            AXIOM EXISTS b:B_2 ()
            AXIOM FORALL b:B_2 ( f_3(b)! )
          END;
IMPORT X INTO
RENAME FUNC g : B -> A TO f IN
CLASS
  SORT B_4
  FUNC g_5 : B_4 -> A_1
  AXIOM FORALL a:A_1 EXISTS b:B_4 ( g_5(b) = a )
END
```

Flattening of the scheme leads to:

```
EXPORT
  SORT A_1,
  SORT B_4,
  FUNC f_5 : B_4 -> A_1
FROM
CLASS
  SORT A_1
  SORT B_2
  FUNC f_3 : B_2 -> A_1
  AXIOM EXISTS b:B_2 ()
  AXIOM FORALL b:B_2 ( f_3(b)! )
```

```
    SORT B4
    FUNC f5 : B4 -> A1
    AXIOM FORALL a:A1 EXISTS b:B4 ( f5(b) = a )
END
```

Elimination of name clashes and removal of origins results in the following normal form of the scheme:

```
EXPORT
  SORT A,
  SORT B,
  FUNC f : B -> A
FROM
CLASS
  SORT A
  SORT B'
  FUNC f' : B' -> A
  AXIOM EXISTS b:B' ()
  AXIOM FORALL b:B' ( f'(b)! )
  SORT B
  FUNC f : B -> A
  AXIOM FORALL a:A EXISTS b:B ( f(b) = a )
END
```

9.6 Comparing two types of models

Recall that in Part I there was a notion of 'model', relating algebras and algebraic specifications, whereas in Part II we introduced a new notion of 'model', relating classes and state-based specifications. It is interesting to compare these notions and to see precisely in which way the new notion is an extension of the old. The following lemma shows how each algebra can be viewed as a particularly simple class.

Lemma. Assume that the algebra A is a model of the normal-form algebraic specification $(\Sigma, \mathcal{D})$. Define the class C_A with

1. **State**$= \{ s_0 \}$ where s_0 has algebra A associated with it,
2. initial state s_0,
3. no transition relations.

Then C_A is a model of $(\Gamma, \mathcal{D})$ with $\Gamma = \Sigma$, i.e. a model of $(\Sigma, \mathcal{D})$ viewed as a state-based specification.

Proof. A is a model of $(\Sigma, \mathcal{D})$ means that there must be an algebra A' such that A was obtained by forgetting the hiddens from A'. Consider $C_{A'}$ defined as the class with **State** $= \{s_0\}$ where s_0 has A' associated with it, initial state $= s_0$ and no transition relations. Verify that

1. $C_{A'}$ satisfies the definitions of $\mathcal{D}$,
2. C_A is obtained from $C_{A'}$ by forgetting the hidden transition relations and the hiddens of each state. □

Next we consider the situation the other way round, viewing certain classes as algebras. This is easy for those classes which arise as models of algebraic specifications.

Lemma. Assume that the class C is a model of the state-based specification $(\Gamma, \mathcal{D})$. Assume that neither Γ nor $\mathcal{D}$ contain procedures and that $\mathcal{D}$ contains no variables; i.e. in fact $(\Gamma, \mathcal{D})$ can be viewed as an algebraic specification. Then there is a standard way to obtain an algebra $A(C)$ from C such that $A(C)$ is a model of the algebraic specification $(\Sigma, \mathcal{D})$ where $\Sigma = \Gamma$.

Proof. Let C be given as the class with

1. set of states **State** where each state s has algebra $A(s)$;
2. initial state s_0;
3. no transition relations.

then take $A(C) := A(s_0)$. □

These lemmas show that the notion of 'model', relating algebras and algebraic specifications, is fully compatible with the new notion of 'model', introduced in Chapter 5, relating classes and state-based specifications.

9.7 The class concept revisited

In this section, let us have a closer look at the class concept. Recall the definition of a 'class', which has a set **State** where each state s has an algebra $A(s)$ associated with it. There seems to be an option to simplify the definition of 'class' by saying that a state *is* an algebra. Yet, if one were to adopt that simplified definition, problems would arise in connection with `EXPORT` since the forgetful mapping $\mathcal{F}$ forgetting the hidden sorts, functions and predicates would lead to an identification of states that were distinct before; more precisely, for states s_1 and s_2 we could have $\mathcal{F}(s_1) = \mathcal{F}(s_2)$ even if $s_1 \neq s_2$. Such identifications may change the state-structure of a class viewed as a state machine, and may even change its observational behaviour. Therefore this simplified definition is *too* simple and must be rejected.

Instead of that, one could identify states when they have the same algebras *and* the same 'transition behaviour'. This can be formalised by using the concept of *bisimulation*. Using this approach one can define a *canonical* form for each class C.

Definition. ($\underline{\leftrightarrow}$) Consider a Γ-class C with set of states **State**, where each state s has an algebra $A(s)$ associated with it, where the initial state is s_0 and where we have transition relations $\mathcal{T}_p$, one for each procedure name $p \in \Gamma$. We say that a relation R on **State** $\times$ **State** is an *auto-bisimulation* if

1. $R(s_0, s_0)$,
2. if $R(s,t)$ then $A(s) = A(t)$,
3. if $(s \rightarrow s')$ is a transition in $\mathcal{T}_p$ and $R(s,t)$, then there is a transition $(t \rightarrow t')$ in $\mathcal{T}_p$ with $R(s', t')$,
4. if $R(s,t)$ then $R(t,s)$.

Note that there is at least one auto-bisimulation and that the union of two or more auto-bisimulations is an auto-bisimulation again and therefore a *maximal* auto-bisimulation exists. We denote it by $\underline{\leftrightarrow}$. □

In the picture below the third clause from the definition of $\underline{\leftrightarrow}$ is illustrated. The picture shows states s, s', t, t' of a class and a number of transitions of a transition relation $\mathcal{T}_p$.

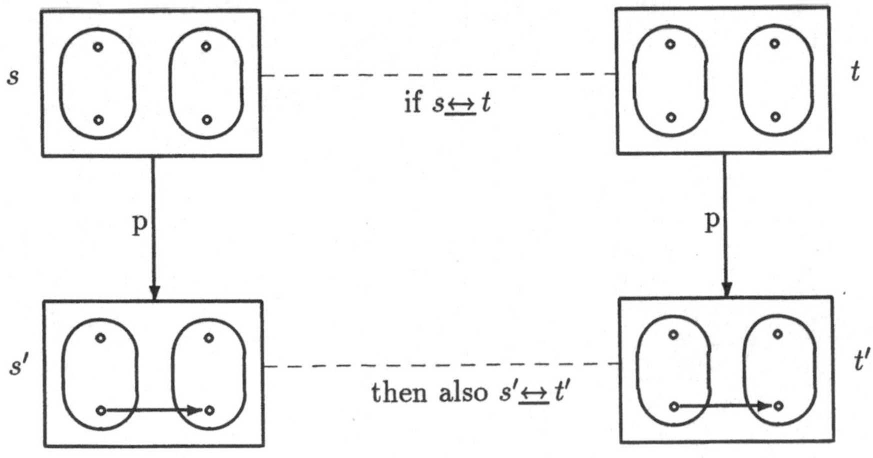

Fig 9.2. Auto-bisimulation $\underline{\leftrightarrow}$.

The relation $\underline{\leftrightarrow}$ is a formalisation of the idea to identify as many states as possible, without however changing the observable behaviour of the class. Note that $\underline{\leftrightarrow}$ is an equivalence relation; therefore we can construct a canonical form for each class by making a new set of states which are the old states modulo $\underline{\leftrightarrow}$. We write $[s]$ for the equivalence class containing s.

Definition. (canonical form of a class). Consider a Γ-class C with set of states **State** as above. We construct a new Γ-class $C/\underline{\leftrightarrow}$ with

- **State**$/\underline{\leftrightarrow}$ as its collection of states, where each $[s]$ has the algebra $A(s)$ associated with it,
- $[s_0]$ as its initial state,
- for each p a transition relation containing all transitions $([s] \rightarrow [s'])$ for which there is a transition $(s \rightarrow s')$ in $\mathcal{T}_p$. □

For more details on auto-bisimulations we refer to [39]. This process of taking canonical forms does not eleminate the need for loose semantics, for in general there are many canonical classes satisfying a given specification. The advantage of constructing canonical classes is that observationally-equivalent classes are identified and replaced by classes whose state-space is as small as possible.

One could go even one step further, constructing *reachable* canonical classes, by removing all states that are not reachable from the initial state.

Chapter 10

Additional language constructs

10.1 Introduction

In this chapter we shall present a number of language constructs which are available in COLD-K but which were not treated in Part I and Part II in order not to complicate the presentation too much. The topics presented in the present chapter can be grouped into three groups. The first of these concerns a single topic, which is a liberal approach to scoping that applies to the expressions and assertions of COLD-K. This is the subject of Section 10.2.

The second group deals with parameterisation and two related language constructs are presented: free definitions and parameterised schemes. These are Sections 10.3 to 10.8.

Finally Sections 10.9 to 10.13 are concerned with a number of closely related topics such as dynamic object creation, procedures with results and a unification of the notions of expression and statement.

10.2 Liberal scope rules

The *scope* of an object name x is the range of text where the name is visible. The usual scope rules of predicate logic imply that a name introduced *in* a construct such as a quantifier is not visible *outside* that construct. But the scope rules for object names in COLD-K are more liberal: the scope of certain object names may extend beyond the assertion or expression C where they are introduced. Such names with an extended scope are said to be *declared* by C. We give some examples:

```
EXISTS n:Nat ( is_in(n,s) ) => is_even(n)

(SOME n:Nat (is_even(n)),add(n,n))
```

The operational intuition is as follows: The names declared by an assertion or expression C correspond with objects *constructed* during the evaluation of C:

- If A is an assertion, then the object names declared by A denote objects whose existence is implied by the *truth* of A. After the truth of A has been established, we may refer to these objects.
- If X is an expression, then the object names declared by X denote objects whose existence is implied by the *success* of X. After X has been successfully evaluated, we may refer to these objects.

The following assertions and expressions introduce object names with an extended scope:

assertions	*expressions*
LET x:T	LET x:T
EXISTS x:T A	SOME x:T A

Table 10.1. Assertions and expressions with extended scope.

The scope of an object name with an extended scope, declared in an assertion A or expression X, extends to an assertion B or expression Y, textually following A or X, in the following cases:

A AND B
A;B
A => B
X,Y

Table 10.2. Constructs where declarations in A extend to B.

The following assertions and expressions are transparent with respect to the object names declared by their constituents:

assertions	*expressions*
A AND B	X,Y
A;B	A?
EXISTS x:T A	SOME x:T A

Table 10.3. Constructs which are transparent for object names.

All other assertions and expressions presented in Part I make the object names declared in their constituents externally invisible. In particular the *block* assertion and expression, which has the following form: BEGIN C END terminates the scope of all object names declared in C (and does nothing else). Note that it is a consequence of this approach that we can treat a declaration such as: LET x:T as a normal assertion or expression – which has the block construct as its counterpart.

There is an interesting analogy with modularisation. A scope extension is very similar to an *export*, i.e., we can interpret an assertion such as:

```
EXISTS m:Nat,n:Nat,p:Nat
( add(sqr(m),sqr(n)) = sqr(p) )
```

as a module exporting the constants m, n and p. The block construct acts as a complete hiding operator. There is no explicit import operator: all externally visible object names are imported automatically into an assertion or expression.

10.3 Free definitions

A *free definition* introduces a sort, predicate or function name with an origin that is as yet unknown. The concept is similar to the *forward* declarations often encountered in programming languages to solve problems arising in connection with recursive definitions and separate compilation. Here we shall explain the concept without reference to linkage editors or compilers and instead employ a generalisation of the origins introduced in Section 9.5.

Free definitions are introduced according to the following syntax:

SORT S FREE
PRED r : S_1 # ... # S_m FREE
FUNC f : S_1 # ... # S_m -> V_1 # ... # V_n FREE

No a priori assumptions about a name introduced by a free definition are made. Names defined by a free definition can be viewed as kinds of parameters for the description they are defined in. This is reflected in the origin assignment process, where a unique *origin variable*, instead of an origin constant, is associated with a free name. If, during the normalization process, such a free name happens to clash with another name, the origin variable will be replaced everywhere in the text by the origin of the latter name, while the free definition 'disappears'. More generally, name clashes lead to the *unification* of the origins of the clashing names – provided that the origin consistency requirement is satisfied. A simple example is provided by the following scheme:

```
IMPORT CLASS
           SORT A   FREE
           FUNC a : -> A
         END
INTO     CLASS
           SORT A
           AXIOM a!
         END
```

After origin assignment we obtain:

```
IMPORT CLASS
           SORT Ax   FREE
           FUNC a1 : -> Ax
         END
INTO     CLASS
           SORT A2
           AXIOM a1!
         END
```

where x is an origin variable. In the normalization process this variable is unified with origin 2, making the free definition vanish:

```
CLASS
  SORT A2
  FUNC a1 : -> A2
  AXIOM a1!
END
```

Thus we obtain the following normal form:

```
EXPORT
  SORT A,
  FUNC a : -> A
FROM
CLASS
  SORT A
  FUNC a : -> A
  AXIOM a!
END
```

Adding a free definition in a flat scheme for a name used but not defined there does not affect the semantics of the scheme. If we do this systematically, the import operator becomes fully symmetric:

IMPORT K INTO L $\equiv$ IMPORT L INTO K

For example:

```
IMPORT CLASS
           SORT A
           FUNC a : -> A
        END
INTO    CLASS
           SORT B
           FUNC f : A -> B
        END
```

is equivalent to:

```
IMPORT CLASS
           SORT A
           FUNC a : -> A
        END
INTO    CLASS
           SORT A    FREE
           SORT B
           FUNC f : A -> B
        END
```

which is equivalent to:

```
IMPORT CLASS
           SORT A    FREE
           SORT B
           FUNC f : A -> B
        END
INTO    CLASS
           SORT A
           FUNC a : -> A
        END
```

10.4 Parameterisation

We have already discussed several data types that are good candidates for being reused in a natural way. In particular sequences, bags, sets, stacks and queues occur frequently in connection with arbitrary data types. It is useful to have a kind of generic description of for example sequences of *items* and the language should provide a facility to apply such a generic description to natural numbers, or Booleans or in fact to any arbitrary data type.

This need has also been recognised in programming languages and has for example led to the inclusion of *generic* packages in Ada. In specification languages it is customary to use the term *parameterised* descriptions. Returning to the example of sequences of items, we view the sort `Item` as a parameter where, roughly speaking, later something else has to replace the sort `Item`. In this section we shall discuss the construct available in COLD-K for setting up parameterised descriptions.

First we shall have a look at a slightly naïve approach to parameterisation, which turns out to be not fully satisfactory. After that we shall present the special facilities of COLD-K. We could define the 'parameterised' scheme `SEQ` of sequences of items by:

```
LET SEQ := EXPORT ... FROM
           CLASS
             SORT Item   FREE
             SORT Seq
             FUNC empty : -> Seq
             FUNC cons  : Item # Seq -> Seq
             ...
           END;
```

and use renamings to derive specifications of different kinds of sequences from this, e.g:

```
LET NAT_SEQ  := RENAME
                  SORT Item TO Nat,
                  SORT Seq  TO Seq_Nat
                IN SEQ;
LET BOOL_SEQ := RENAME
                  SORT Item TO Bool,
                  SORT Seq  TO Seq_Bool
                IN SEQ;
```

However, this approach has a number of inherent problems. First of all, it conflicts with the origin consistency requirement: `Nat` and `Bool` above have the same origin, which leads to origin inconsistency if they clash with the 'real' `Nat` and `Bool`. More precisely, if `NAT` is imported into `NAT_SEQ` and `BOOL` is imported into `BOOL_SEQ`, then the origin unification procedure fails. To see this, suppose that `Item` has been labelled as $\mathtt{Item}_x$, `Nat` has been labelled as $\mathtt{Nat}_1$ and `Bool` has been labelled as $\mathtt{Bool}_2$, then x must be instantiated to become both 1 and 2, which is impossible.

Also, all definitions of 'sequence sorts' such as `Seq_Nat` and `Seq_Bool` would get the same origin. Finally, we are unable to express restrictions on the parameters, such as the fact that a certain sort parameter is supposed to be a partial order.

In the next sections we present a much more powerful approach to writing parameterised descriptions. The approach is to employ formal parameters ranging over schemes. Mathematically speaking, the technique is to employ a special lambda calculus (called $\lambda\pi$-calculus) as explained in [19]. The basic idea is very simple viz. that the definition of the sort `Item` should be packaged in a separate scheme, which (at the time of writing the scheme of sequences) is as yet unknown; therefore we can use a variable `X`, say, instead of the actual scheme. This `X` is imported into the scheme of sequences as if it were a normal description:

```
IMPORT
  X
INTO
CLASS
  SORT Seq
  FUNC empty : -> Seq
  FUNC cons  : Item # Seq -> Seq
  ...
END
```

This is the basic idea. In the next section we shall give more details and we shall also indicate how to express parameter restrictions.

We now give an overview of the kinds of schemes introduced in Part I and to be introduced here. In the table below, $D_1 \ldots D_n$ are definitions, K and L are schemes, Σ is a signature, ρ is a renaming and finally z is a scheme name.

CLASS D_1 ... D_n END IMPORT K INTO L EXPORT Σ FROM K RENAME ρ IN K
LET z := K ; L z
(K)
LAMBDA z:K OF L APPLY K TO L

Table 10.4. Survey of all schemes.

10.5 Abstraction schemes

What we need are *generic* or *parameterised* specifications, from which new specifications can be generated by *instantiating* them with actual parameters. To get started we could write

LAMBDA x OF $L(x)$

where x is a formal parameter and $L(x)$ is a scheme which may contain free occurrences of x. The use of the symbol LAMBDA is nothing but a compact way of saying: *here comes the unknown*. It is taken from a special branch of mathematical logic called lambda-calculus [40] and is usually written as λ.

Although this is the basic idea, the approach still needs refinement: the problem is that we must make sure that the formal parameter x provides the sorts and operations expected from it. Therefore we introduce 'parameter descriptions', which are nothing but schemes written in COLD-K again. A parameter description serves as a *specification* of the formal parameter. A parameterised specification is also called an *abstraction scheme* and has the following form:

LAMBDA x : K OF $L(x)$

where x is a formal parameter (a scheme name), K is a scheme not containing free occurrences of x and finally $L(x)$ is a scheme which may contain free occurrences of x.

It can be viewed as a partial function mapping a scheme x to the scheme $L(x)$. The domain of this partial function is defined by the *parameter restriction* K and consists of the set of all *implementations* of the scheme K. In Section 8.8 we discussed what we mean when one scheme is an implementation of another.

In most cases K is an axiomatic specification without hidden names. Checking that A is an implementation of K can then be done by checking the signature inclusion and verifying that the axioms of K are theorems in A.

The approach to parameterisation by means of *lambda abstraction* is similar to the approach of the algebraic specification language ASL [6]. Just as in the λ-abstractions of COLD-K, parameter restrictions are allowed in ASL.

Now we can give an example showing the parameterised description of sequences. Note the keyword `LAMBDA` followed by the parameter `X` – which is the 'unknown'. Later, when instantiating this description, other schemes like `NAT` will be used to instantiate `X`. After the `X` and the '`:`' symbol we see a kind of mini-scheme `CLASS SORT Item END` which is the specification of `X`.

```
LAMBDA X : CLASS
             SORT Item
           END
OF
EXPORT ... FROM
IMPORT X INTO
CLASS
  SORT Seq
  FUNC empty : -> Seq
  FUNC cons  : Item # Seq -> Seq
  ...
END;
```

Since we are introducing new scheme operators, we shall have to extend the normalization procedure. We adopt the same syntactical approach of assigning a meaning to schemes, where we first reduce the schemes to normal-form specifications – if possible. This will be presented in Section 10.7.

10.6 Application schemes

A parameterised scheme P can be instantiated by providing it with an actual parameter A satisfying the parameter restriction. The corresponding construct is called an *application scheme* and has the following form:

```
APPLY P TO A
```

In order to explain the meaning of this construct, we take an abstraction scheme for P:

```
APPLY (LAMBDA x : K OF L(x)) TO A
```

Provided that A is indeed an implementation of K, this scheme is equivalent to the scheme $L(A)$, i.e., the scheme $L(x)$ with A substituted everywhere for x.

In order to make the formal parameter of a parameterised specification 'fit' the actual parameter, it may be necessary to rename some of the names in the formal parameter. For that purpose, renamings are extended to parameterised schemes in the obvious way. Consider the example given at the end of Section 10.5 and assume that it is abbreviated as SEQ. Using a renaming, we can define sequences of natural numbers by instantiating the parameterised scheme SEQ as follows:

```
LET NAT_SEQ := APPLY
                 RENAME
                   SORT Item TO Nat,
                   SORT Seq  TO Seq_Nat
                 IN SEQ
               TO NAT;
```

The actual parameter NAT of (the renamed version of) SEQ satisfies the parameter restriction of SEQ.

10.7 Extending the normalization procedure

The normalization procedure for schemes containing applications of parameterised schemes can be the same as before, except for the following two changes:

1. the origin assignment process has to be refined;
2. a new reduction rule has to be added.

For more information about origins we refer to Section 9.5 and Section 10.3. We adopt the following refinement of the origin assignment process. First, associate a unique 'origin parameter' (i.e., an origin variable) with each visible name in the parameter restriction of an abstraction scheme and assign an origin-tuple of the form $\langle c, x_1, \ldots, x_n \rangle$ to each name u defined in the body of the abstraction scheme, where c is a unique value identifying the definition of u and $x_1, \ldots, x_n$ are the origin parameters of the scheme. Now when the parameterised scheme is instantiated, the corresponding origins $a_1, \ldots, a_n$ of the names in the actual parameter are substituted for the origin parameters $x_1, \ldots, x_n$, thus turning the origin of u into $\langle c, a_1, \ldots, a_n \rangle$.

The additional reduction rule applies under the proviso that the actual parameter satisfies the parameter restriction. More precisely: provided that A is an implementation of K, the following scheme:

APPLY (LAMBDA x : K OF $L(x)$) TO A

reduces (after origin assignment) to the scheme $L(x)$ with A substituted for x and the origins of the names in A substituted for the corresponding origin parameters of the names in K (everywhere in $L(x)$).

We exemplify the extended normalization procedure by showing how the definition of sequences of natural numbers as given before is reduced to normal form. First we give the 'complete' definition:

```
LET NAT := EXPORT ... FROM
           CLASS
             SORT Nat
             ...
           END;
LET SEQ := LAMBDA X : CLASS
                        SORT Item
                      END
           OF
           EXPORT ... FROM
           IMPORT X INTO
           CLASS
             SORT Seq
             FUNC empty : -> Seq
             FUNC cons  : Item # Seq -> Seq
             ...
           END;
LET NAT_SEQ := APPLY
                 RENAME
                   SORT Item TO Nat,
                   SORT Seq  TO Seq_Nat
                 IN SEQ
               TO NAT;
NAT_SEQ
```

Using x as the origin parameter associated with the name Item in the parameter restriction of SEQ, this leads after origin assignment to:

```
LET NAT := EXPORT ... FROM
           CLASS
             SORT Nat₁
             ...
           END;
LET SEQ := LAMBDA X : CLASS
                        SORT Item₂
                      END
           OF
           EXPORT ... FROM
           IMPORT X INTO
           CLASS
             SORT Seq⟨3,x⟩
             FUNC empty⟨4,x⟩ : -> Seq⟨3,x⟩
             FUNC cons⟨5,x⟩ : Itemₓ # Seq⟨3,x⟩ -> Seq⟨3,x⟩
             ...
           END;
LET NAT_SEQ := APPLY
                 RENAME
                   SORT Item TO Nat,
                   SORT Seq  TO Seq_Nat
                 IN SEQ
               TO NAT;
NAT_SEQ
```

It should be noted that the origin of `Item` in the body of `SEQ` is the origin parameter associated with `Item` and *not* the origin of `Item` in the parameter restriction. Expanding all abbreviations and applying the renaming leads to:

```
APPLY
  LAMBDA X : CLASS
               SORT Nat₂
             END
             OF
  EXPORT ... FROM
  IMPORT X INTO
  CLASS
    SORT Seq_Nat⟨3,x⟩
    FUNC empty⟨4,x⟩ : -> Seq_Nat⟨3,x⟩
    FUNC cons⟨5,x⟩ : Natₓ # Seq_Nat⟨3,x⟩ -> Seq_Nat⟨3,x⟩
    ...
  END
TO EXPORT ... FROM
   CLASS
     SORT Nat₁
```

```
    ...
  END
```

In order to further reduce this scheme we have to check that the actual parameter is an implementation of the parameter restriction. For that purpose, the actual parameter and the parameter restriction should first be reduced to normal form.

The check of the implementation relation is simple in this case and the subsequent reductions bring the scheme into the following normal form:

```
EXPORT ... FROM
CLASS
  SORT Nat₁
  ...
  SORT Seq_Nat⟨3,1⟩
  FUNC empty⟨4,1⟩ : -> Seq_Nat⟨3,1⟩
  FUNC cons⟨5,1⟩ : Nat₁ # Seq_Nat⟨3,1⟩ -> Seq_Nat⟨3,1⟩
  ...
END
```

The last steps of the normalization procedure (name clash elimination and origin removal) are simple now and will be omitted.

It should be noted that the origin of **Nat** in this specification is that of the original sort **Nat** and the origin of **Seq_Nat** will be different from the origin of any other sequence sort derived from **SEQ**. If we were to instantiate **SEQ** in exactly the same way at some other place, the sort **Seq_Nat** would get the same origin as before, which is precisely what we want.

10.8 More complex parameter restrictions

We give an example: defining a scheme with a 'sort' operation.

```
LET ORDER := CLASS
               SORT Item
               PRED r : Item # Item
               AXIOM  FORALL i:Item,j:Item,k:Item (
               {ORD1} NOT r(i,i);
               {ORD2} r(i,j) AND r(j,k) => r(i,k);
               {ORD3} r(i,j) OR i = j OR r(j,i) )
             END;

LET LSORT := LAMBDA X : ORDER OF
             EXPORT
```

```
    SORT Seq,
    FUNC sort : Seq -> Seq
  FROM
  IMPORT X INTO
  IMPORT (APPLY SEQ TO X) INTO
  CLASS
    FUNC sort : Seq -> Seq
    ...
  END;
```

In instantiating the scheme LSORT, any scheme A can be provided as an actual parameter that is an implementation of ORDER, e.g:

```
LET SORT_NAT := APPLY
                  RENAME
                    SORT Item            TO Nat,
                    PRED r : Item # Item TO less
                  IN LSORT
                TO NAT;
```

It is also allowed for parameterised schemes to have parameters that are themselves parameterised. The use of these 'higher order' parameters requires an extension of the implementation relation to parameterised schemes.

Not only the renaming and abbreviation operators have extensions to parameterised schemes, but also the other two modularisation operators (export and import), each with their own reduction rules. These extensions are not discussed here. We also mention that a number of special operators dealing with signatures are available, such as SIG K denoting the signature of K and Σ_1 + Σ_2 denoting the union of Σ_1 and Σ_2. Similarly Σ_1 & Σ_2 denotes the intersection of Σ_1 and Σ_2. If ρ is a renaming, then: ρ @ Σ denotes the signature Σ' obtained by renaming all names in Σ according to ρ. Finally u ^ Σ is the signature obtained by removing the name u from Σ.

There is also one operation on renamings available: ρ_1 $ ρ_2 denotes functional composition of two renamings. Most of these operators on signatures and renamings are not often needed but we mention them for completeness.

10.9 Object creation and procedures with results

The most general notion of procedure name in COLD-K has not only a domain type, but also a range type. This can be used when a procedure must yield a result in addition to establishing a certain side-effect. The notation for such a procedure name is

$$\texttt{PROC}\ p\ :\ S_1\ \texttt{\#}\ \ldots\ \texttt{\#}\ S_m\ \texttt{->}\ V_1\ \texttt{\#}\ \ldots\ \texttt{\#}\ V_n.$$

Of course when we allow for procedure result parameters, the restriction that the body X of a procedure has the empty type should be dropped: in this case its type must match the range type of the procedure.

COLD-K has in fact a more powerful notion of class than that used throughout part II. The 'constant sorts' restriction on classes can be relaxed. In this case sorts can be variable, just like functions and predicates. Instead of the constant sorts restriction, a monotonicity requirement is adopted which states that sorts cannot shrink (in the approach of [19] this is formalised by having more than one $\perp$-object for each sort).

When allowing procedures with a non-empty range type and when introducing the option of variable sorts, the definition of a 'transition relation' must be replaced by

Definition For a procedure name p with type S_1 # ... # S_m -> V_1 # ... # V_n, a *transition relation* for p is an $m+n+2$-ary relation $\mathcal{T}_p$ on

$$\mathsf{State} \times S_1 \times \ldots \times S_m \times \mathsf{State} \times V_1 \times \ldots \times V_n$$

such that the following holds for each transition $(s, x \rightarrow t, y)$ in it:

- x is a tuple of objects existing in $S_1^{A(s)}, \ldots, S_m^{A(s)}$;
- y is a tuple of objects existing in $V_1^{A(t)}, \ldots, V_n^{A(t)}$;
- each sort in $A(s)$ is a subset of the corresponding sort in $A(t)$, i.e. $S^{A(s)} \subseteq S^{A(t)}$; this constraint expresses the requirement that sorts cannot shrink. □

We give an example where the dynamic object creation feature is used. We assume the following class signature for Γ:

```
SORT Atom
PROC create: ->
```

Fig 10.1. Class signature with one sort and one procedure.

There is a Σ-algebra associated with each state, where Σ contains only `SORT Atom`. In the Γ-class shown below there are infinitely many states. We show only three of them. The transitions of the transition relation corresponding with the `create` procedure have been labelled `create`.

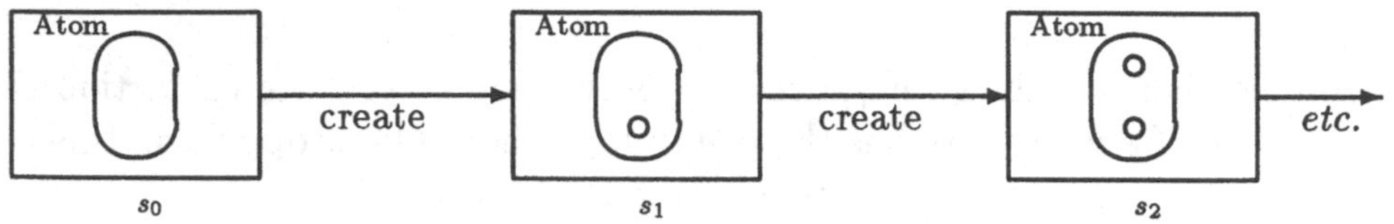

Fig 10.2. Class with dynamic object creation.

In this example all states have algebras with the same signature – but with different sets for the sort `Atom`. Let $\mathtt{Atom}^s$ denote the set corresponding with `Atom` in state s, then $\mathtt{Atom}^{s_0} = \emptyset \subseteq \mathtt{Atom}^{s_1} \subseteq \mathtt{Atom}^{s_2} \subseteq \ \ldots$.

10.10 Variable sort definitions

A *variable sort definition* defines a sort which can grow dynamically:

```
SORT T VAR
```

Recall the built-in restriction on state transitions: once an object has been created, it cannot be removed anymore. It is not yet specified if and how the sort will grow dynamically. State transformations due to procedure calls will be subject to conditions related to the modification rights. In typical applications, the objects to be created are parts of data structures which are constructed dynamically. Examples are nodes and leaves of tree structures, and cells in linked lists.

Below we summarise the various ways of defining sorts. The free definitions serve to introduce a sort, predicate or function defined elsewhere. Inductive and algorithmic definitions have been discussed already in Part I. The keyword `DEP` refers to dependent sorts, which will be introduced in the next section.

body	*keyword*
empty	
free	`FREE`
variable	`VAR`
dependent	`DEP`

Table 10.5. Survey of sort definitions.

When using variable sorts and dynamic object creation, there is a typical way of using the previously assertion which we shall now show. The example concerns the variable sort `Atom`.

```
SORT Atom VAR
PROC new: -> Atom MOD Atom
AXIOM [ LET a:Atom; a := new ] a! AND PREV NOT a!
```

This axiom says that if `new` succeeds, it yields an object of sort `Atom` which did not exist in the previous state. As the axiom in this example shows, a liberal notion of scoping – like the one presented in Section 10.2 – applies to the always assertion. It also applies to the sometimes assertion.

10.11 Dependent definitions

There are two ways of introducing sorts, predicates and functions that may vary from state to state, viz. *variables* (keyword `VAR`) and *dependents* (keyword `DEP`). State components are generally divided into *variable* and *dependent* state components. The variable state components can be viewed as independent variables spanning the state space of a class. The dependent state components depend on these variables in the sense that they are left unmodified if the variables are left unmodified and so they cannot vary independently of the variables. If we specify the dependency of each dependent state component on the other state components explicitly, then it suffices to mention the modified variables in the modification rights of a procedure. The other state components modified by the procedure can be reconstructed by means of the specified dependencies. If we add a new dependent state component, we need only specify its dependencies and no old definitions have to be modified. Note that in explicit definitions of state components (such as inductive and algorithmic predicate and function definitions), there is no need to specify the dependencies: they can be derived from the body of the definition.

A dependent sort definition introduces a sort that can grow dynamically, but the growth of the sort is connected with the growth or modification of other sorts, predicates or functions. Its general structure is as follows:

SORT T DEP $V_1, \ldots, V_k$

where each V_i is a sort, predicate or function name. The meaning of this definition is as follows: if in a state transition none of the sorts, predicates and functions $V_1, \ldots, V_k$ is modified, then neither is T. In the example below we have a sort `Pair` whose objects can be viewed as pairs of atoms.

```
SORT Atom VAR
SORT Xyz  VAR
SORT Pair DEP Atom

FUNC pair : Atom # Atom -> Pair

PRED is_gen : Pair
IND  FORALL a:Atom, b:Atom
     ( is_gen(pair(a,b)) )

AXIOM   FORALL a:Atom, c:Atom, b:Atom, d:Atom (
{PAIR1} pair(a,b)!;
{PAIR2} pair(a,b) = pair(c,d) => a = c AND b = d );
{PAIR3} FORALL t:Pair ( is_gen(t) )
```

The sort `Atom` itself is variable. Furthermore there is another sort `Xyz`. The function `pair`, the predicate `is_gen` and the three axioms guarantee that the sort `Pair` contains exactly all pairs of atoms. When more atoms are created, more pairs can come into existence; but when `Xyz` grows and `Atom` does not, then `Pair` will not grow. An empty body denotes a 'constant' sort which can be viewed as a special case of a dependent sort. In particular, `SORT` T `DEP NONE` introduces T as a sort which cannot be modified. `SORT` T is just a shorthand for this.

A dependent predicate definition defines a predicate with a truth value that may vary from state to state, but the modifications are connected with the growth or modification of other sorts, predicates or functions. Its general structure is as follows.

`PRED` r `:` S_1 `#` ... `#` S_m `DEP` $V_1, \ldots, V_k$

where each V_i is a sort, predicate or function name. The meaning of this definition is as follows: if in a state transition none of the V_i are modified, then neither is r. Again, `DEP NONE` may be omitted to indicate a 'constant' predicate.

A dependent function definition defines a function with a value that may vary from state to state. Again the modifications are connected with the growth or modification of other sorts, predicates or functions. Its general structure is as follows.

`FUNC` f `:` S_1 `#` ... `#` S_m `->` T_1 `#` ... `#` T_n `DEP` $V_1, \ldots, V_k$

where each V_i is a sort, predicate or function name. The meaning of this definition is analogous to that of a dependent predicate definition: if in a state transition none of the V_i are modified, then neither is f.

We give a small example. In this example we have the sorts **Nat** and **Index** and the variable function **array** as before. Furthermore there is a simple programming variable **xyz** which we assume to be unrelated to **array**. Now assume that one frequently needs the *squares* of the numbers stored in the array. Of course these can be calculated as $\mathtt{array}(i) \times \mathtt{array}(i)$ but for efficiency reasons it is a useful idea to store these squares in a separate array called **squares**. Clearly, **array** must be in the dependency list of **squares**. We shall also need procedures modifying these variable functions and maintaining the invariant $\mathtt{squares}(i) = \mathtt{array}(i) \times \mathtt{array}(i)$ but we do not show such procedures here. The fact that **xyz** is unrelated to **array** is modelled very well by the definitions of this example because, due to the meaning of the **DEP** clause, modifying **xyz** leaves **squares** unaffected.

```
SORT Index
SORT Nat
FUNC xyz : -> Nat  VAR
FUNC array : Index -> Nat  VAR
FUNC squares : Index -> Nat  DEP array
```

As before we can add axioms to further specify the precise nature of the dependency between **array** and **squares**; one could add the following axiom:

```
AXIOM  FORALL i:Index ( squares(i) = mul(array(i),array(i)) )
```

There is a point worth mentioning concerning the modification of functions and predicates. Assume a variable sort `S` and a variable function, `f : S -> Nat`, then extension of `S` (by dynamic object creation) is *not* viewed as a modification of `f`, although of course the domain of `f` is extended. The same view applies to predicates. As a simple example, consider

```
SORT Atom VAR
SORT Nat

PROC new : -> Atom MOD Atom
FUNC value : Atom -> Nat VAR
```

Because of the modification rights, invoking **new** does not modify the function **value**. Yet, according to our interpreation of the notion of 'modification', it is possible for **new** to create new atoms. We do not need any axiom stating that for all existing atoms a after execution of **new** the value of **value**(a) is left unchanged.

10.12 Example: specification of instances

In this section we shall specify a variable sort named `Inst`. The creation which is modelled by the `create` procedure has the effect of modifying this sort. We shall build the specification in an incremental manner, mixing formal and informal texts and beginning with a version which is somewhat too naïve. Then we gradually introduce the more subtle aspects of the specification.

```
LET INST :=
EXPORT
  SORT Inst,
  PROC create: -> Inst
FROM
CLASS

  SORT Inst  VAR

  AXIOM {INST1} INIT => NOT EXISTS a:Inst ()

  PROC create: -> Inst  MOD Inst

  AXIOM {INST2} < create > TRUE

  AXIOM {INST3} [ LET i:Inst; i := create ] ( i! )
```

Actually, the definedness of `i` is redundant, so in fact the last axiom says nothing; but mentioning `i!` does no harm either. There is a problem because `create` may yield an 'old' instance. Therefore we propose the following 'improved' version of axiom `INST3`.

```
% correction (1)

AXIOM {INST3} [ LET i:Inst; i := create ]
              ( i! AND (PREV NOT i!) )
```

We must explain the clause `PREV NOT i!` which we have added to the post-condition in `INST3`. It states that `i` is *new*, because in the *previous* state (i.e before execution of `LET i:Inst; i := create`) it was not yet defined.

There is still a problem with the above axiom: it is too weak because it does not guarantee that `i` is the only new instance created. This makes it hard to maintain invariants when *using* instances. Therefore we propose the following final version of axiom **INST3**.

```
  % correction (2)

  AXIOM {INST3} [ LET i:Inst; i := create ]
                ( i! AND (PREV NOT i!) AND
                  FORALL j:Inst ( (PREV NOT j!) => j = i ) )

END {INST}
```

The clause `FORALL j:Inst ( (PREV NOT j!) => j = i )` which we added in **INST3** can be explained as follows: first note that the assertion `PREV NOT j!` means that `j` is *new*, therefore the added `FORALL` clause says that any new `j` equals `i`; in other words: `i` is the *only* new instance.

10.13 Unifying expressions and statements

In this section we generalise the interpretation of expressions to include the concept of *side-effect* without introducing statements as a separate syntactical category. The meaning of an expression X with type S_1 # ... # S_m becomes a transition relation $\mathcal{T}_X$ which is an $m+2$-ary relation on

$$\textsf{State} \times \textsf{State} \times S_1 \times \ldots \times S_m.$$

The meaning of the composition expression X , Y is changed. In particular, X , Y denotes the sequential composition of X and Y where the result is obtained by concatenation of the results yielded by X and Y. Formally, if X has type S_1 # ... # S_m and Y has type V_1 # ... # V_n then X , Y denotes an $m+n+2$-ary transition relation $\mathcal{T}_{X,Y}$ on

$$\textsf{State} \times \textsf{State} \times S_1 \times \ldots \times S_m \times V_1 \times \ldots \times V_n.$$

$\mathcal{T}_{X,Y}$ contains precisely the transitions $(s \to t, x, y)$ for which there exists an intermediate state s' such that the interpretation $\mathcal{T}_X$ of X contains a transition $(s \to s', x)$ and the interpretation $\mathcal{T}_Y$ of Y contains a transition $(s' \to t, y)$.

The interpretations of the function expression $f\,X$, the parenthesized expression (X) and the empty tuple expression () do not change. The other composition expression X ; Y is the same as the first composition expression.

The interpretations of the guard expression A ? and the choice expression X | Y only change in the sense that they include guarding a state transition and choosing between state transitions. The interpretation of the selection expression SOME x : T A, the declaration expression LET x : T, the binding expression x := Y and the block expression BEGIN X END do not change.

If p : S_1 # ... # S_m -> V_1 # ... # V_n is a procedure name and X is an expression of type S_1 # ... # S_m, then

$p\,X$

is an expression of type V_1 # ... # V_n. The interpretation of $p\,X$ is an $n+2$-ary transition relation $\mathcal{T}_{pX}$ on State $\times$ State $\times\, V_1 \times \ldots \times V_n$. The relation $\mathcal{T}_{pX}$ contains precisely the transitions $(s \rightarrow t, y)$ for which there exist an intermediate state s' and intermediate results x such that the interpretation $\mathcal{T}_X$ of X contains a transition $(s \rightarrow s', x)$ and the interpretation $\mathcal{T}_p$ of p contains a transition $(s', x \rightarrow t, y)$.

We also present one new kind of expression: the *flush expression* serves to discard the result of an expression, preserving its side-effect. One could call this 'voiding'. If X is an expression of arbitrary type, then

FLUSH X

is an expression of the empty type. Formally, the interpretation of FLUSH X is a binary transition relation on State $\times$ State which contains the transitions $(s \rightarrow t)$ such that the interpretation $\mathcal{T}_X$ of X contains a transition $(s \rightarrow t, x)$. Sometimes it has to be used in connection with invariance axioms, as in the example below:

```
FUNC v1 : -> Nat VAR
FUNC v2 : -> Nat VAR

PROC p1 : -> MOD v1,v2
PROC p2 : -> Bool MOD  v1,v2

PROC some_p : ->
DEF  ( p1
     | FLUSH p2
     )

PRED PI : DEP v1,v2

AXIOM PI => [ some_p ] PI
```

In this example a typing error would occur if we defined `some_p` by a `DEF` clause `( p1 | p2 )` because `p1` and `p2` do not have the same (empty) type.

Let us have a look at the mechanisms for introducing algorithmic functions; this was already done in Part I, but in view of the unification of expressions and statements, we must have another look at algorithmic function definitions.

The notation for an *algorithmic function* definition is:

FUNC f : S_1 # ... # S_m -> V_1 # ... # V_n
PAR $x_1 : S_1, \ldots, x_m : S_m$
DEF X

Consider the function f with the above input types and result types and with body DEF X. In a given state s it denotes a function which maps input values $x_1, \ldots, x_n$ to the unique tuple $y_1, \ldots, y_n$ for which there exists a state t such that $(s \rightarrow t, y_1, \ldots, y_n)$ is contained in $\mathcal{T}_{X(x_1,\ldots,x_m)}$. Here $\mathcal{T}_{X(x_1,\ldots,x_m)}$ is the $n+2$-ary transition relation on State × State × $V_1 \times \ldots \times V_n$ that is the interpretation of X for the given $x_1, \ldots, x_m$ values. If no such unique $y_1, \ldots, y_n$ values exist, then the result is undefined. We refer to this situation by saying that the *term interpretation* of an expression should be used, which means that its result is required to be unique.

In the example below we introduce three simple functions `f`, `g` and `h`. Their defining bodies refer to a function `v` which is variable. We assume `Nat`, `0`, `1`, `succ` and `lss` from the standard class description `NAT`.

```
FUNC v: -> Nat VAR

FUNC f: -> Nat
DEF  MOD v END;
     v

FUNC g: -> Nat
DEF  MOD v END;
     ( v = 0      ?; succ(v)
     | NOT v = 0 ?; 1
     )

FUNC h: -> Nat
DEF  SOME n:Nat
     ( lss(n,v) )
```

The function `f` is undefined because its defining body `DEF MOD v END; v` does not yield a unique value. The function `g` is defined however and we have `g` $= 1$ because for all states resulting from `MOD v END` we find that `( v = 0 ?; succ(v) | NOT v = 0 ?; 1 )` yields the unique result 1. The function `h` is undefined in those states where `v` $\neq 1$ because for `v` $= 0$ no `n` with `n` $<$ `v` exists and for `v` > 1 several values for `n` with `n` $<$ `v` exists. When we are in a state where `v` $= 1$, we find that `h` is defined and then `h` $= 0$.

Let us also have another look at the mechanisms for introducing algorithmic procedures. An *algorithmic procedure* introduces a transition relation given by an expression. The notation for an algorithmic procedure definition is:

```
PROC p : S1 # ... # Sm -> V1 # ... # Vn
PAR  x1:S1,...,xm:Sm
DEF  X
```

p denotes the $m+n+2$-ary transition relation on $\mathsf{State} \times S_1 \times \ldots \times S_m \times \mathsf{State} \times V_1 \times \ldots \times V_n$ containing the transitions $(s, x_1, \ldots, x_m \to t, y_1, \ldots, y_n)$ for which $(s \to t, y_1, \ldots, y_n)$ is contained in $\mathcal{T}_{X(x_1,\ldots,x_m)}$, i.e. in the transition relation that is the interpretation of X. The type of X must be V_1 `#` $\ldots$ `#` V_n.

Chapter 11

Towards large systems

11.1 Introduction

All the previous chapters are about techniques for unambiguously specifying hardware/software systems and transforming abstract specifications into efficient programs. One important motivation for presenting these techniques is the fact that it is often useful to have a distinction between the external view and the internal view of a system. The external view can take the form of a formal specification and it can be optimised with respect to abstractness, compactness and clarity. The internal view is a program which is devised with efficiency in mind. To have two descriptions corresponding to these two views can be considered as a separation of concerns: it helps to manage the complexity of large systems.

This approach introduces *additional formal texts* when compared with the older approaches dealing mostly with programs. As a consequence, care is needed to maintain the *overview* of all formal texts that arise when designing large systems.

This chapter presents two techniques developed in the context of COLD-K which serve for keeping this overview. These are certainly not the only useful techniques; they should be complemented with additional graphical techniques and classical software engineering techniques for configuration management, project management, etc. The first technique is to use simple pictures showing the modular structure of a formal specification. This is the topic of Section 11.2. The second technique is to add structure, putting specifications and implementations together in simple language constructs called *components* and *designs*. This is the topic of Section 11.3. Finally, Sections 11.4 and 11.5 present a number of applications as well as some concluding remarks.

11.2 Graphical representation of modules

Recall that COLD-K modular schemes are constructed from flat schemes by means of binary operators (import, export, renaming) as well as a simple mechanism for associating names with modules and for using these names. The fact that the module composition mechanisms are operators makes it possible to employ an old idea embodied in the well-known Nassi-Shneidermann diagrams [41]: predefined shapes and templates can be used for putting other pictures together, thus modelling operators from the language by means of predefined shapes.

These diagrams have become rather popular since the time that structured programming reduced programming constructs to a few operators such as the ternary **if** ␣ **then** ␣ **else** ␣ and the binary **while** ␣ **do** ␣ and ␣ ; ␣. By employing a similar approach *at the level of modules* instead of at the level of the program statements, the pictures provide for a true abstraction step. The pictures are much smaller in size than the formal text they represent. This is achieved by using a forgetful mapping when generating the pictures from COLD-K. In [42] a graphical language called POLAR is presented. Its syntax, well-formedness and semantics have been described formally – using COLD-K as a specification language. We briefly present it here.

A flat scheme of the form `CLASS` D_1 ... D_n `END` is represented by an envelope-like box. No further details are visible, so each envelope could be the representation of any flat scheme.

Fig 11.1. Graphical representation of `CLASS` D_1 ... D_n `END`.

A scheme of the form `IMPORT` K `INTO` L is represented by the representation of K stacked on top of the representation of L. A scheme of the form `EXPORT` Σ `FROM` K is represented by a shaded area enclosing two smaller boxes: viz. a box for the signature as well as a box representing K. A signature is always represented by the Greek letter Σ. The representation of the signature is placed *above* the representation of the scheme K. A scheme of the form `RENAME` ρ `IN` K is represented by two boxes stacked horizontally. The representation of K is placed at the left of the representation of the renaming. The renaming itself is shown as the Greek letter ρ.

A scheme fragment of the form `LET` z `:=` K is represented by two vertically stacked boxes. The upper box has a two-line boundary and contains the identifier z and the lower box represents K. When representing a scheme of the form LET z := K ; L, the relative positions of the pictures for LET z := K and for L are left unspecified. These may depend upon the page layout. A scheme of the form z, where z is an identifier, is represented by a box containing the identifier z. Finally a scheme (K) is represented by the picture of K. The pictures can be nested, just like the operators IMPORT ␣ INTO ␣ , EXPORT ␣ FROM ␣ etc. For example, a scheme fragment of the form

LET EXPERIMENT_SPEC :=
EXPORT Σ FROM
EXPORT Σ' FROM
EXPORT Σ'' FROM
IMPORT CLASS D_1 ... D_k END INTO
IMPORT CLASS D_1' ... D_n' END INTO
RENAME ρ IN
CLASS D_1'' ... D_m'' END

is represented by the following picture:

Fig 11.2. Nested import/export structure.

We conclude this section by showing a larger example. Below we give the graphical representation of the various schemes that occurred in the editor example presented previously.

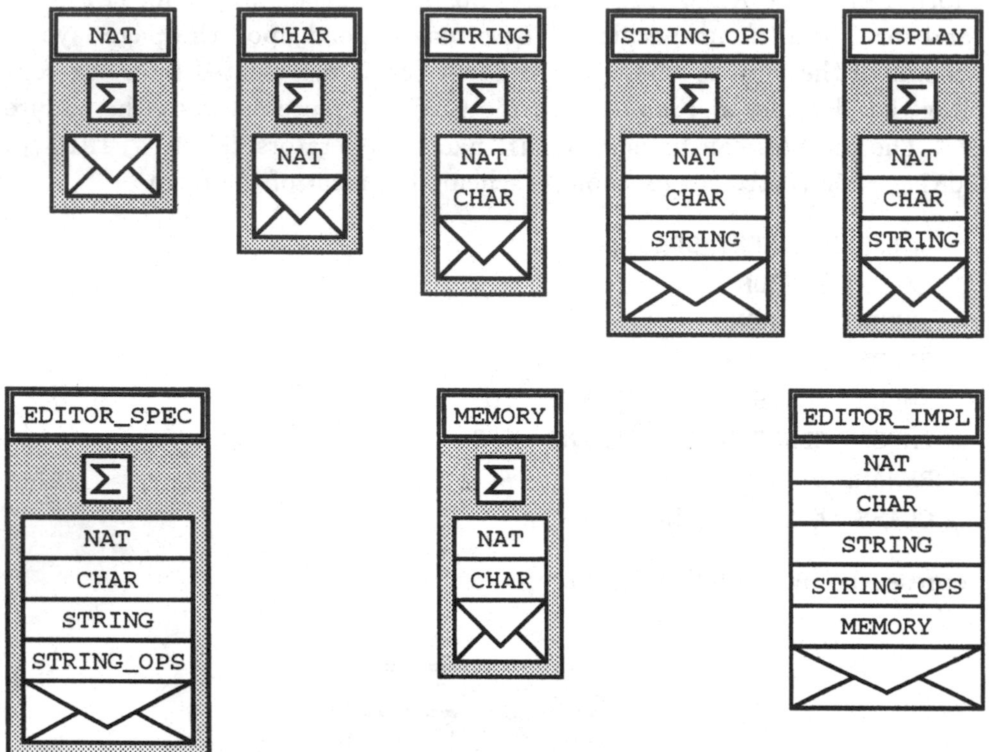

Fig 11.3. Overview of the editor (first part).

A tool generating POLAR pictures from COLD-K texts has been developed as well as a prototype of an interactive editor combining POLAR pictures and COLD-K texts. The pictorial representation by POLAR has been used to represent the modular structure of specifications of up to 5000 lines.

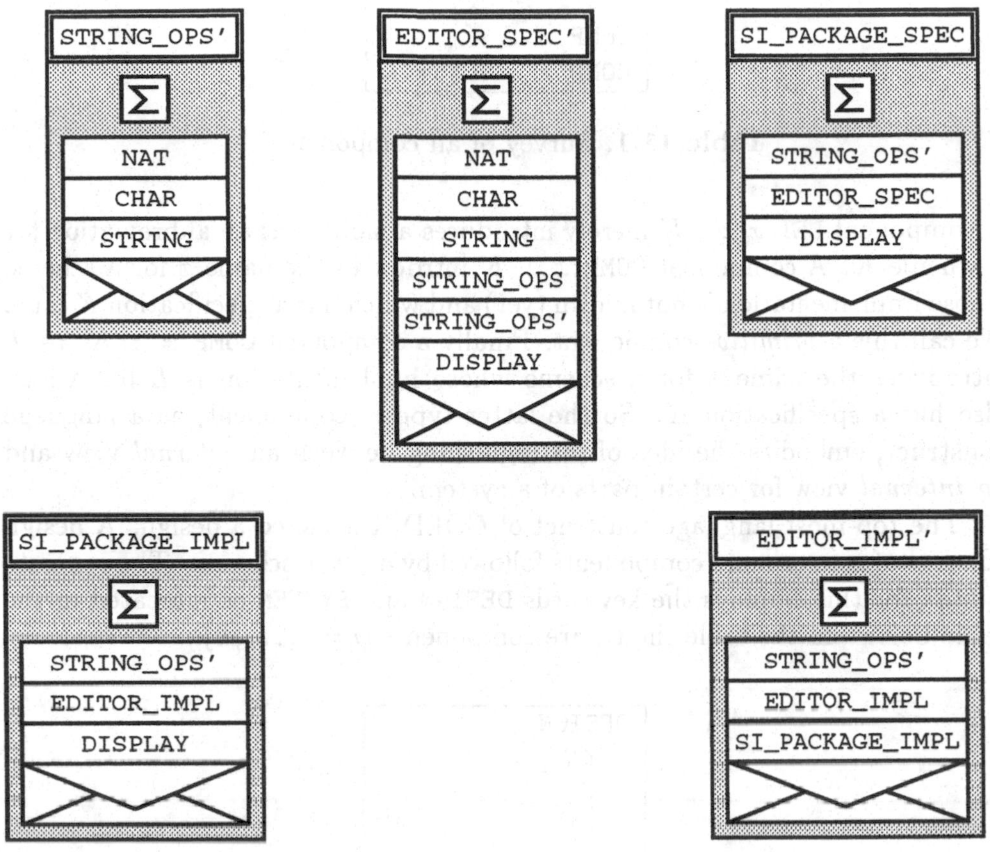

Fig 11.4. Overview of the editor (display-oriented features).

11.3 Components and designs

A formal description can occur in at least two distinct roles: as a *specification* and as an *implementation*. In COLD-K there is no a priori distinction between specifications and implementations: both are described by schemes.

It is useful therefore to have special language constructs for indicating the roles that the various descriptions play and to indicate their relationships. We present language constructs for *components* and *designs* which are available in COLD-K. Speaking in intuitive terms, a design can be viewed as a collection of components, where each component has a specification and an optional implementation associated with it. Furthermore, components have names. There are three types of components, summarised in the table below.

LET x := K
COMP x : K
COMP x : K := L

Table 11.1. Survey of all components.

A component LET x := K merely introduces a name x as an abbreviation for a scheme K. A component COMP x : K introduces the name x for a scheme whose implementation is not known (yet) and which has a specification K only. We call this a *primitive* component. Finally a component COMP x : K := L introduces the name x for a scheme whose implementation is L but which also has a specification K. So the latter type of component, as a language construct, embodies the idea of distinguishing between an *external* view and an *internal* view for certain parts of a system.

The top-most language construct of COLD-K is called a design. A design consists of zero or more components followed by a list of schemes. The concrete syntax for this employs the keywords DESIGN and SYSTEM as indicated in the table below. In the table the C_i are components ($i = 1, \ldots, k$).

```
DESIGN
   C_1 ;
   ⋮
   C_{k-1};
   C_k
SYSTEM K_1,...,K_n
```

Table 11.2. Designs.

There is a well-formedness rule that applies to designs: all component names must be introduced before use. So if the i-th component introduces x_i as a component name, x_i may occur in the specifications and implementations of the subsequent components C_{i+1} ... C_k and of the system schemes K_1 ... K_n, but x_i cannot occur in the specifications and implementations of the components C_1 ... C_{i-1} that precede it, nor in its own specification and implementation.

A design can be viewed as a notation for a list of schemes. Referring to Table 11.2 these are the schemes $K_1 \ldots K_n$ where all occurrences of the component names have been replaced by their implementation schemes. When there are primitive components, they should be viewed as parameters of the design – and hence of the schemes it represents. Components may be shared and therefore the process of origin labelling should be done *before* the process of replacing component names – similar to the approach for the LET construct at the scheme level.

For example if we put the various bits and pieces of the line-editor example together (see Section 8.7), we get the following design:

```
DESIGN {d-editor}

  LET NAT       := ... ;
  LET CHAR      := ... ;
  LET STRING    := ... ;

  LET STRING_OPS    := ... ;
  LET DISPLAY       := ... ;
  LET EDITOR_SPEC   := ... ;
  LET MEMORY        := ... ;
  LET EDITOR_IMPL   := ... ;

  COMP EDITOR : EDITOR_SPEC := EDITOR_IMPL;

  LET STRING_OPS'       := ... ;
  LET EDITOR_SPEC'      := ... ;
  LET SI_PACKAGE_SPEC := ... ;
  LET SI_PACKAGE_IMPL := ... ;

  COMP SI_PACKAGE : SI_PACKAGE_SPEC := SI_PACKAGE_IMPL;

  LET EDITOR_IMPL' := ... ;

  COMP EDITOR' : EDITOR_SPEC' := EDITOR_IMPL'

SYSTEM EDITOR
```

In addition to the well-formedness rule that applies to designs, there are two stronger notions of correctness which we call *glass box correctness* and *black box correctness*. A design is correct if for each component COMP x_i : K_i := L_i we find that L_i is an implementation of K_i. Or, using the $\sqsubseteq$ notation introduced in Section 8.8, that

$$L_i \sqsubseteq K_i.$$

Here the subtle point arises that there are at least two possible *contexts* in which the proposition $L_i \sqsubseteq K_i$ can be considered. This is because the i-th component must be considered in a context derived from the $i-1$ components preceding it.

If we consider the correctness of the i-th component under the assumption that all preceding components are given by their implementations, this is called *glass box correctness.* In that case its context is given as the set of equations $x_1 = L_1, \ldots, x_{i-1} = L_{i-1}$.

If we consider the correctness of the i-th component under the assumption that all preceding components are given by their specification only, we call it *black box correctness.* In that case its context is given as the set of assumptions $x_1 \sqsubseteq K_1, \ldots, x_{i-1} \sqsubseteq K_{i-1}$. Using the latter notion of correctness means adopting a certain type of information hiding: the actual implementations $L_1 \ldots L_{i-1}$ are considered hidden information.

From a methodological point of view, black box correctness is often to be preferred over glass box correctness. This is because the information hiding gives rise to a certain implementation freedom which can be very useful when modifying the design in a later phase of its development.

To illustrate these concepts, we give an example showing a number of related (extremely simple) designs. In particular we shall show a design d_1 which is glass box correct but not black box correct, a design d_2 which is completely incorrect and a design d_3 which is both glass box correct and black box correct. These designs must provide the user with an implementation of an enumerated data type with a kind of toggle function. Consider the following design d_1:

```
DESIGN {d1}

  LET ENUM_SPEC :=
  CLASS

    SORT Enum
    FUNC enum1 : -> Enum
    FUNC enum2 : -> Enum

    AXIOM enum1!; enum2!;  NOT enum1 = enum2

  END;

  LET BOOL_BASED_ENUM_IMPL :=
  RENAME
    SORT Bool              TO Enum,
    FUNC false : -> Bool TO enum2,
    FUNC true  : -> Bool TO enum1
  IN BOOL;
```

```
COMP ENUM : ENUM_SPEC := BOOL_BASED_ENUM_IMPL;

LET TOGGLE_SPEC :=
IMPORT ENUM_SPEC INTO
CLASS

  FUNC toggle : Enum -> Enum

  AXIOM toggle(enum1) = enum2;
        toggle(enum2) = enum1;
        FORALL x:Enum ( toggle(x)! )

END;

LET TOGGLE_IMPL :=
IMPORT ENUM INTO
CLASS

  FUNC toggle : Enum -> Enum
  PAR  x:Enum
  DEF  ( x = enum1 ?, enum2
       | x = enum2 ?, enum1
       )

END;

COMP TOGGLE  : TOGGLE_SPEC := TOGGLE_IMPL

SYSTEM TOGGLE
```

d_1 introduces ENUM_SPEC which is concerned with an enumerated data type Enum – however without a no-junk property. The only requirement specified is that there are at least two distinct values enum1 and enum2. The implementation part of the component ENUM is BOOL_BASED_ENUM_IMPL which uses the Booleans by means of a renaming. BOOL is supposed to be taken from the appendix.

The specification TOGGLE_SPEC adds to the requirements on Enum a toggle satisfying toggle(enum1) = enum2 and toggle(enum2) = enum1. Furthermore it is required to be a total function. In the component TOGGLE it is implemented as TOGGLE_IMPL which is an import of the component ENUM in combination with an algorithmic definition of the function toggle.

d_1 is glass box correct but is not black box correct. First we shall show that it is glass box correct. This means that we must verify the correctness of two components. Note that the component named ENUM is correct because BOOL_BASED_ENUM_IMPL $\sqsubseteq$ ENUM_SPEC. The component named TOGGLE is also correct, for if we use the assumption:

ENUM = BOOL_BASED_ENUM_IMPL

it is easily verified that TOGGLE_IMPL $\sqsubseteq$ TOGGLE_SPEC. But the above design is not black box correct! To see this, note that the component TOGGLE is not correct when only using the assumption

ENUM $\sqsubseteq$ ENUM_SPEC.

In particular it cannot be verified that `toggle` is a total function. One would like to reason by cases – saying x is either enum1 or enum2 – but this reasoning is not justified in view of the rather weak specification ENUM_SPEC.

Now we shall turn our attention to a second design d_2, which is obtained as a modification of d_1. The modification concerns the implementation part of the component named ENUM.

```
DESIGN {d2}

  LET ENUM_SPEC :=
  CLASS
    % as in d1
  END;

  LET NAT_BASED_ENUM_IMPL :=
  IMPORT RENAME
    SORT Nat                TO Enum,
    FUNC zero : -> Nat      TO enum1
  IN NAT INTO
  CLASS

    FUNC enum2 : -> Enum
    DEF  succ(succ(enum1))

  END;

  COMP ENUM : ENUM_SPEC := NAT_BASED_ENUM_IMPL;

  LET TOGGLE_SPEC :=
  IMPORT ENUM_SPEC INTO
  CLASS
```

```
    % as in d1
  END;

  LET TOGGLE_IMPL :=
  IMPORT ENUM INTO
  CLASS
    % as in d1
  END;

  COMP TOGGLE   : TOGGLE_SPEC := TOGGLE_IMPL

SYSTEM TOGGLE
```

As we shall see, the above design d_2 is neither glass box correct nor black box correct. Yet it was the result of a local modification of the first component which did not affect the correctness of this first component.

First we shall show that d_2 is not glass box correct. Again we must analyse the correctness of two components. Note that the new component named ENUM is still correct because NAT_BASED_ENUM_IMPL $\sqsubseteq$ ENUM_SPEC. The component named TOGGLE is not correct, for if we use the assumption:

ENUM = NAT_BASED_ENUM_IMPL

it is easily shown that TOGGLE_IMPL $\sqsubseteq$ TOGGLE_SPEC does not hold. The function `toggle` is not total: it yields undefined when applied to the Enum objects `succ(enum1)` or `succ(succ(succ(enum1)))`, etc. It is also not black box correct, because – as before – when using the assumption ENUM $\sqsubseteq$ ENUM_SPEC, it cannot be verified that `toggle` is a total function.

Now we shall turn our attention to a third design d_3, which is both glass box correct and black box correct.

```
DESIGN {d3}

  LET ENUM_SPEC :=
  CLASS
    % as in d2
  END;

  LET NAT_BASED_ENUM_IMPL :=
  IMPORT RENAME
    SORT Nat              TO Enum,
    FUNC zero : -> Nat    TO enum1
  IN NAT INTO
```

```
    CLASS
      % as in d2
    END;

    COMP ENUM : ENUM_SPEC := NAT_BASED_ENUM_IMPL;

    LET TOGGLE_SPEC :=
    IMPORT ENUM_SPEC INTO
    CLASS
      % as in d2
    END;

    LET NEW_TOGGLE_IMPL :=
    IMPORT ENUM INTO
    CLASS

      FUNC toggle : Enum -> Enum
      PAR  x:Enum
      DEF  ( x = enum1     ?, enum2
           | NOT x = enum1 ?, enum1
           )

    END;

    COMP TOGGLE  : TOGGLE_SPEC := NEW_TOGGLE_IMPL

  SYSTEM TOGGLE
```

First we shall show that d_3 is glass box correct. This means that we must verify the correctness of two components. Of course ENUM is correct again. The component named TOGGLE is also correct, for if we use the assumption:

ENUM = NAT_BASED_ENUM_IMPL

it can be verified that TOGGLE_IMPL $\sqsubseteq$ TOGGLE_SPEC. Now toggle is a total function. We can reason by cases: either $x =$ enum1 or $x \neq$ enum1. To see that d_3 is also black box correct, note that the component TOGGLE is already correct when only using the assumption

ENUM $\sqsubseteq$ ENUM_SPEC.

When going through the various versions of the above design, a number of observations already made can be generalised, leading to the proposition given below. It tells us that black box correctness is harder to obtain than glass box correctness, but also that once black box correctness has been achieved, the design is much more robust for certain typical kinds of modifications. From a methodological point of view these are important insights and it is useful to make them explicit.

Proposition. Consider a well-formed design *d*. The following properties hold:

1. if *d* is black box correct, then it is glass box correct.
2. if *d* is black box correct and *d'* has been obtained from *d* by modifying the implementation of one component which after the modification is still correct (in the black box sense), then *d'* is black box correct. □

The converse of the first clause from the proposition does not hold in general. Also the analogon of the second clause for glass box correctness does not hold. For the rigorous formulation and the proofs of the propositions we refer to [35].

The example also shows that glass box correctness is an absolutely *minimal* requirement: a design which is not even glass box correct is intuitively just wrong. A design which is glass box correct but not black box correct is not really wrong: it is a situation arising quite often in practical situations when using specifications – either in COLD-K or in any other language. But special care is needed when modifying such a design: no provisions for implementation freedom have been built-in to the design and a seemingly innocent change in some low level component can cause the higher levels of the design to break down.

There is a rich and useful theory concerning designs and their correctness. For more details we refer to [35], [43] or [44].

11.4 Applications

The language COLD has been applied in the following areas:

- database design,
- systems software,
- computer graphics,
- medical image processing,
- computer-aided design (CAD for image tubes),
- consumer electronics (user interfaces of TV sets),
- computer-integrated manufacturing (CIM for component placement).

Most of these applications have taken place within Philips. Let us discuss some applications briefly.

The database design application reported in [45] was done for the GAK which is a Dutch administrative organisation in the area of social security. An experimental design was made, providing a special interface to a classical database management system to be used by application programs written in an object-oriented programming language. In particular, an SQL-based INGRES system was made available to Eiffel programs. The interface was formally described using COLD.

In the area of systems software we mention two applications. The first of these is concerned with a distributed real-time systems architecture with a non-conventional message communication facility. COLD was used in the phases of system-conception and design. There was not just one formal specification, but a number of them were developed in parallel and in interaction with the conception of the system. The formal specifications served as a means of communication. After the formal specification was finished and stabilised, the system was implemented using C (many thousands of lines of code).

The second systems software application took place in the context of mini-computer systems development. A formal specification of a so-called Document Distribution System (DDS) was made. This DDS adds a layer of higher-level concepts like 'container' and 'document', on top of an optical-disk based file-system.

The medical image processing application was done in a business unit whose main activity is to develop, manufacture and market medical systems such as Nuclear Magnetic Resonance (NMR) scanners. In an NMR scanner, a complex physical measurement set-up produces data which can be transformed into images for medical diagnostic purposes – a process called image reconstruction. To complement the existing design documentation of the image reconstruction, several COLD descriptions were constructed – at various levels of abstraction. The relation between these descriptions was made by means of abstraction functions. The aim of the application was to bridge the gap between existing design documentation and actual program code.

A computer-aided design application was done in cooperation with the automation-department of a business unit developing display-components. The project was concerned with the specification and construction of a dedicated CAD package for 'shadow-mask design' – which is a relevant topic when designing high-resolution electron-beam based colour image tubes. A non-trivial optimisation criterion had to be formulated. This application showed that an extensive application-domain formalisation may be required before the actual problem at hand can be addressed. Starting from the question 'what must be described?', the objects to be described were identified such as mechanical filters based on point-sets, curved surfaces which are intersected by a light beam, light sources, reference planes, symmetry axes, etc. From a mathematical point of view these appeared as classical geometric concepts: planes, lines in 2 and 3 dimensions, (curved) surfaces, curved lines, curved-line families, vectors in 2 and 3 dimensions, inner and outer products and matrices with matrix addition, products and determinants. Using this machinery, a formulation of the kernel problem of shadow-mask design has been obtained using COLD. Another project in the same business unit is described in [46].

The consumer electronics application was done in a business unit whose main activity is to develop, manufacture and market consumer-electronics equipment. There was a programmable and reconfigurable set-up of a variety of audio-video components such as a monitor, a video tape deck, a tuner, a remote-control receiver, loudspeakers, etc. This was intended to provide a *fast simulation service* of the user-interface control for any audio-video configuration. COLD was used here essentially for two purposes: (1) to describe the 'modes' and 'keybindings' of the control system, and (2) to identify and formally specify the control aspects of the various reusable building blocks – both the software interface and the relevant aspects of 'real audio-video behaviour'.

A CIM application was conducted in a business unit whose main activity is to make Modular Component-placement Machines (MCM). These machines serve for mounting electronic components on 'printed-circuit boards' (PCBs). An MCM is essentially a flow line where each PCB passes one or more 'placement stations'. Each placement station can pick up, move and put components (chips, resistors, etc.) in certain locations. It does so by means of grip arms and pipettes, possibly doing certain things in parallel. This means that there is a complex optimisation problem, optimising the throughput, with a large number of boundary conditions such as the limitations of the MCM and the fact that the PCBs must be populated in the right way. The use of COLD was concerned with the formal specification of this optimisation problem. For the details we refer to [47]. In another project, the heuristic rules used in practice to arrive at reasonable approximations of the optimal solution, which can be calculated in reasonable time, were described using COLD.

Aspects of COLD-K also served as input for the design of other languages, notably Middelburg's VVSL [48], [49] where VDM, temporal logic and COLD-K are combined and Akkerman's CoDDLe [50] where COLD-K and SDL are combined.

11.5 Concluding remarks

As shown by the applications mentioned in the previous section, one of the main benefits of using COLD is the fact that essential parts of complex systems can be well documented and thus become well understood. Using formal specifications makes it possible to encapsulate algorithms and data structures in reusable components.

A reusable component is a piece of software P which has a precise specification S, say. 'P satisfies S' is a clear statement that can be shown by reasoning or that can be falsified by testing; users of P can read S and rely on it and the designer of P has a clearly formulated task. The notion of a *design* presented in Section 11.3 provides a rigorous framework for structuring systems into reusable components.

The price to be paid for the better understanding of complex software systems and for their improved structure is that one must invest in writing formal specifications: this is what the techniques presented in this text are meant for. The text offers a rich collection of notations and techniques for writing formal specifications. Moreover the notations shown are not just ad-hoc notations: in the language COLD-K they have been put together in a consistent way. Each language construct has its syntax and its semantics and these are explained using semantical concepts – the many-sorted algebras presented in Part I and the classes presented in Part II.

The text provides a large number of examples and guidelines as well as a number of advanced techniques (part III). Learning to write formal specifications requires investments but these will pay off because of the better software that can be made by using these specifications.

Industrial applicability has been one of the central goals in the design of COLD and the applications indicate that this requirement has been met. The language can interface with the current practice of software development and because of the wide-spectrum nature of the language, its users are not forced into a narrow formalism but are given the freedom to express their intuition, using familiar concepts such as states and invariants. The language does not presuppose the existence of a new implementation technology either. As shown by the examples in the text and by the applications, the language can be used for the development of programs in existing programming languages.

References [1, 10, 19, 20, 30, 33, 34, 35, 42, 43, 44, 45, 46, 47, 50] together with [52, 53, 54, 55, 56, 57, 58] constitute a COLD(-K) bibliography.

Recall that the language presented in this text is a kernel language, which means that it is intended to be used as the basis of more user-oriented languages by syntactic extensions, sometimes called syntactic sugar. For instance, a user-oriented language version called COLD-1 has been developed by Jonkers [29] and tools for it have been constructed in the context of the ESPRIT project ATMOSPHERE 2565. Also an executable subset of COLD-1 called PROTOCOLD [51] has been defined and an experimental compiler for it exists.

Due to the formal nature of the language, a wide range of supporting tools can be conceived, varying from simple text editors to advanced design knowledge bases. A considerable improvement in the quality of industrial software is already obtained if the language is used in combination with relatively simple tools such as a type checker and a picture generator.

Bibliography

[1] H.B.M. Jonkers. An introduction to COLD-K, in: M. Wirsing, J.A. Bergstra (Eds.), Algebraic Methods: Theory, Tools and Applications, Springer-Verlag LNCS 394, pp. 139-205 (1989).

[2] C.B. Jones. Systematic software development using VDM, Prentice-Hall International, ISBN 0-13-880725-6 (1986).

[3] D. Björner, C.B. Jones (Eds.). The Vienna Development Method: the meta-language, Springer-Verlag LNCS 61 (1978).

[4] I. Hayes (Ed.). Specification case studies. Prentice-Hall International series in computer science, ISBN 0-13-826579-8 (1987).

[5] J.M. Spivey. Understanding Z, a specification language and its formal semantics, Cambridge Tracts in Theoretical Computer Science 3, ISBN 0-521-33429-2 (1988).

[6] M. Wirsing. Structured algebraic specifications: a kernel language, Habilitation thesis, Technische Universität München (1983).

[7] J.A. Bergstra, J. Heering, P. Klint. Module algebra, JACM Vol. 37 No. 2, pp. 335-372 (1990).

[8] D. Harel. Dynamic logic, in: D. Gabbay, F. Guenther (Eds.), Handbook of philosophical logic, Vol. II, pp. 497-604, D. Reidel Publishing Company, ISBN 90-277-1604-8 (1984).

[9] D.S. Scott. Existence and description in formal logic, in R. Schoenman (Ed.), Bertrand Russell, Philosopher of the Century, Allen & Unwin, London, pp. 181-200 (1967).

[10] C.P.J. Koymans, G.R. Renardel de Lavalette. The logic MPL_ω, in: M. Wirsing, J.A. Bergstra (Eds.), Algebraic Methods: Theory, Tools and Applications, Springer-Verlag LNCS 394, pp. 247-282 (1989).

[11] CRI, CISI Ingenerie, and Matra. HOOD: Hierarchical Object-Oriented Design, Paris, France (June 1987).

[12] Ludwig Wittgenstein. Tractatus logico-philosophicus, (citation 4.1), Athenaeum - Polak & Van Gennep, ISBN 90-253-1534-8 (1922).

[13] J.A. Bergstra, J. Heering, P. Klint. Algebraic specification, ACM Press, Frontier Series, Addison-Wesley (1989).

[14] M.C. Gaudel. Towards structured algebraic specifications, in: ESPRIT'85: Status Report of Continuing Work, Part 1, North Holland, pp. 439-510 (1986).

[15] R.M. Burstall, J.A. Goguen. Semantics of CLEAR, a specification language, in: Björner (ed.), Abstract software specifications, Proceedings of the Copenhagen winter school, Springer-Verlag LNCS 86, pp. 292-332 (1980).

[16] H. Ehrig, B. Mahr. Fundamentals of algebraic specifications, Vol. 1, Equations and initial semantics, Springer-Verlag (1985).

[17] K. Futatsugi, J.A. Goguen, J.P. Jouannaud, J. Meseguer. Principles of OBJ-2, in: proceedings of the 12th POPL, ACM, pp. 52-66 (1985).

[18] E.T. Bell. The development of mathematics, McGraw-Hill p.170 (1945).

[19] L.M.G. Feijs, H.B.M. Jonkers, C.P.J. Koymans, G.R. Renardel de Lavalette. Formal definition of the design language COLD-K. Revised Edition, ESPRIT document METEOR/t7/PRLE/7 (Oct. 1987).

[20] C.P.J. Koymans, G.R. Renardel de Lavalette. Inductive Definitions in COLD-K. Logic Group reprint series No. 50, Department of Philosophy, University of Utrecht (Sept. 1989).

[21] J. Hagelstein, F. Ponsaert. Introducing formal requirements into industry, in: J.A. Bergstra, L.M.G. Feijs (Eds.), Algebraic Methods: Theory, Tools and Applications Part II, Springer-Verlag LNCS 490, pp. 129-141 (1991).

[22] C. Weissman. LISP 1.5 Primer, Dickenson Publishing Company, Inc., Belmont, California (1967).

[23] K. Jensen, N. Wirth. PASCAL user manual and report, Springer-Verlag, Berlin (1974).

[24] R.W. Floyd. Assigning meaning to programs, Proc. Amer. Math. Soc. Symposia in Applied Mathematics, Vol. 19, pp. 19-31 (1967).

[25] C.A.R. Hoare. An axiomatic basis for computer programming, Communications of the ACM, Vol. 12, No. 10, pp. 576-580,583 (1969).

[26] E.W. Dijkstra. A discipline of programming, Prentice Hall, ISBN 0-13-215871-X (1976).

[27] A. Salwicki. Formalized algorithmic languages, Bull. Acad. Polon. Sci., Ser. Sci. Math. Astron. phys. 18 pp. 227-232 (1970).

[28] G. Mirkowska. Algorithmic logic with nondeterministic programs, Fund. Informaticae 3, pp. 45-64 (1980).

[29] H.B.M. Jonkers. Description of COLD-1, Philips IST Report RWR-513-hj-91020-hj (March 1991).

[30] W.E. Baats, L.M.G. Feijs, J.H.A. Gelissen. A formal specification of INGRES, in: M. Wirsing, J.A. Bergstra (Eds.), Algebraic Methods: Theory, Tools and Applications, Springer-Verlag LNCS 394, pp. 207-245 (1989).

[31] E.F. Codd. A relational model for large shared data banks, Communications of the ACM 13:6, pp. 377-387 (1970).

[32] R. Epstein. A Tutorial On INGRES, Memorandum No. ERL - M77 25, (Revised), Electronics Research Laboratory, College Of Engineering, University Of California, Berkeley, 94720 (Dec. 1977).

[33] M.E.A. Corthout, H.B.M. Jonkers. The transformational development of a new point containment algorithm, Philips Journal of Research 41, pp. 83-174 (1986).

[34] M.E.A. Corthout, H.B.M. Jonkers. A new point containment algorithm for B-regions in the discrete plane, Proceedings of the NATO Conference on Theoretical Foundations of Computer Graphics and CAD, Italy (1987).

[35] L.M.G. Feijs. A formalisation of design methods, a λ-calculus approach to system design with an application to text editing, Ph. D. Thesis Technical University Eindhoven (1990).

[36] D. Gries. The science of programming, Springer-Verlag, ISBN 0-387-90641-X (1981).

[37] J. Barwise. An introduction to first-order logic, in: J. Barwise (Ed.) Handbook of mathematical logic, North-Holland pp. 5-46, (1977).

[38] H.A. Klaeren. Algebraische Spezifikation, eine Einführung, Springer-Verlag (1983).

[39] J.C.M. Baeten, W.P. Weijland. Process algebra, Cambridge Tracts in Theoretical Computer Science 18, ISBN-0-512-400431-0.

[40] H. Barendregt. The lambda calculus, its syntax and semantics, North Holland, Amsterdam (revised edition), ISBN 0-444-867481 (1984).

[41] I. Nassi, B. Shneidermann. Flowchart techniques for structured programming. ACM SIGPLAN Not. 8:8, pp. 12-16 (1973).

[42] R.D. van den Bos, L.M.G. Feijs, R.C. van Ommering. POLAR, a picture-oriented language for abstract representations, in: J.A. Bergstra, L.M.G. Feijs (Eds.), Algebraic methods: Theory, Tools and Applications Part II Springer-Verlag LNCS 490, pp. 233-276 (1991).

[43] L.M.G. Feijs, H.B.M. Jonkers, J.H. Obbink, C.P.J. Koymans, G.R. Renardel de Lavalette, P.H. Rodenburg. A survey of the design language COLD, in: ESPRIT '86: Results and Achievements, Elsevier Science Publishers B.V. (North Holland), pp. 631-644 (1986).

[44] L.M.G. Feijs, A formalisation of design structures, COMPEURO-87, pp. 214-229, IEEE Society Press (1987).

[45] J.M. Grewer. Design of an interface between an object-oriented environment and the RDBMS system (in Dutch). GAK report, Thesis University of Amsterdam (1990).

[46] F.J. Van der Linden. Specification in COLD-1 of a CAD package for drawing shadow masks, in: A. van Lamsweerde, A. Fugetta (Eds.), ESEC '91, Springer-Verlag LNCS 550, pp. 101-121 (1991).

[47] A. de Bunje, L.M.G. Feijs. Formal specifications applied in industry: a case study using COLD, Proceedings of the third international workshop on software engineering and its applications, Toulouse, EC2 (269-287 rue de la Garenne, 92024 Nanterre Cedex France) ISBN 2-906899-48-8, pp. 649-669 (Dec. 1990).

[48] C.A. Middelburg. Syntax and semantics of VVSL, Ph. D. Thesis, University of Amsterdam (1990).

[49] C.A. Middelburg. Experiences with combining formalisms in VVSL, in: J.A. Bergstra, L.M.G. Feijs (Eds.), Algebraic Methods: Theory, Tools and Applications Part II, Springer-Verlag LNCS 490, pp. 83-103 (1991).

[50] G.J. Akkerman. CoDDLe: Common Design and Description Language, SERC Report RP/mod-89/9. Software Engineering Research Centre. Utrecht, The Netherlands (Nov. 89).

[51] H.B.M. Jonkers. PROTOCOLD 1.1 User manual, Philips IST Report RWR-513-hj-91080-hj (Aug. 1991).

[52] L.M.G. Feijs, H.B.M. Jonkers. Transformational design: an annotated example, Proceedings of the IFIP TC 2 Working Conference on Program Specification and Transformation, Bad Toelz, Elsevier Science Publishers pp. 89-112, (1987).

[53] L.M.G. Feijs, H.B.M. Jonkers. METEOR and beyond: industrialising formal methods, in: K.H. Bennett (Ed.), Software Engineering Environments: Research and Practice, Ellis Horwood Limited, pp. 255-274 (1989).

[54] H.B.M. Jonkers. Description algebra, in: M. Wirsing, J.A. Bergstra (Eds.), Algebraic Methods: Theory, Tools and Applications, Springer-Verlag LNCS 394, pp. 283-305 (1989).

[55] L.M.G. Feijs. The calculus $\lambda\pi$, in: M. Wirsing, J.A. Bergstra (Eds.), Algebraic Methods: Theory, Tools and Applications, Springer-Verlag LNCS 394, pp. 307-328 (1989).

[56] H.B.M. Jonkers. Inheritance in COLD, in: J.A. Bergstra, L.M.G. Feijs (Eds.), Algebraic Methods: Theory, Tools and Applications Part II, Springer-Verlag LNCS 490, pp. 277-301 (1991).

[57] L.M.G. Feijs. Norman's database modularised in COLD-K, in: J.A. Bergstra, L.M.G. Feijs (Eds.), Algebraic Methods: Theory, Tools and Applications Part II, Springer-Verlag LNCS 490, pp. 205-231 (1991).

[58] J.C.M. Baeten, J.A. Bergstra, S. Mauw, G.J. Veltink. A process specification formalism based on static COLD, in: J.A. Bergstra, L.M.G. Feijs (Eds.), Algebraic Methods: Theory, Tools and Applications Part II, Springer-Verlag LNCS 490, pp. 303-335 (1991).

Appendix A

Syntax

A.1 General

In this appendix a concrete syntax for COLD-K is defined. It is concerned with the full language, including the constructs presented in Chapter 10 and 11. The notions of term, expression and statement are integrated into a single syntactical category called <expression>. We give an (extended) BNF grammar defining a set of strings of ASCII characters which are used as concrete representations of the COLD-K constructs.

For user convenience, it is allowed to omit redundant type information. In the applied occurrence of a name the associated type information is generally omitted (otherwise the use of names would become very clumsy). Though in many situations the missing type information can be reconstructed from the context, there are situations where ambiguities may occur. We leave it to the parser to report such ambiguities; there is a special syntactic operator (the *cast*) to disambiguate the type of an expression.

In the concrete syntax defined here prefix, infix and postfix notations are used for the built-in operators of the language. For the user-defined operators (predicates, functions, procedures) only a prefix notation is provided. The main reason for not introducing infix, postfix or mixfix notations for the latter is simplicity. The possibility to define special notations for user-defined operators is typical for user-oriented versions of COLD, which can be defined as a kind of macro-extension of COLD-K.

A.2 Concrete syntax

We define the concrete syntax of COLD-K by means of a context free grammar and priority and associativity rules for the built-in operators. Below we shall define the lexical elements (tokens). In Section A.6 we give the context free syntax for the language using extended BNF notation. The priorities and associativities of the built-in operators are defined in Section A.7.

Throughout the rest of this appendix we shall use typewriter face to denote concrete representations of COLD-K constructs. The characters of this type face are listed below:

```
  ! " # $ % & ' ( ) * + , - . / 0 1 2 3 4 5 6 7 8 9 : ; < = > ?
@ A B C D E F G H I J K L M N O P Q R S T U V W X Y Z [ \ ] ^ _
` a b c d e f g h i j k l m n o p q r s t u v w x y z { | } ~
```

A.3 Tokens

A terminal production of the concrete syntax of COLD-K is a sequence of tokens, where each token is a sequence of ASCII characters. In a given string of ASCII characters, tokens are recognised on the basis of left to right reading, taking the longest possible match. Spaces and new lines act as separators. The tokens are subdivided into identifiers, keywords and comments, to be discussed in the following subsections.

Identifiers are arbitrary non-empty strings of letters, digits and the following six special characters:

```
" ' . / \ _
```

excluding those strings which are keywords (see Section A.4 below).

A.4 Keywords

A *keyword* is one of the following sequences of characters:

```
AND       FUNC      RENAME    +
APPLY     IMPORT    SIG       ,
AXIOM     IN        SKIP      ->
BEGIN     IND       SOME      :
CLASS     INIT      SORT      :=
COMP      INTO      SYSTEM    ;
DEF       LAMBDA    TO        <
DEP       LET       TRUE      <=>
DESIGN    MOD       USE       =
END       NONE      VAR       =>
EXISTS    NOT       !         >
EXPORT    OF        #         ?
```

```
FALSE     OR      $      @
FLUSH     PAR     &      [
FORALL    PRED    (      ]
FREE      PREV    )      ^
FROM      PROC    *      |
```

A.5 Comments

Comments may be inserted anywhere between two tokens and have no meaning in terms of the abstract syntax, hence they are ignored in the grammar in Section A.6. Two comment facilities are provided. The first is the use of the comment brackets `{` and `}`, which turn the enclosed text (not containing a `}`) into a comment:

```
{ This is comment }
```

The comment brackets cannot be nested. The second is the use of a `%`-sign, which turns the rest of the line into a comment:

```
% This is comment
```

A.6 Grammar

In this section we present the concrete syntax of COLD-K by means of a context free grammar. The actual set of syntactically correct COLD-K constructs is a subset of the set of constructs defined by this grammar (see A.7). The notation used is extended Backus-Naur form with the following conventions:

1. All characters in typewriter face are terminal symbols.
2. $[X]$ in a production rule denotes X or the empty string.
3. $\{X\}$ in a production rule denotes an arbitary sequence of X s, including the empty sequence.

The start symbol of the grammar is the nonterminal <design>. The nonterminal <identifier> has no production rule in the grammar and denotes an arbitrary identifier.

<design> ::= `DESIGN` <component list> `SYSTEM` <scheme list>
<component list> ::= `NONE`
    | <component> { `;` <component> }
<component> ::= `COMP` <identifier> `:` <scheme>
    | `COMP` <identifier> `:` <scheme> `:=` <scheme>

```
      | LET <identifier> := <scheme>
<scheme list> ::= NONE
      | <scheme> { , <scheme> }
<scheme> ::= CLASS <definition set> END
      | RENAME <renaming> IN <scheme>
      | IMPORT <scheme> INTO <scheme>
      | EXPORT <signature> FROM <scheme>
      | LAMBDA <identifier> : <scheme> OF <scheme>
      | APPLY <scheme> TO <scheme>
      | LET <identifier> := <scheme> ; <scheme>
      | <identifier>
      | ( <scheme> )
<definition set> ::= NONE
      | <definition> { <definition> }
<renaming> ::= <pair set>
      | <renaming> $ <renaming>
      | ( <renaming> )
<pair set> ::= NONE
      | <pair> { , <pair> }
<pair> ::= <item> TO [ <identifier> ]
<signature> ::= <item set>
      | <renaming> @ <signature>
      | <signature> + <signature>
      | <signature> & <signature>
      | <item> ^ <signature>
      | SIG <scheme>
      | ( <signature> )
<item set> ::= NONE
      | <item> { , <item> }
<item> ::= SORT <identifier>
      | PRED <identifier> : <domain>
      | FUNC <identifier> : <domain> -> <domain>
      | PROC <identifier> : <domain> -> <domain>
<domain> ::= [ <identifier> { # <identifier> } ]
<definition> ::= SORT <identifier> <sort body>
      | PRED <identifier> : <domain> <predicate body>
      | FUNC <identifier> : <domain> -> <domain> <function body>
      | PROC <identifier> : <domain> -> <domain> <procedure body>
      | AXIOM <assertion>
<sort body> ::= FREE
      | VAR
      | [ DEP <entity set> ]
```

```
<predicate body> ::= FREE
    | VAR
    | [ DEP <entity set> ]
    | IND <assertion>
    | [ PAR <object list> ] DEF <assertion>
<function body> ::= FREE
    | VAR
    | [ DEP <entity set> ]
    | IND <assertion>
    | [ PAR <object list> ] DEF <expression>
<procedure body> ::= FREE
    | [ MOD <entity set> ] [ USE <procedure set> ]
    | [ PAR <object list> ] DEF <expression>
<entity set> ::= NONE
    | <entity> { , <entity> }
<entity> ::= <identifier> [ : <domain> [ -> <domain> ] ]
<procedure set> ::= NONE
    | <procedure> { , <procedure> }
<procedure> ::= <identifier> [ : <domain> -> <domain> ]
<object list> ::= NONE
    | <object> { , <object> }
<object> ::= <identifier> : <sort list>
<sort list> ::= NONE
    | <identifier> { # <identifier> }
<assertion> ::= <expression> !
    | <expression> = <expression>
    | <identifier> [ <expression> ]
    | TRUE
    | FALSE
    | NOT <assertion>
    | <assertion> AND <assertion>
    | <assertion> ; <assertion>
    | <assertion> , <assertion>
    | <assertion> OR <assertion>
    | <assertion> => <assertion>
    | <assertion> <=> <assertion>
    | FORALL <object list> <assertion>
    | EXISTS <object list> <assertion>
    | INIT
    | [ <expression> ] <assertion>
    | < <expression> > <assertion>
    | PREV <assertion>
```

```
           | LET <object list>
           | <identifier list> := <expression>
           | BEGIN <assertion> END
           | ( [ <assertion> ] )
<expression> ::= <identifier>
           | SOME <object list> <assertion>
           | SKIP
           | <assertion> ?
           | <expression> <expression>
           | <expression> ; <expression>
           | <expression> , <expression>
           | <expression> | <expression>
           | <expression> *
           | MOD <entity set> [ USE <procedure set> ] END
           | USE <procedure set> END
           | FLUSH <expression>
           | PREV <expression>
           | LET <object list>
           | <identifier list> := <expression>
           | BEGIN <expression> END
           | <expression> : <sort list>
           | ( [ <expression> ] )
     <identifier list> ::= NONE
           | <identifier> { , <identifier> }
```

A.7 Operator priorities and associativities

In the following two sections we give tables defining the priorities and associativities of the various operators in renamings and signatures, and in assertions and expressions. We distinguish nullary, unary and binary operators, where operators may consist of more than one token (as indicated by the tables). Unary operators can be prefix or postfix, while binary operators are always infix. The holes for the arguments of the operators are indicated by bullets (•). Increasing priority corresponds with increasing binding strength.

The operators at a given priority level are either all nullary, unary or binary. The only exception seems to be priority level 14 in assertions and expressions, which contains the operators for expression composition and operation application. This is due to the fact that, from the semantic point of view, the operators at this level have different arities. From a purely syntactic point of view they can all be viewed as binary operators, represented by empty strings.

The priorities and associativities (L for left and R for right) are used to associate a unique parse tree with each renaming/signature and assertion/expression produced by the ambiguous grammar presented in A.6. The parse tree associated with a construct is defined as the tree obtained by parsing the construct in accordance with the strict priority and associativity rules. The tree obtained this way need not be a legal parse tree of the grammar defined in A.6, in which case the construct is considered syntactically incorrect. Hence the set of syntactically correct COLD-K constructs is the set of terminal productions of grammar A.6 which have a legal parse tree (as defined above) associated with them.

As an example, consider the following assertion, which is a terminal production of the nonterminal <assertion>:

```
FORALL x:T x = x
```

This assertion is not syntactically correct since it would be parsed as: `(FORALL x:T x) = x` which is not a legal assertion. Problems such as the one above can occur only in constructs containing both assertions and expressions as subconstructs (and even then only in a limited number of cases). They can be solved in a simple way by adding parentheses at the proper places. For example, for the assertion above the problems would be solved by writing it as: `FORALL x:T (x = x)`.

The advantage of the above approach is that the set of syntactically correct COLD-K constructs can be described by an LALR(1) grammar, in contrast with the full language defined by A.6. This makes it possible to construct an efficient parser for the language. The LALR(1) grammar could have been presented as the context-free syntax of COLD-K, but it is less readable than the given grammar (at least for the syntax of renamings, signatures, assertions and expressions).

A.7.1 Operators in renamings and signatures

Operator	*Pri*	*Ass*	*Construct name*
• + •	1	L	union signature
• & •	2	L	intersection signature
• @ •	3	-	renaming signature
• $ •	4	R	composition renaming
... ^ •	5	-	deletion signature
...	6	-	constant renaming/signature
SIG ...	6	-	scheme signature
(...)	6	-	parentheses

A.7.2 Operators in assertions and expressions

<table>
<tr><th>Operator</th><th>Pri</th><th>Ass</th><th>Construct name</th></tr>
<tr><td>• | •</td><td>1</td><td>L</td><td>choice expression</td></tr>
<tr><td>• ; •</td><td>2</td><td>L</td><td>conjunction assertion / composition expression</td></tr>
<tr><td>• , •</td><td>2</td><td>L</td><td>conjunction assertion / composition expression</td></tr>
<tr><td>[...] •</td><td>3</td><td>-</td><td>always assertion</td></tr>
<tr><td><...> •</td><td>3</td><td>-</td><td>sometimes assertion</td></tr>
<tr><td>• ?</td><td>4</td><td>-</td><td>guard expression</td></tr>
<tr><td>• *</td><td>4</td><td>-</td><td>repetition expression</td></tr>
<tr><td>PREV •</td><td>5</td><td>-</td><td>previously assertion/expression</td></tr>
<tr><td>• <=> •</td><td>6</td><td>R</td><td>equivalence assertion</td></tr>
<tr><td>• => •</td><td>7</td><td>R</td><td>implication assertion</td></tr>
<tr><td>• OR •</td><td>8</td><td>L</td><td>disjunction assertion</td></tr>
<tr><td>• AND •</td><td>9</td><td>L</td><td>conjunction assertion</td></tr>
<tr><td>NOT •</td><td>10</td><td>-</td><td>negation assertion</td></tr>
<tr><td>• = •</td><td>11</td><td>-</td><td>equality assertion</td></tr>
<tr><td>• !</td><td>12</td><td>-</td><td>definedness assertion</td></tr>
<tr><td>FORALL ... •</td><td>13</td><td>-</td><td>forall assertion</td></tr>
<tr><td>EXISTS ... •</td><td>13</td><td>-</td><td>exists assertion</td></tr>
<tr><td>SOME ... •</td><td>13</td><td>-</td><td>selection expression</td></tr>
<tr><td>FLUSH •</td><td>13</td><td>-</td><td>flush expression</td></tr>
<tr><td>... := •</td><td>13</td><td>-</td><td>binding assertion/expression</td></tr>
<tr><td>• •</td><td>14</td><td>R</td><td>composition expression</td></tr>
<tr><td>... •</td><td>14</td><td>-</td><td>predicate assertion</td></tr>
<tr><td>... •</td><td>14</td><td>-</td><td>function expression</td></tr>
<tr><td>... •</td><td>14</td><td>-</td><td>procedure expression</td></tr>
<tr><td>• : ...</td><td>15</td><td>-</td><td>cast</td></tr>
<tr><td>...</td><td>16</td><td>-</td><td>reference expression</td></tr>
<tr><td>TRUE</td><td>16</td><td>-</td><td>true assertion</td></tr>
<tr><td>FALSE</td><td>16</td><td>-</td><td>false assertion</td></tr>
<tr><td>INIT</td><td>16</td><td>-</td><td>initially assertion</td></tr>
<tr><td>SKIP</td><td>16</td><td>-</td><td>skip expression</td></tr>
<tr><td>MOD ... USE ... END</td><td>16</td><td>-</td><td>modification expression</td></tr>
<tr><td>MOD ... END</td><td>16</td><td>-</td><td>modification expression</td></tr>
<tr><td>USE ... END</td><td>16</td><td>-</td><td>modification expression</td></tr>
<tr><td>LET ...</td><td>16</td><td>-</td><td>declaration assertion/expression</td></tr>
<tr><td>BEGIN ... END</td><td>16</td><td>-</td><td>block assertion/expression</td></tr>
<tr><td>(...)</td><td>16</td><td>-</td><td>parentheses</td></tr>
</table>

Appendix B

Standard library

In this appendix a number of class descriptions are given which constitute a 'standard library'. They can be copied and re-used in many typical formal specification tasks. They are given as modular schemes, that is, without using the advanced parameterisation constructs presented in Part III. A number of class descriptions have already been worked out (more or less) in the text – like NAT in Chapters 1 and 2.

B.1 Booleans

```
% BOOL specifies the data type of boolean values.
%
% Interpretation (b,c:Bool):
%
% Bool      : the set of boolean values;
% true      : the boolean value 'true';
% false     : the boolean value 'false';
% not(b)    : the negation of b;
% and(b,c)  : the conjunction of b and c;
% or(b,c)   : the disjunction of b and c;
% imp(b,c)  : the implication of b and c;
% eqv(b,c)  : the equivalence of b and c;
% xor(b,c)  : the 'exclusive or' of b and c.

LET BOOL :=
EXPORT
  SORT Bool,
  FUNC true  :               -> Bool,
  FUNC false :               -> Bool,
  FUNC not   : Bool          -> Bool,
  FUNC and   : Bool # Bool -> Bool,
  FUNC or    : Bool # Bool -> Bool,
  FUNC imp   : Bool # Bool -> Bool,
  FUNC eqv   : Bool # Bool -> Bool,
```

```
  FUNC xor   : Bool # Bool -> Bool
FROM
CLASS

  SORT Bool
  FUNC true  : -> Bool
  FUNC false : -> Bool

  PRED is_gen : Bool
  IND  is_gen(true);
       is_gen(false)

  AXIOM {BOOL1} true!;
        {BOOL2} false!;
        {BOOL3} NOT true = false;
        {BOOL4} FORALL b:Bool ( is_gen(b) )

  FUNC not : Bool -> Bool
  IND  not(true ) = false;
       not(false) = true

  FUNC and : Bool # Bool -> Bool
  IND  FORALL x:Bool
       ( and(false,x) = false;
         and(true ,x) = x )

  FUNC or : Bool # Bool -> Bool
  IND  FORALL x:Bool
       ( or(false,x) = x;
         or(true ,x) = true )

  FUNC imp : Bool # Bool -> Bool
  IND  FORALL x:Bool
       ( imp(false,x) = true;
         imp(true ,x) = x )

  FUNC eqv : Bool # Bool -> Bool
  IND  FORALL x:Bool
       ( eqv(x,x) = true;
         eqv(x,not(x)) = false )

  FUNC xor : Bool # Bool -> Bool
  IND  FORALL x:Bool
       ( xor(x,x) = false;
         xor(x,not(x)) = true )

END;
```

B.2 Natural numbers

```
% NAT specifies the data type of natural numbers.
%
% Interpretation (m,n:Nat):
%
% Nat      : the set of natural numbers;
% zero     : the natural number 'zero';
% succ(m)  : the successor of m (= m + 1);
% pred(m)  : the predecessor of m ( = m - 1);
% lss(m,n) : m is less than n;
% leq(m,n) : m is less than or equal to n;
% gtr(m,n) : m is greater than n;
% geq(m,n) : m is greater than or equal to n;
% add(m,n) : the sum of m and n;
% sub(m,n) : the difference of m and n;
% mul(m,n) : the product of m and n;
% div(m,n) : the integer quotient of m and n;
% mod(m,n) : the rest of m when divided by n;
% exp(m,n) : m to the power of n;
% log(m,n) : the integer m-logarithm of n;
% max(m,n) : the maximum of m and n;
% min(m,n) : the minimum of m and n.

LET NAT :=
EXPORT
  SORT Nat,
  FUNC zero : -> Nat,
  FUNC succ : Nat -> Nat,
  FUNC pred : Nat -> Nat,
  PRED lss : Nat # Nat,
  PRED leq : Nat # Nat,
  PRED gtr : Nat # Nat,
  PRED geq : Nat # Nat,
  FUNC add : Nat # Nat -> Nat,
  FUNC sub : Nat # Nat -> Nat,
  FUNC mul : Nat # Nat -> Nat,
  FUNC div : Nat # Nat -> Nat,
  FUNC mod : Nat # Nat -> Nat,
  FUNC exp : Nat # Nat -> Nat,
  FUNC log : Nat # Nat -> Nat,
  FUNC max : Nat # Nat -> Nat,
  FUNC min : Nat # Nat -> Nat
FROM
CLASS

  SORT Nat
  FUNC zero : -> Nat
  FUNC succ : Nat -> Nat
```

```
PRED is_gen : Nat
IND  is_gen(zero);
     FORALL m:Nat
     ( is_gen(m) => is_gen(succ(m)) )

AXIOM
{NAT1} zero!;
       FORALL m:Nat,n:Nat (
{NAT2} succ(m)!;
{NAT3} NOT succ(m) = zero;
{NAT4} succ(m) = succ(n) => m = n );
{NAT5} FORALL n:Nat ( is_gen(n) )

FUNC pred : Nat -> Nat
IND  FORALL n:Nat
     ( pred(succ(n)) = n )

PRED lss : Nat # Nat
IND  FORALL m:Nat,n:Nat
     ( lss(m,succ(m));
       lss(m,n) => lss(m,succ(n)) )

PRED leq : Nat # Nat
IND  FORALL m:Nat,n:Nat
     ( leq(m,m);
       leq(m,n) => leq(m,succ(n)) )

PRED gtr : Nat # Nat
IND  FORALL m:Nat,n:Nat
     ( gtr(succ(m),m);
       gtr(m,n) => gtr(succ(m),n) )

PRED geq : Nat # Nat
IND  FORALL m:Nat,n:Nat
     ( geq(m,m);
       geq(m,n) => geq(succ(m),n) )

FUNC add : Nat # Nat -> Nat
IND  FORALL m:Nat,n:Nat
     ( add(m,zero) = m;
       add(m,succ(n)) = succ(add(m,n)) )

FUNC sub : Nat # Nat -> Nat
IND  FORALL m:Nat,n:Nat
     ( sub(m,zero) = m;
       gtr(m,n) => sub(m,succ(n)) = pred(sub(m,n)) )

FUNC mul : Nat # Nat -> Nat
IND  FORALL m:Nat,n:Nat
     ( mul(m,zero) = zero;
       mul(m,succ(n)) = add(mul(m,n),m) )
```

```
  FUNC div : Nat # Nat -> Nat
  IND  FORALL m:Nat,n:Nat,q:Nat,r:Nat
       ( m = add(mul(n,q),r) AND lss(r,n) => div(m,n) = q )

  FUNC mod : Nat # Nat -> Nat
  IND  FORALL m:Nat,n:Nat,q:Nat,r:Nat
       ( m = add(mul(n,q),r) AND lss(r,n) => mod(m,n) = r )

  FUNC exp : Nat # Nat -> Nat
  IND  FORALL m:Nat,n:Nat
       ( exp(m,zero) = succ(zero);
         exp(m,succ(n)) = mul(m,exp(m,n)) )

  FUNC log : Nat # Nat -> Nat
  IND  FORALL m:Nat,n:Nat,p:Nat
       ( leq(exp(m,p),n) AND lss(n,exp(m,succ(p))) => log(m,n) = p )

  FUNC max : Nat # Nat -> Nat
  IND  FORALL m:Nat,n:Nat
       ( geq(m,n) => max(m,n) = m;
         leq(m,n) => max(m,n) = n )

  FUNC min : Nat # Nat -> Nat
  IND  FORALL m:Nat,n:Nat
       ( leq(m,n) => min(m,n) = m;
         geq(m,n) => min(m,n) = n )

END;
```

B.3 Characters

```
% CHAR specifies the data type of characters.
%
% Interpretation (n:Nat, c:Char)
%
% Char      : the set of characters;
% chr(n)    : the character corresponding to n;
% ord(c)    : the natural number corresponding to c;
% minchar   : the minimum character (as ordered by lsschar);
% maxchar   : the maximum character (as ordered by lsschar);
% lsschar   : the ordering induced by 'lss'.

LET CHAR :=
EXPORT
  SORT Char,
  SORT Nat,
  FUNC chr : Nat -> Char,
  FUNC ord : Char -> Nat,
```

```
  FUNC minchar : -> Char,
  FUNC maxchar : -> Char,
  PRED lsschar : Char # Char
FROM
IMPORT NAT INTO
CLASS

  SORT Char
  FUNC min : -> Nat
  FUNC max : -> Nat

  FUNC chr : Nat -> Char
  FUNC ord : Char -> Nat

  PRED dom : Nat
  PAR  m:Nat
  DEF  leq(min,m) AND leq(m,max)

  AXIOM
  {CHAR1} lss(min,max);
          FORALL m:Nat (
  {CHAR2} chr(m)! <=> dom(m);
  {CHAR3} dom(m) => ord(chr(m)) = m )

  PRED is_gen : Char
  IND  FORALL m:Nat ( dom(m) => is_gen(chr(m)) )

  AXIOM {CHAR4} FORALL c:Char ( is_gen(c) )

  FUNC minchar : -> Char DEF chr(min)
  FUNC maxchar : -> Char DEF chr(max)

  PRED lsschar : Char # Char
  PAR  c:Char, d:Char
  DEF  lss(ord(c),ord(d))

END;
```

B.4 Tuples

```
% TUP2 specifies the data type of 2-tuples.
%
% Interpretation (i1:Item1, i2:Item2, t:Tup2):
%
% Item1       : the set of objects acting as the first elements of tuples;
% Item2       : the set of objects acting as the second elements of tuples;
% Tup2        : the set of tuples of objects of types Item1 and Item2;
% tup(i1,i2)  : the tuple consisting of i1 and i2;
% proj1(t)    : the first element of tuple t;
```

```
% proj2(t)    : the second element of tuple t.
%
% Note: this data type can be generalised in a straightforward
% way to the case of n-tuples (n > 0).

LET TUP2 :=
EXPORT
  SORT Tup,
  SORT Item1,
  SORT Item2,
  FUNC tup   : Item1 # Item2 -> Tup,
  FUNC proj1 : Tup           -> Item1,
  FUNC proj2 : Tup           -> Item2
FROM
CLASS

  SORT Item1
  SORT Item2

  SORT Tup
  FUNC tup : Item1 # Item2 -> Tup

  PRED is_gen : Tup
  IND  FORALL i1:Item1,i2:Item2
       ( is_gen(tup(i1,i2)) )

  AXIOM  FORALL i1:Item1,j1:Item1,i2:Item2,j2:Item2 (
  {TUP1} tup(i1,i2)!;
  {TUP2} tup(i1,i2) = tup(j1,j2) => i1 = j1 AND i2 = j2 );
  {TUP3} FORALL t:Tup ( is_gen(t) )

  FUNC proj1 : Tup -> Item1
  IND  FORALL i1:Item1,i2:Item2
       ( proj1(tup(i1,i2)) = i1 )

  FUNC proj2 : Tup -> Item2
  IND  FORALL i1:Item1,i2:Item2
       ( proj2(tup(i1,i2)) = i2 )

END;
```

B.5 Finite sets

```
% SET specifies the data type of finite sets.
%
% Interpretation (i:Item, s,t:Set):
%
% Item          : the set of objects contained in sets;
% Set           : the set of finite sets of objects of type Item;
```

```
% is_in(i,s)   : i is an element of s;
% empty        : the empty set;
% ins(i,s)     : the set s with i inserted;
% rem(i,s)     : the set s with i removed;
% union(s,t)   : the union of s and t;
% isect(s,t)   : the intersection of s and t;
% diff(s,t)    : the difference of s and t;
% subset(s,t)  : s is a subset of t;
% card(s)      : the cardinality of s.

LET SET :=
EXPORT
  SORT Item,
  SORT Nat,
  SORT Set,
  PRED is_in  : Item # Set,
  FUNC empty  : -> Set,
  FUNC ins    : Item # Set -> Set,
  FUNC rem    : Item # Set -> Set,
  FUNC union  : Set  # Set -> Set,
  FUNC isect  : Set  # Set -> Set,
  FUNC diff   : Set  # Set -> Set,
  PRED subset : Set  # Set,
  FUNC card   : Set        -> Nat
FROM
IMPORT NAT INTO
CLASS

  SORT Item
  SORT Set
  PRED is_in : Item # Set
  FUNC empty : -> Set
  FUNC ins   : Item # Set -> Set

  PRED is_gen : Set
  IND  is_gen(empty);
       FORALL i:Item,s:Set
       ( is_gen(s) => is_gen(ins(i,s)) )

  AXIOM
  {SET1} empty!;
         FORALL i:Item,j:Item,s:Set (
  {SET2} ins(i,s)!;
  {SET3} NOT is_in(i,empty);
  {SET4} is_in(i,ins(j,s)) <=> i = j OR is_in(i,s);
  {SET5} ins(i,ins(j,s)) = ins(j,ins(i,s));
  {SET6} ins(i,ins(i,s)) = ins(i,s) );
  {SET7} FORALL s:Set ( is_gen(s) )

  FUNC rem : Item # Set -> Set
  IND  FORALL i:Item,j:Item,s:Set
```

```
       ( rem(i,empty) = empty;
         rem(i,ins(i,s)) = rem(i,s);
         NOT i = j => rem(i,ins(j,s)) = ins(j,rem(i,s)) )

  FUNC union : Set # Set -> Set
  IND  FORALL s:Set
       ( union(s,empty) = s );
       FORALL i:Item,s:Set,t:Set
       ( union(s,ins(i,t)) = ins(i,union(s,t)) )

  FUNC isect : Set # Set -> Set
  IND  FORALL s:Set
       ( isect(s,empty) = empty );
       FORALL i:Item,s:Set,t:Set
       ( is_in(i,s) => isect(s,ins(i,t)) = ins(i,isect(s,t));
         NOT is_in(i,s) => isect(s,ins(i,t)) = isect(s,t) )

  FUNC diff : Set # Set -> Set
  IND  FORALL s:Set
       ( diff(s,empty) = s );
       FORALL i:Item,s:Set,t:Set
       ( diff(s,ins(i,t)) = rem(i,diff(s,t)) )

  PRED subset : Set # Set
  IND  FORALL s:Set
       ( subset(s,s) );
       FORALL i:Item,s:Set,t:Set
       ( subset(s,t) => subset(s,ins(i,t)) )

  FUNC card : Set -> Nat
  IND  card(empty) = zero;
       FORALL i:Item,s:Set
       ( NOT is_in(i,s) => card(ins(i,s)) = succ(card(s)) )

END;
```

B.6 Finite bags

```
% BAG specifies the data type of finite bags (= multisets).
%
% Interpretation (i:Item, b,c:Bag):
%
% Item          : the set of objects contained in bags;
% Bag           : the set of finite bags of objects of type Item;
% is_in(i,b)    : i occurs at least once in b;
% empty         : the empty bag;
% ins(i,b)      : the bag b with one occurrence of i inserted;
% rem(i,b)      : the bag b with one occurrence of i removed;
% union(b,c)    : the union of b and c;
```

```
% isect(b,c)  : the intersection of b and c;
% diff(b,c)   : the difference of b and c;
% subbag(b,c) : b is a subbag of c;
% mult(i,b)   : the number of occurrences (multiplicity) of i in b.

LET BAG :=
EXPORT
  SORT Item,
  SORT Nat,
  SORT Bag,
  PRED is_in  : Item # Bag,
  FUNC empty  : -> Bag,
  FUNC ins    : Item # Bag -> Bag,
  FUNC rem    : Item # Bag -> Bag,
  FUNC union  : Bag  # Bag -> Bag,
  FUNC isect  : Bag  # Bag -> Bag,
  FUNC diff   : Bag  # Bag -> Bag,
  PRED subbag : Bag  # Bag,
  FUNC mult   : Item # Bag -> Nat
FROM
IMPORT NAT INTO
CLASS

  SORT Item
  SORT Bag
  PRED is_in : Item # Bag
  FUNC empty : -> Bag
  FUNC ins   : Item # Bag -> Bag

  PRED is_gen : Bag
  IND  is_gen(empty);
       FORALL i:Item,b:Bag
       ( is_gen(b) => is_gen(ins(i,b)) )

  AXIOM
  {BAG1} empty!;
         FORALL i:Item,j:Item,b:Bag,c:Bag (
  {BAG2} ins(i,b)!;
  {BAG3} NOT is_in(i,empty);
  {BAG4} is_in(i,ins(j,b)) <=> i = j OR is_in(i,b);
  {BAG5} ins(i,ins(j,b)) = ins(j,ins(i,b));
  {BAG6} ins(i,b) = ins(i,c) => b = c );
  {BAG7} FORALL b:Bag ( is_gen(b) )

  FUNC rem : Item # Bag -> Bag
  IND  FORALL i:Item,j:Item,b:Bag
       ( rem(i,empty) = empty;
         rem(i,ins(i,b)) = b;
         NOT i = j => rem(i,ins(j,b)) = ins(j,rem(i,b)) )

  FUNC union : Bag # Bag -> Bag
```

```
IND  FORALL b:Bag
     ( union(b,empty) = b );
     FORALL i:Item,b:Bag,c:Bag
     ( union(b,ins(i,c)) = ins(i,union(b,c)) )

FUNC isect : Bag # Bag -> Bag
IND  FORALL b:Bag
     ( isect(b,empty) = empty );
     FORALL i:Item,b:Bag,c:Bag
     ( isect(ins(i,b),ins(i,c)) = ins(i,isect(b,c));
       NOT is_in(i,b) => isect(b,ins(i,c)) = isect(b,c) )

FUNC diff : Bag # Bag -> Bag
IND  FORALL b:Bag
     ( diff(b,empty) = b );
     FORALL i:Item,b:Bag,c:Bag
     ( diff(b,ins(i,c)) = rem(i,diff(b,c)) )

PRED subbag : Bag # Bag
IND  FORALL b:Bag
     ( subbag(b,b) );
     FORALL i:Item,b:Bag,c:Bag
     ( subbag(b,c) => subbag(b,ins(i,c)) )

FUNC mult : Item # Bag -> Nat
IND  FORALL i:Item,j:Item,b:Bag
     ( mult(i,empty) = zero;
       mult(i,ins(i,b)) = succ(mult(i,b));
       NOT i = j => mult(i,ins(j,b)) = mult(i,b) )

END;
```

B.7 Finite sequences

```
% SEQ specifies the data type of finite sequences.
%
% Interpretation (i:Item, s,t:Seq, m:Nat):
%
% Item      : the set of objects contained in sequences;
% Seq       : the set of finite sequences of objects of type Item;
% empty     : the empty sequence;
% cons(i,s) : the sequence s with i appended at the head of s;
% hd(s)     : the head of s (= element with index 0);
% tl(s)     : the tail of s (= s with its head removed);
% len(s)    : the length of s (= number of elements of s);
% sel(s,m)  : the element of s with index m;
% cat(s,t)  : the concatenation of s and t;
% rev(s)    : the sequence s with its elements in reverse order.
```

```
LET SEQ :=
EXPORT
  SORT Item,
  SORT Nat,
  SORT Seq,
  FUNC empty : -> Seq,
  FUNC cons  : Item # Seq -> Seq,
  FUNC hd    : Seq        -> Item,
  FUNC tl    : Seq        -> Seq,
  FUNC len   : Seq        -> Nat,
  FUNC sel   : Seq # Nat  -> Item,
  FUNC cat   : Seq # Seq  -> Seq,
  FUNC rev   : Seq        -> Seq
FROM
IMPORT NAT INTO
CLASS

  SORT Item
  SORT Seq
  FUNC empty : -> Seq
  FUNC cons  : Item # Seq -> Seq

  PRED is_gen : Seq
  IND  is_gen(empty);
       FORALL i:Item,s:Seq
       ( is_gen(s) => is_gen(cons(i,s)) )

  AXIOM
  {SEQ1} empty!;
         FORALL i:Item,j:Item,s:Seq,t:Seq  (
  {SEQ2} cons(i,s)!;
  {SEQ3} NOT cons(i,s) = empty;
  {SEQ4} cons(i,s) = cons(j,t) => i = j AND s = t );
  {SEQ5} FORALL s:Seq ( is_gen(s) )

  FUNC hd : Seq -> Item
  IND  FORALL i:Item,s:Seq
       ( hd(cons(i,s)) = i )

  FUNC tl : Seq -> Seq
  IND  FORALL i:Item,s:Seq
       ( tl(cons(i,s)) = s )

  FUNC len : Seq -> Nat
  IND  len(empty) = zero;
       FORALL i:Item,s:Seq
       ( len(cons(i,s)) = succ(len(s)) )

  FUNC sel : Seq # Nat -> Item
  IND  FORALL i:Item,j:Item,s:Seq,n:Nat
       ( sel(cons(i,s),zero) = i;
```

```
        sel(s,n) = j => sel(cons(i,s),succ(n)) = j )

  FUNC cat : Seq # Seq -> Seq
  IND  FORALL s:Seq
       ( cat(empty,s) = s );
       FORALL i:Item,s:Seq,t:Seq
       ( cat(cons(i,s),t) = cons(i,cat(s,t)) )

  FUNC rev : Seq -> Seq
  IND  rev(empty) = empty;
       FORALL i:Item,s:Seq
       ( rev(cons(i,s)) = cat(rev(s),cons(i,empty)) )

END;
```

B.8 Finite maps

```
% MAP specifies the data type of finite maps.
%
% Interpretation (m:Map, x:Item1, v:Item2):
%
% Item1       : the set of objects acting as arguments of maps;
% Item2       : the set of objects acting as values of maps;
% Set1        : the set of finite sets of objects of type Item1;
% Set2        : the set of finite sets of objects of type Item2;
% Map         : the set of finite maps;
% empty       : the empty map (= map with empty domain);
% add(m,x,v)  : the map m with the value of argument x replaced by v;
% rem(m,x)    : the map m with x removed from the domain;
% app(m,x)    : the value of map m applied to argument x;
% dom(m)      : the domain of the map m;
% ran(m)      : the range of the map m.

LET SET1 :=
EXPORT
  SORT Item1,
  SORT Nat,
  SORT Set1,
  PRED is_in  : Item1 # Set1,
  FUNC empty  : -> Set1,
  FUNC ins    : Item1 # Set1 -> Set1,
  FUNC rem    : Item1 # Set1 -> Set1,
  FUNC union  : Set1  # Set1 -> Set1,
  FUNC isect  : Set1  # Set1 -> Set1,
  FUNC diff   : Set1  # Set1 -> Set1,
  PRED subset : Set1  # Set1,
  FUNC card   : Set1          -> Nat
FROM
IMPORT NAT INTO
```

```
CLASS

  SORT Item1
  SORT Set1
  PRED is_in : Item1 # Set1
  FUNC empty : -> Set1
  FUNC ins   : Item1 # Set1 -> Set1
  % ... as SET

END;

LET SET2 :=
EXPORT
  SORT Item2,
  SORT Nat,
  SORT Set2,
  PRED is_in  : Item2 # Set2,
  FUNC empty  : -> Set2,
  FUNC ins    : Item2 # Set2 -> Set2,
  FUNC rem    : Item2 # Set2 -> Set2,
  FUNC union  : Set2  # Set2 -> Set2,
  FUNC isect  : Set2  # Set2 -> Set2,
  FUNC diff   : Set2  # Set2 -> Set2,
  PRED subset : Set2  # Set2,
  FUNC card   : Set2         -> Nat
FROM
IMPORT NAT INTO
CLASS

  SORT Item2
  SORT Set2
  PRED is_in : Item2 # Set2
  FUNC empty : -> Set2
  FUNC ins   : Item2 # Set2 -> Set2
  % ... as SET

END;

LET MAP :=
EXPORT
  SORT Item1,
  SORT Item2,
  SORT Set1,
  SORT Set2,
  SORT Map,
  FUNC empty : -> Map,
  FUNC add   : Map # Item1 # Item2 -> Map,
  FUNC rem   : Map # Item1         -> Map,
  FUNC app   : Map # Item1         -> Item2,
  FUNC dom   : Map                 -> Set1,
  FUNC ran   : Map                 -> Set2
FROM
```

```
IMPORT SET1 INTO
IMPORT SET2 INTO
CLASS

  SORT Map
  FUNC empty : -> Map
  FUNC add   : Map # Item1 # Item2 -> Map
  FUNC app   : Map # Item1         -> Item2

  PRED is_gen : Map
  IND  is_gen(empty);
       FORALL m:Map,i:Item1,v:Item2
       ( is_gen(m) => is_gen(add(m,i,v)) )

  AXIOM
  {MAP1} empty:Map!;
         FORALL i:Item1,j:Item1,v:Item2,w:Item2,m:Map  (
  {MAP2} add(m,i,v)!;
  {MAP3} NOT app(empty,i)!;
  {MAP4} app(add(m,i,v),j) = w <=>
         ( (i = j AND v = w) OR (NOT i = j AND app(m,j) = w) );
  {MAP5} NOT i = j => add(add(m,i,v),j,w) = add(add(m,j,w),i,v);
  {MAP6} add(add(m,i,v),i,w) = add(m,i,w) );
  {MAP7} FORALL m:Map ( is_gen(m) )

  FUNC rem : Map # Item1 -> Map
  IND  FORALL i:Item1
       ( rem(empty,i) = empty );
       FORALL m:Map,i:Item1,j:Item1,v:Item2 (
         rem(add(m,i,v),i) = rem(m,i);
         NOT i = j => rem(add(m,i,v),j) = add(rem(m,j),i,v) )

  FUNC dom : Map -> Set1
  IND  dom(empty) = empty;
       FORALL m:Map,i:Item1,v:Item2
       ( dom(add(m,i,v)) = ins(i,dom(m)) )

  FUNC ran : Map -> Set2
  IND  ran(empty) = empty;
       FORALL m:Map,i:Item1,v:Item2
       ( ran(add(m,i,v)) = ins(v,ran(rem(m,i))) )

END;
```

Index

Printed in the United States
By Bookmasters